PATENT SHOCK SERIES ®

WHITE SPACE PATENTING

DRAFTING GREAT PATENT APPLICATIONS

Third Edition

ROBERT D. FISH, ESQ.

Printed in the United States of America
ISBN 979-8-9876415-1-4
March 2023

Considerable precaution has been taken to ensure that
the information presented in this book is accurate. Nevertheless, neither the author nor the publisher shall have
any liability to any person or entity for loss or damage
caused or alleged to be caused, directly or indirectly, by
the information contained within, or referenced by, this
work. The information is presented on an "as is" basis,
without any warranty.

The information contained within, or referenced by, this
work is not legal advice. One should consult an attorney
for legal advice.

To Julie and Sky, for their
unending patience and support.

Additional thanks to Dave Walston for his
incredible drawings, and to many individuals
at Fish IP Law, LLP for their ideas and
inspiration.

Table of Contents

PREFACE

This book is directed at anyone who is drafting patent applications, as well as anyone who wants to work more efficiently and cost-effectively with patent counsel. Unlike other books that merely teach the mechanics of patent drafting, this book focuses on strategy.

Why is strategy important? Strategy is important because without it, most inventors are just wasting their money. It is said that fully 80% of patents are never commercialized at all, and at least 95% of patent applicants never make back the money they spent on their patent attorney.

The biggest problem with most patent drafting efforts is that the drafter is focusing on specific embodiments of ideas rather than the underlying ideas, and specific technologies rather than markets for the claimed products or processes. Most inventors and patent counsel start with what the inventor considers to be the "invention", and then branch out as far as they can until they run into the prior art. That yields an "invention centered" application; one that covers the invention but not the marketplace.

Instead of focusing on "what the invention is", they should be asking "what do you want to stop others from doing?" That latter question is "market centered", and ends up claiming far more than what the inventor thinks he invented.

Now, how is that accomplished?

Chapters I and II of this book graphically depict the concept of market-centered, white space patenting, and describe how one can use patentability searching to brainstorm the available white space.

Chapter III provides guidelines for drafting good patent applications. For those relying on patent counsel to draft their applications, Chapter III explains how to distinguish between those who write "good" patents and those who write "bad" patents. This is a highly abstract discussion, but one that should be read to place the remainder of the book in perspective.

Chapter IV addresses the *mechanics* of patent claims, including the different formats in common use, differences between structure and method claims, Markush and Jepson claims, and so forth.

Chapter V moves on to claiming strategies. Topics include the importance of using market-centered claiming as opposed to invention-centered claiming, how to best use independent and dependent claims, target claiming, special aspects of claiming in various fields (biomedical, electrical, mechanical), and portfolio building.

Perhaps most importantly, White Space Patenting explains how to draft broad scope claims that nevertheless fall within the confines dictated by important Supreme Court cases, *KSR*, *Bilski*, *Alice*, *Mayo*, *Myriad*, *Ariosa*, and others.

Chapter VI walks the reader through the various parts of a specification, from title through abstract and drawing. The main emphasis is on drafting these sections in a manner that supports the claims, while avoiding the most common pitfalls in writing style.

Note that there is a detailed index and table of authorities. For ease of reading, claim text is marked out in blue frames, and specification text is marked out in green frames.

Chapter I - What Is White Space Patenting?

As practiced in our office,[1] white space patenting is the process of claiming what the inventor thinks he or she invented, *plus whatever commercially viable alternatives can be claimed*, while still falling within the confines dictated by recent Supreme Court and Federal Circuit precedents.

Management and marketing people get this concept immediately. They are not so much interested in what the inventor invented, but in what sort of monopoly can be obtained, i.e., commercial value. Consequently, the question they ask is not what was invented, but what a patent can stop the competitors from doing. This may sound like the same thing, but it is not. The traditional approach is invention- or technology-oriented, whereas the true white space patenting approach is market-oriented. This can be readily appreciated using the Venn diagrams shown below.

> **The main focus of white space patenting is blocking out the competition**

A) Invention-Oriented Approach Versus Market-Oriented Claiming

(1) Market-Oriented Approach Yields Broader Claims

Every invention is really a solution to a problem. Ideally, the inventor would claim every commercially viable solution, which in the following diagram would be the entire space.

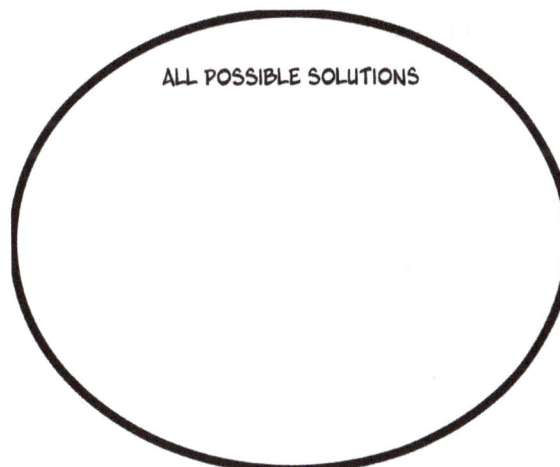

ALL POSSIBLE SOLUTIONS

1   Fish IP Law, 19900 MacArthur Blvd. Suite 810, Irvine CA 92612; www.FishIPLaw.com; 949-943-8300.

It would be nice to claim all possible solutions to a problem, but in most cases that is just not possible. Almost every inventive space is already occupied by at least some prior art[2] (represented by the rectangles) that precludes the inventor from capturing the entire space.

ALL POSSIBLE SOLUTIONS

PRIOR ART   PRIOR ART

PRIOR ART

In the diagram below, the invention is shown as a light bulb. The inventor could, of course, simply claim the area occupied by the light bulb. But that is usually a very bad idea because the claimed subject matter is much too small.

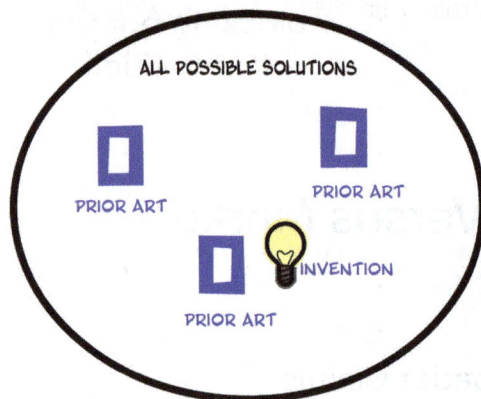

ALL POSSIBLE SOLUTIONS

PRIOR ART   PRIOR ART

INVENTION

PRIOR ART

The better idea is to broaden the claims out beyond the inventor's *preferred embodiments* as far as one can go, until the "invention" runs into the prior art. But that still leaves a lot of patentable subject matter on the table.

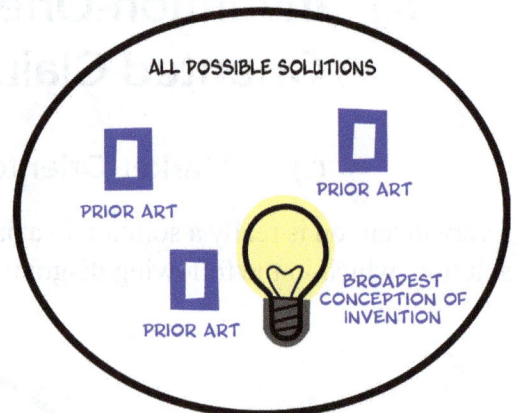

ALL POSSIBLE SOLUTIONS

PRIOR ART   PRIOR ART

PRIOR ART

BROADEST CONCEPTION OF INVENTION

PRIOR ART

At Fish IP Law, LLP, what we think of as white space patenting is not merely fluffing out the preferred embodiments, but (1) figuring out *all of the commercially viable alternatives that are not already disclosed* by, or obvious over, the prior art, (2) devising solutions that cover those alternatives, and then (3) writing claims that cover the preferred embodiments, plus variations of those embodiments, plus everything else of commercial significance that's available to be claimed.

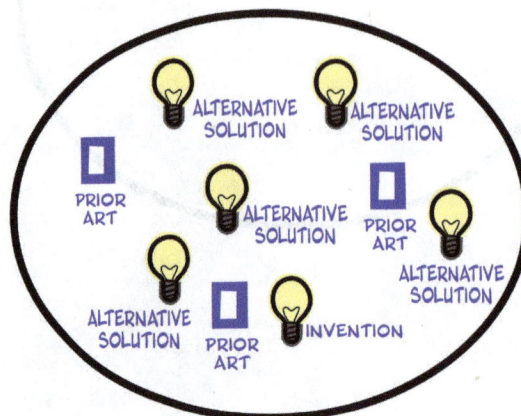

ALTERNATIVE SOLUTION   ALTERNATIVE SOLUTION

PRIOR ART

ALTERNATIVE SOLUTION

PRIOR ART

ALTERNATIVE SOLUTION

ALTERNATIVE SOLUTION   PRIOR ART   INVENTION

---

2   In the patent world, prior art is all information that should be considered when determining the scope of the claims of a patent or patent application. 35 U.S.C §§ 102 and 103.

Does that make the patent drafter a co-inventor? Some people think so. But the fact is that if the person drafting the patent application can devise all these other solutions from the one solution developed by the inventor, then those other solutions are *inherent* in the inventor's conception. And the patent drafter should not be considered a co-inventor.

Of course, covering the true white space can be a difficult task. It requires the patent drafter to be extremely creative, good at brainstorming and drafting claims, and be a good communicator to boot. Conceptually, the coverage resulting from market-oriented white space patenting should look like a bird's eye view of a golf course, with the claims covering all of the available subject matter.

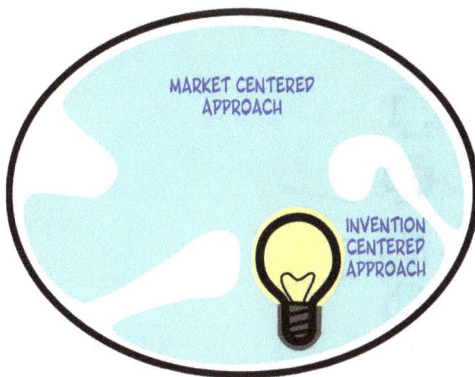

The point is that the market-oriented approach to patenting is simply better than the invention-oriented approach because it produces broader claims. Would you rather have protection for the small region covered by the light bulb, or the broader regions covered by the golf course?

Now it is true that claiming broadly from a market perspective can lead to problems with enablement. Whenever a patent drafter is trying to cover everything in the field other than what is already known, they will almost certainly wind up claiming things that are not readily manufactured using known technology. But that is where the *art* of patenting comes into play. The application should include real or imagined experiments that enable the far-flung reaches of the claimed subject matter. It should also identify texts and articles that assist in enablement, and incorporate them by reference into the specification.

> Writing claims using a market-oriented approach is almost always better than using an invention-centered approach

It is also true that claiming too broadly can run afoul of the case law, *Alice v. CLS Bank*[3], *Mayo v. Prometheus*[4], and *Ass'n for Mol. Pathology v. Myriad*[5]. At this point in the discussion, however, is suffices to say that claiming with a market-oriented approach is almost always better that claiming from an invention-centered approach.

---

3   *Alice Corp. Pty. Ltd. v. CLS Bank Int'l*, (2014) 134 S. Ct. 2347.
4   *Mayo Collaborative Servs. v. Prometheus Labs., Inc.*, (2012) 132 S. Ct. 1289.
5   *Ass'n for Molecular Pathology v. Myriad Genetics, Inc.*, (2013) 133 S. Ct. 2107.

(2)   Market-Oriented Approach Provides Clear Strategy To Creating A Patent Thicket

One very useful strategy for market-oriented claiming is to view the technology *metaphorically*, as fitting somewhere along a generalized flow from raw materials to one or more distributed products. This may seem a bit odd, but even services such as that provided by real estate agents can be viewed as "products". In that case, the raw materials are listings and potential consumers, and the products are closed sales.

Using an appropriate metaphor, the patent drafter should be able to use a schematic such as that shown in the figure below to identify the technology space that is at least potentially subject to patenting. The trick is to *assume* that the technology has a counterpart to every portion of the conceptual structure, and then figure out what those counterparts must be.

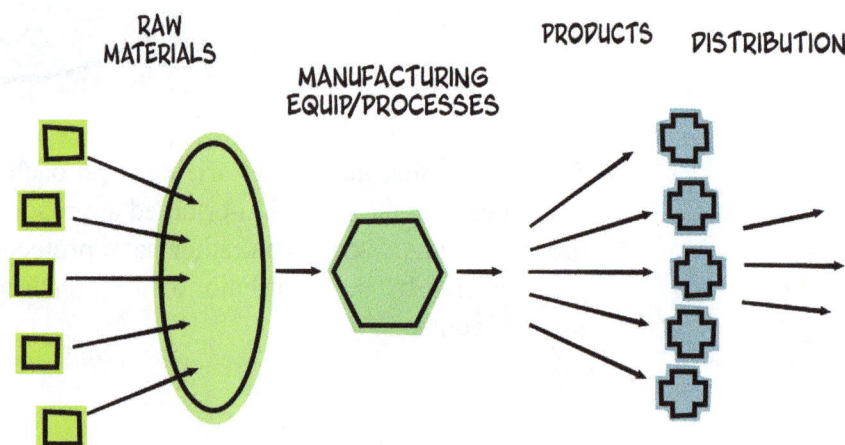

Figure - Generalized Schematic Of Technology Space

The next step is to consider all of those various counterparts as potential "choke points" where the competition could be kept at bay. By way of example, consider the technology relating to synthetic threads.

From a materials standpoint, there are many different compositions that could be used to make a synthetic thread. This is depicted graphically below, with patent numbers of exemplary patents in the field.

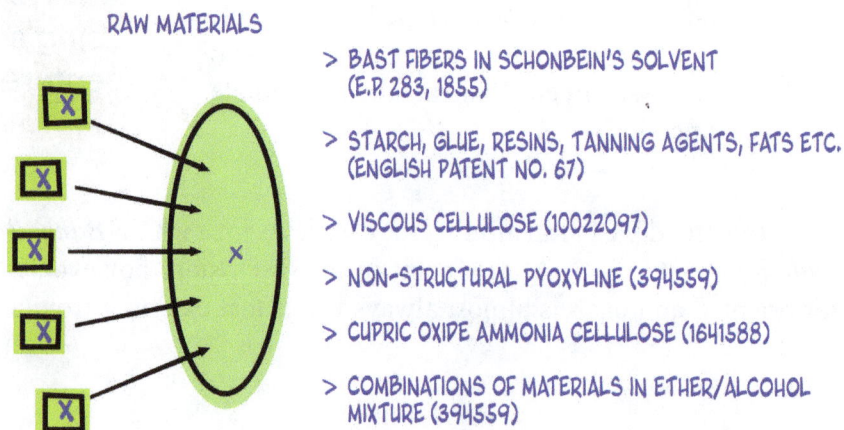

RAW MATERIALS

> BAST FIBERS IN SCHONBEIN'S SOLVENT (E.P. 283, 1855)

> STARCH, GLUE, RESINS, TANNING AGENTS, FATS ETC. (ENGLISH PATENT NO. 67)

> VISCOUS CELLULOSE (10022097)

> NON-STRUCTURAL PYOXYLINE (394559)

> CUPRIC OXIDE AMMONIA CELLULOSE (1641588)

> COMBINATIONS OF MATERIALS IN ETHER/ALCOHOL MIXTURE (394559)

Figure - Potential "Choke Points" For Raw Materials

When viewed in this way, the reader should immediately appreciate that the various inventors secured their patents using an invention-oriented approach. Any one of them could have locked up the entire field by contemplating, and then claiming, all the various possible classes of raw materials. That would have involved patenting from a market-oriented approach -- but no one did that. They could also have used the market-oriented approach to lock up all commercially viable manufacturing equipment and processes, final products, distribution schemes, and so forth. But they didn't do that either. Instead, they narrowly focused on specific inventions.

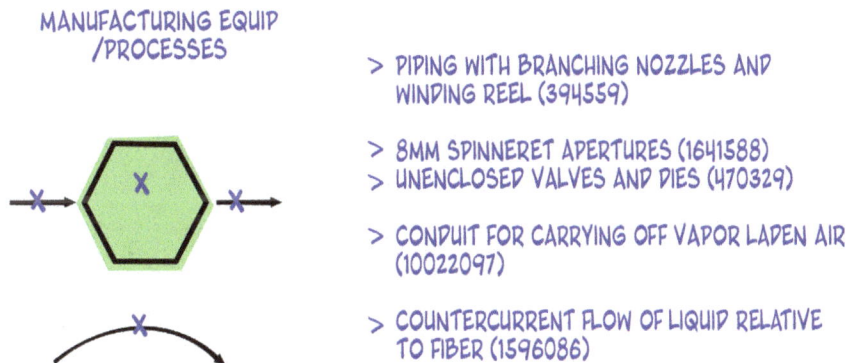

MANUFACTURING EQUIP
/PROCESSES

> PIPING WITH BRANCHING NOZZLES AND
  WINDING REEL (394559)

> 8MM SPINNERET APERTURES (1641588)
> UNENCLOSED VALVES AND DIES (470329)

> CONDUIT FOR CARRYING OFF VAPOR LADEN AIR
  (10022097)

> COUNTERCURRENT FLOW OF LIQUID RELATIVE
  TO FIBER (1596086)

Figure - Potential "Choke Points" For Manufacturing

The bottom line is that in drafting patent applications, one should view any given invention as a piece of a much larger technology space. One should map out the entire space from raw materials to distributed end product, figure out all of the remaining patentable "white space", and then claim everything that remains to be claimed. That is the essence of true white space, (i.e., market-oriented) claiming.

(3)   It Is Not Necessary To Cover Every Possible Embodiment

One important caveat here. Although it is nice to write patent claims that cover every possible embodiment in the white space, it is not always necessary to do so. First, the primary goal of patenting is merely to cover commercially significant embodiments. Second, even if claims fail to cover *all* such embodiments, it often suffices if they cover *some* embodiments that are especially desired by the marketplace. For example, assume that someone invents an automated license plate reader for use on highway patrol cars. If the prior art systems can read license plates on cars moving in the same lane as the patrol car, or on parked cars in adjacent lanes, an applicant cannot now claim a system that covers all license plate readers. But he doesn't have to. All he has to do is claim systems that read license plates on cars (1) moving (2) in other lanes. Given a choice of the prior art system or the new system, police departments will very likely choose the latter.

Now, should the applicant *also* include a dependent claim to additionally read plates in the same lane? Yes, absolutely. That way, a competitor would infringe the independent claim for a system that read plates only in moving cars in adjacent lanes, and he would infringe both independent and dependent claims for a system that read faces in moving cars in both adjacent and same lanes.

Chapter II - Search Patentability To Brainstorm The Available White Space

How is it that good patent drafter can often devise white space claims in a few hours, whereas it may have taken the inventor months or years to come up with the invention? Why is it that the most effective patent counsel is often someone who is not an expert in the particular field of the invention? The answer is that a good patent drafter (A) understands what constitutes a patentable invention, (B) performs a decent prior art search, and (C) employs a lot of creativity and brainstorming during the searching process to find and fill the white space. This chapter shows how each of those steps is done.

A) Understanding What Constitutes A Patentable Invention.

To secure a patent from the U.S. Patent Office, one must be able to describe an invention that is (1) new, (2) useful and (3) non-obvious.

The "new" part of patentability is called "novelty", and is usually fairly easy to satisfy. As long as neither the inventor nor anyone else has ever put the claimed product on the market (or used the steps of a method), and the concept was never disclosed or suggested in a book, magazine, or anywhere else, then the inventor probably has a novel idea. In the past, an inventor could rely on date of conception to establish priority. However, the U.S. is now on a "first to file" system, which basically means a race to the patent office. Yes, it is possible to obtain patent rights when someone else files first, but proving that the other person stole the idea, or otherwise improperly filed, is a hard sell.

> The U.S. has moved to a "first to file" system, which basically amounts to a race to the patent office

The main things to watch out for in searching novelty are: (1) that the idea is novel *throughout the world*; and (2) that the idea was novel *at all previous times*. If an idea was publicly disclosed in a patent application in Germany, it is not novel in the U.S. under the AIA rules[6]. If the idea was disclosed in an old patent that has now expired, it is not novel. Even if the idea was publicly disclosed but never patented, it is not novel. With some exceptions, the proper test for determining novelty is a comparison of the claims against what is already known anywhere in the world at any time. The test is definitely not comparing the claims against what has been patented.

Patent Beast © FISH 2007

I HAVE THE WORLD'S GREATEST INVENTION. | THERE IS A ONE YEAR WINDOW FROM THE FIRST SALE. | BUT I'VE BEEN SELLING IT FOR FIVE YEARS...... | DO I HAVE TO TELL THE PATENT OFFICE?

As with other aspects of patent law, the Patent Beast™[7] comic strip (www.patentbeast.com) captures some of the more humorous aspects of novelty. Some of those comics are included in this book.

> **It is usually better for the person drafting the patent application to run his/her own patent searches**

The "useful" part of determining patentability is also usually quite easy to satisfy. If a new idea were not useful, one wouldn't be spending the time or money trying to get a patent. Indeed, the standard of usefulness is so low it doesn't have anything to do with commercializability. What, for example, is the commercial benefit of patenting a comb-over to cover a bald spot, (see U.S. 4022227 to Frank and Donald Smith, 1977), or a method of swinging on a swing, (see U.S. 6368227 to Steven Olson, 2002)? Such patents could never be enforced. These and many other essentially worthless patents can be found at the Totally Absurd Archives.[8]

Just about the only time applicants get rejections on the grounds of non-usefulness is when the claimed invention appears to be inconsistent with the accepted laws of physics[9]. Perpetual motion machines, for example, are almost always rejected,[10] as are cold-fusion related inventions.

The kicker is usually obviousness of the invention. A ballpoint pen with a single red dot on the barrel may be novel, but it is merely an obvious design choice. By contrast, the use of a sodium nitride ball in a pen was definitely inventive, and patentable, as were pens that spool out writing paper.

There will be quite a bit more to say about obviousness later on in the book in the discussion on claim drafting. Suffice it to say at this stage that to get a decent patent, one needs to come up with something that is non-obvious to a Person of Ordinary Skill in the Art (a POSITA or PHOSITA). And that usually means claiming something that is more than a *mere design choice*.

(1)   "The Invention" Is Not The Same Thing As A "Preferred Embodiment"

Inventors often get into trouble by confusing their "preferred embodiments" with their "inventions". Preferred embodiments are merely *examples* of the invention. This is a critical distinction.

---

7   https://www.patentbeast.com/

8   www.totallyabsurd.com/inventionsarchive.htm

9   *Bilski v. Kappos*, 130 S. Ct. 3218, 177 L. Ed. 2d 792 (1010)

10   Every once in awhile the patent office does issue a patent on perpetual motion. See e.g., U.S. 257103 (Apr. 1882) "Perpetual Motion Machine"

Focusing on preferred embodiments rather than inventions has two very undesirable consequences. First, inventors tend to focus their patentability searches too narrowly, and end up wasting a lot of money on patent applications that should never have been filed. Second, claiming preferred embodiments, rather than the underlying concepts, often produces claims that are essentially unenforceable. It is said that 80% of patents are never commercialized at all, and perhaps 95% of patent applicants never make back the money they paid for filing and prosecution of the applications. Those horrible statistics result directly from the fact that many patent claims are way too narrow.

If one is going to get a commercially significant patent, one needs to figure out the core inventive concept, and then figure out the choke points for applying that concept in the marketplace. That means doing the heavy mental lifting of figuring out all of the commercially viable alternatives, and finding a common thread that passes through all of them. Thus, if one invents a new type of serration for a steel knife, one should claim the concept broadly enough to encompass all markets that might have use for the new type of serration. That would include plastic and even wooden knives, as well as squared cutting surfaces that might not even be considered knives.

Some inventors are quite good at figuring out what the core concept is. But more often than not, they are "tree" people rather than "forest" people, and tend to get stuck on the details. Most inventors should seek guidance of patent counsel who not only understands the technology, but who is also good at seeing the big picture.

B)   Performing A Good Prior Art Search

Effective prior art searching is absolutely critical to white space patenting. Indeed, this provides one very quick way to separate better patent counsel from mediocre or poor counsel. Patent counsel who thinks they can write good claims without searching the prior art, should probably be avoided.

The fact is that until one understands what is known in the field, one cannot realistically figure out where the white space is. A good searching strategy involves conscious decisions about when to search, what kind of search to perform, and how deep the search should go. Those decisions involve many different factors, from susceptibility of the field to keyword searching, to the impact of the search on research and development efforts.

In searching the white space, one should be careful about using outside searching services. Even if the service does a thorough job, it is the *searcher* who grasps the overall landscape of the available white space. It is the searcher who develops new ideas for improving the invention, and understands the right-to-practice issues. By and large, the person writing the patent claims should be the person conducting the search.

There are two important caveats. First, some consumer products have so many prior art hits, that it is not cost-effective for patent counsel to run the search. Second, in some technologies there is a lot of critical prior art that can only be found in foreign languages. In either of those cases, it can be very desirable to use an outside searching service. Some of the services that we have found to produce good results, and be cost-effective, is Cardinal IP[11], Gray B[12], and Patexia[13].

(1)   You Don't Know What's In The Prior Art

It is impossible for any inventor to know everything of relevance (i.e., all of the "prior art") in the field of the invention. Reviewing patents on Google, and surfing the web for products, are just not adequate search strategies. Nor is experience gleaned from spending many years in the technology space. This is especially true under the new AIA version of 35 U.S.C. § 102, in which prior art includes anything "described in a printed publication, or in public use, on sale, or otherwise available to the public before the effective filing date of the claimed invention", with very few exceptions.

As noted above, a great deal of information is available only in foreign patents and applications, and in journals and other non-patent literature. In addition, both U.S. and foreign patent applications are generally held in confidence by the patent office for 18 months, so that a patentability search likely won't find a competitor's disclosure that was filed only a year ago. Still another reason that an inventor can't know everything of relevance is that what counts as prior art against an applicant is determined by what is claimed in that application. Since the claims almost invariable amended during prosecution before the US Patent and Trademark office, what counts as prior art often changes during prosecution. The fact is that neither an inventor nor his or her patent counsel, nor even the world's best searcher, can possibly know everything that is prior art.

11   https://cardinal-ip.com/
12   https://www.greyb.com/
13   https://www.patexia.com/

What is prior art anyway? For most purposes since 2013[14], prior art is the following, modified from 35 U.S.C. § 102 (a): Prior art is anything that is patented, described in a printed publication, or in public use, on sale, or otherwise available to the public before the effective filing date of the claimed invention.

That's the law in the United States, and for the most part that's also the law in other countries. The text looks simple enough, but appearances here are deceiving. What, for example, is meant by "printed publication", "public use", "on sale", "otherwise available" or even "the invention"? The complexity is such that the Patent Office devotes numerous sections (§2121 - § 2138) of the Manual of Patent Examining Procedure (MPEP) trying to explain to patent examiners how to apply the law[15].

> **With minor exceptions, prior art can include anything that is known anywhere in the world, prior to the filing date of the patent application**

There are three big exceptions to the general prior art rule of AIA § 102(a).

The first exception is that under AIA § 102(b)(1)(A), an inventor *theoretically* has one year from the time he discloses an invention within which to file his patent application. But inventors should not rely on that window. Under USPTO's Rules For The "First-to-File" System, an inventor can only prevail against an earlier filer if the subject matters of their respective disclosures is *substantially identical*. And that, of course, is very unlikely. The U.S. system now embodies "race to the patent office".

The second exception has to do with child applications. A child of an earlier filed application can usually take as its priority date the filing date of the parent, grandparent, great-grandparent, etc. For CIP (Continuation-In-Part) applications, in which additional matter is added in the child application, there are two priority dates; the earlier filing date, and the filing date that the additional material was added.

The third exception is patent application disclosures are not prior art if either the subject matter was obtained directly from the inventor or a joint inventor, or there is common ownership or a joint research agreement.

> **Once a patent or patent application is published, it becomes prior art as of its filing date**

Inventors sometimes think that U.S. patents are only considered prior art as of their issue date. The fact is that U.S. published patent applications and issued patents are considered prior art effect as of the filing date of the application. The rule is different for foreign applications, whether filed in English or another language, Which are only given prior art effect as of the publication date of the application.

There used to be a distinction between anticipation (35 U.S.C. § 102 prior art) and obviousness (35 U.S.C. § 103 prior art). That distinction was eliminated by the AIA, §3.

One often needs to resolve whether or not information constitutes a printed publication. For example, is a Ph.D. thesis in a major university considered a printed publication for purposes of 35 U.S.C. § 102(a) under the AIA? What about a mere term paper? Actually, the distinction has nothing to do with the sophistication of the publication or the context in which it was created, but instead has everything to do with whether the document was "publicly accessible".

---

14   The law was changed by the America Invents Act of 2011 (the AIA)
15   Start at www.uspto.gov/web/offices/pac/mpep/s2121.html

A reference is "publicly accessible" whenever:

> "… persons interested and ordinarily skilled in the subject matter . . . exercising reasonable diligence, can locate it and recognize and comprehend there from the essentials of the claimed invention without need of further research or experimentation".[16]

Several cases have required that for a publication to provide prior art effect, the publication must allow those interested in the art a sufficient amount of time to "capture, process and retain the information conveyed by the reference", or to locate the material "in a meaningful way"[17].

Even canceled drawing figures in a Canadian patent application can count as prior art in a U.S. patent

It turns out those tests are fairly easy to satisfy because they merely address technical accessibility. In *Bruckelmyer v. Ground Heaters, Inc.*,[18] for example, the Federal Circuit found that canceled drawing figures in a Canadian patent application were publicly accessible even though neither the figures nor even the application had been specifically indexed, and there were no copies known to have been made or sent outside the Canadian patent office during the prior art period. In that instance the figures were considered to be prior art merely because the Canadian prosecution file had technically been open to the public more than a year before the inventor filed his U.S. application. The bottom line is that, at least during the searching process, one should assume that any relevant documents that the searcher can find will be considered publicly accessible.

Another factor to consider is that inventors often become unnecessarily discouraged by wild-eyed teachings or suggestions in the prior art. Even under the AIA, disclosures that fail to teach how to make and use what they are describing are "not enabled", and cannot validly be used by the Patent Office against a patent application.

(2)   Choose An Appropriate Search Strategy

With all this in mind, the next steps in searching the prior art are to figure out how much effort to put into the search, and how to go about doing the search. The answer depends entirely upon the specific circumstances.

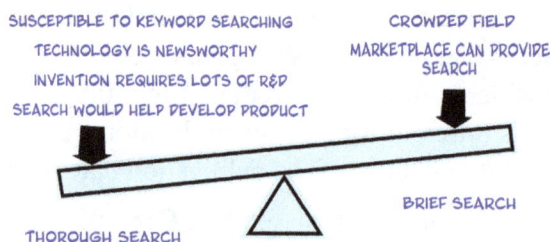

SUSCEPTIBLE TO KEYWORD SEARCHING
TECHNOLOGY IS NEWSWORTHY
INVENTION REQUIRES LOTS OF R&D
SEARCH WOULD HELP DEVELOP PRODUCT

CROWDED FIELD
MARKETPLACE CAN PROVIDE SEARCH

BRIEF SEARCH

THOROUGH SEARCH

- Is the search readily susceptible to keyword searching? Keyword searching works best where the invention can be readily described with a few *distinctive* words. Thus, a clothing perspiration shield that sticks to the skin would be readily searchable, because the searcher could simply search for a combination of perspire*, shield or cover, and adhere* or stick*, where the asterisks indicate a symbol for a wild card. Searching for suntan lotion packaged in single use packets the way mustard and ketchup are sold is also readily searchable. The searcher would simply search for a combination of the terms suntan, packet, and possibly single-use. But searching for an

16   *In re Wyer*, 655 F.2d 221, 226 (C.C.P.A. 1981); see also MPEP §2128, https://www.uspto.gov/web/offices/pac/mpep/s2128.html
17   *In re Klopfenstein*, 380 F.3d 1345, 1350 (Fed. Cir. 2004); *In re Cronyn*, 890 F.2d at 1158, 1161 (Fed. Cir. 1989)
18   *Bruckelmyer v. Ground Heaters, Inc.*, 2006 U.S. App. LEXIS 9853 (Fed. Cir. 2006)

internet invention that uses a database to store information is very difficult to search. Terms such as server, database, and user interface can pull up millions of hits.

• Is the field crowded? Patentability searching often works poorly in crowded fields, even if the invention is readily described by distinctive keywords. For example, a searcher should probably invest minimal time searching a baby toy in which shaped pieces are inserted into correspondingly shaped holes. There is so much prior art that anything more than a quick search is probably a waste of money.

• Would a thorough search help in developing the product? Sometimes it is useful to conduct a very thorough search, even though the subject matter is difficult to search and the field is crowded. The benefit lies less in determining if the idea is patentable than in guiding the R&D effort by identifying what is known in the field. The evolution of technology is like building an arch. No matter how many blocks are used to build the foundation of the arch, it won't stand up by itself until someone inserts the keystone at the top. In technology, there may be hundreds or even thousands of people working on a project, each adding to the foundation. But the person who adds that last missing piece gets the patent *and all the credit,* even though that keystone piece is almost always quite small compared to the whole. A good search can go a long way towards finding that keystone.

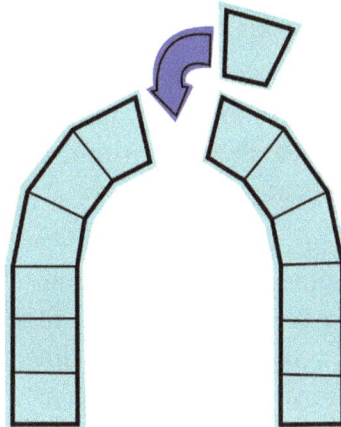

Figure - The One Who Adds The Keystone Gets All The Credit

• Is the technology likely or unlikely to be published? The various keyword databases are only useful in searching inventions that are published. For example, using keywords to search for the use of a particular sewing stitch on the hem of a swimsuit would be almost impossible. Swimsuits have been manufactured for well over a hundred years, with different manufactures trying out new stitches without ever publishing information on what they are doing. Use of one stitch rather than another would likely never find its way into the local newspaper, in a patent, or in any publication for that matter.

• Does the invention require a lot of R&D? In some instances, a company is planning to spend hundreds of thousands or even millions of dollars on R&D for a product. Knowing early on that the product is unpatentable can save huge sums of money, or at least re-direct that money to something more worthwhile. In those instances, the cost-effective approach is to invest in a thorough search as soon as possible, and update the search as the research develops.

• Can the marketplace provide the search? If the invention is fairly simple, and there is little or no additional conceptualization to be done, then the most cost-effective strategy is probably to file an inexpensive provisional application to secure patent pending status, and then go out into the marketplace to try to find a licensee or customer. If the product is old, those people will surely say so, and the application can be abandoned. If everyone loves the invention, then it is probably cost-effective to run a more thorough search, and file a formal patent application (utility application or PCT).

Of course, the filing costs and prosecution speed should be taken into account. The out of pocket filing costs for filing a U.S. utility application runs about $2,000 for a large entity (in general, at least 500 employees) and takes about 18-20 months for the applicant to receive the first substantive office action. Small entities pay half that, and under the America Invents Act, micro entities pay only a quarter of the large entity fees for filing and certain other charges. See additional details in Chapter V, section G(1).

Pendencies fluctuate somewhat. As of May 2022 the pendency is around 20 months. Pendencies and other interesting information can be viewed in graphical form at the USPTO Data Visualization Center[19]. To the right is an example of their pendency dashboard.

Filing costs for a PCT (Patent Cooperation Treaty- International application) application through the U.S. receiving office runs about $3,500, and a PCT filing through the International Bureau (where searching is done by the European Patent office) runs about $4,000. But while the out of pocket costs are greater, the searches are faster. Where the PCT is filed with no prior priority claim, the applicant is supposed to receive a search report within 9 months of the filing date, and where the PCT claims priority to an earlier application, the applicant is supposed to receive a search report within 16 months of the filing date of that earlier application.

In deciding on an appropriate search strategy, one should focus on both patent and non-patent materials. In some fields, such as computer science, this is especially critical because a great deal of the prior art never makes it into patent publications. As a result, time and money are wasted on patent applications that have no chance whatsoever of being issued as a valid patent with broad claims.

And yet, such applications are filed all the time. Below is a claim from U.S. 6874084[20] assigned to IBM™ with a priority claim to May 2000.

> 1. A method for creating a secure connection to a server, comprising:
>   within a platform independent applet, initializing a secure socket
>   connection request via HyperText Transport Protocol (HTTP);
>   using a certificate database to authenticate the server; and
>   creating the secure connection between the platform independent applet
>   and the server using HyperText Transport Protocol Secure
>   (HTTPS) if the server is authenticated, wherein the secure
>   connection between the platform independent applet and the server
>   is created without intervention by a Web browser.

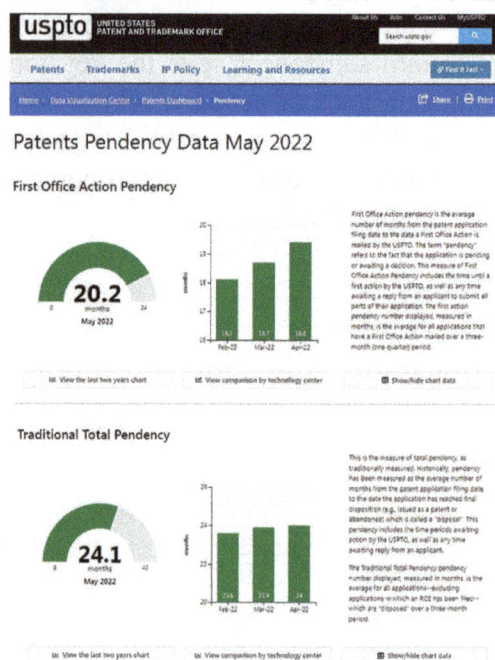

---

19   https://www.uspto.gov/dashboard/patents/
20   U.S. 6874084 (Mar. 2005) "Method and apparatus for establishing a secure communication connection between a java application and secure server"

The patent lists only three U.S. patents references, and no references outside the patent literature. If the patent drafter or the examiner had just spent even a short time looking for references outside the patent literature, the patent would never have been issued. The patent was still in force at the end of in 2015, and one can only hope that IBM won't ever waste anyone's time trying to enforce it.

The Internet is such a treasure trove of information, many people wonder whether they can access historical "snapshots" of web pages to use in prior art searching. It turns out that one can do so through the WayBack Machine.[21]

> **Withdrawn Internet pages can often be accessed using the WayBack Machine**

(3)   Tailor The Searching Effort To The Purpose

The first rule is to tailor the searching effort to the needs of the application. Below is a diagram of a broad patentability search, in which the arrows represent searching efforts going off in many different directions, and the squares represent the patents or other documents being sought. The search here is wasteful because it goes off in way too many directions (lacks focus), and several of the searches go deeper into the field (are much longer) than is necessary.

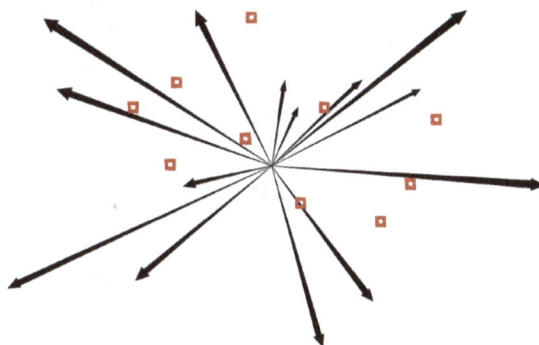

Figure - Wasteful Search

If the goal is to find out whether an idea is worth pursuing, the better approach is to narrow the search. The reason is that the searcher need only find one piece of invalidating prior art to support a conclusion that the invention is old. Drowning in ten feet of water is the same as drowning in 100 feet of water – the person is still dead.

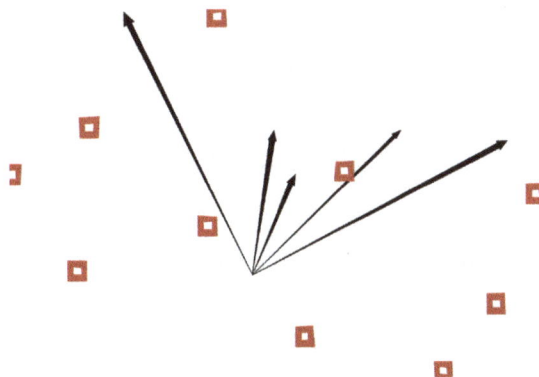

Figure - Sometimes a Simple Search Will Suffice

21   www.archive.org/web/web.php.

(4)   Iterative Searching

Probably the best strategy is to run searches iteratively, i.e. in stages. Start with very specific keywords in a proximity-based system to see if there is an easy match. When searching for a screw with interleaved threads, for example, one should search for a patent where the terms "screw", "inter*", and "thread" are all in the same sentence, or within 10 words of each other. If the searcher finds just what they are looking for, then the search is over. If they don't, then they need to keep broadening the scope (usually by removing keywords from the search) until they find at least a few patents or other prior references that match. This works on paid services such as Lexis™ Total Patent™[22], Delphion™,[23] and Westlaw™,[24] and on some free search engines including Google Patents[25] WebCrawler,[26] FreePatentsOnline,[27] and Patent Lens.[28]

Unfortunately, with Google™ and most of the other free search engines, the only proximity searching available is exact matches, e.g., "cancer treatment" or "brake pads".

Search iteratively, using keywords from one document to find another document

The second step in iterative searching is to examine the documents that were found in the first step, and then use them to refine the keywords. People use a great many terms and phrases to describe the same thing. A sawhorse may be described in one reference as a sawhorse, but in another reference as a cutting or sawing table. Similarly, the Internet may be alternatively described as a global network, or as a package switched network. One should definitely look in each new reference for keywords that the searcher hadn't thought of in the first place. In addition to identifying new words, it may be necessary to search for plural terms as well as singular terms. By properly refining keywords, the searches are both broader (in terms of using more alternatives) and more focused (because the searcher can combine more search terms into a given search).

I filed a patent application several years ago on a searching system that simplifies iterative searching, by providing a user with a concordance of nearby words and phrases.[29]

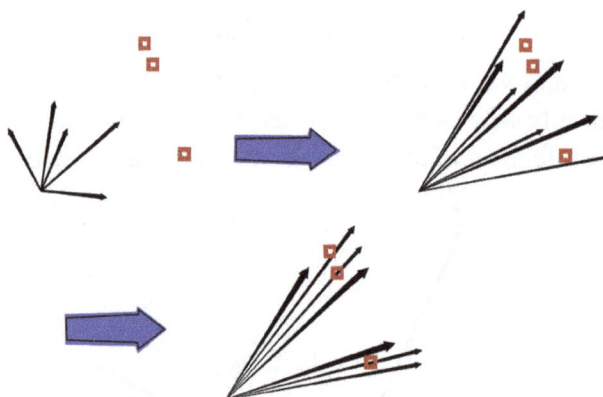

Figure - Iterative Keyword Searching Focuses the Effort

22   www.lexisnexis.com/totalpatent.
23   www.delphion.com.
24   www.westlaw.com.
25   https://patents.google.com/.
26   www.webcrawler.com.
27   www.freepatentsonline.com.
28   https://www.lens.org/
29   U.S. 2007/0219983 (Sept. 2007) " Methods & App. For Facilitating Context Searching".

An alternative to iterative *keyword* searching is iterative *parent/child* searching. Once a searcher finds patents or applications in step one (the parents), they look at all the references cited *in* those patents and applications (the children). That second-generation search will likely widen the catch to at least 40 or 50 references. The next step is to examine all those references to find the closest ones, and then look at children and parents of that second generation of references to find a third generation. Repeat that process until the subsequent searches find only references that were already identified.

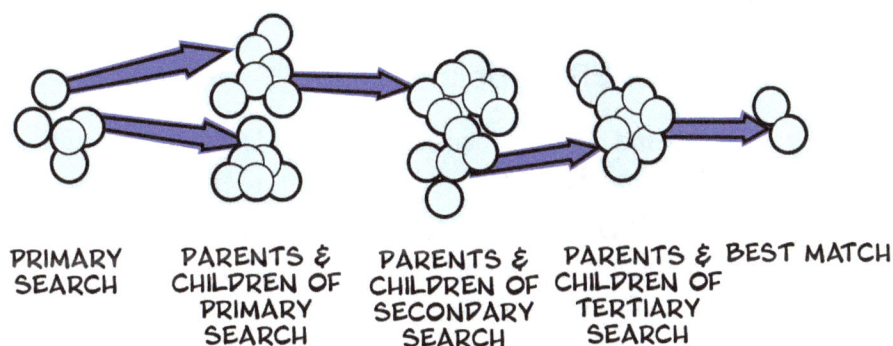

PRIMARY
SEARCH

PARENTS &
CHILDREN OF
PRIMARY
SEARCH

PARENTS &
CHILDREN OF
SECONDARY
SEARCH

PARENTS & BEST MATCH
CHILDREN OF
TERTIARY
SEARCH

Figure - Iterative Parent/Child Searching Is Also Extremely Effective

(5)   Use The Most Cost-Effective Sources For Searching

No matter what level of search is undertaken, and what strategies are decided upon, it is extremely important to choose the *right* information sources. It therefore behooves a prior art searcher to choose the very best search engine for the job, and indeed to use multiple search engines. This section addresses strengths and weaknesses of specific search engines. Additional information is available on the Internet in a well-researched article put out by Cambia.[30]

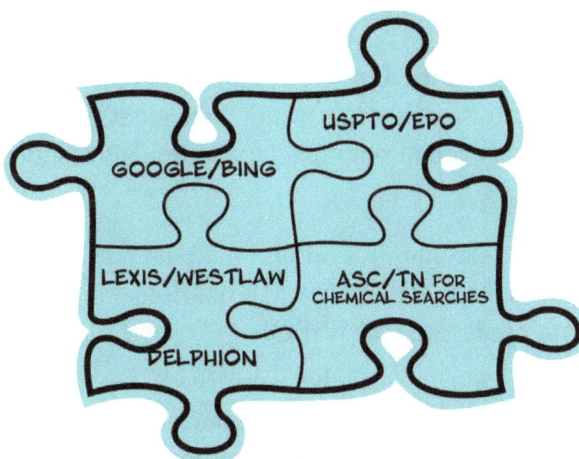

USPTO/EPO

GOOGLE/BING

LEXIS/WESTLAW

ASC/TN FOR
CHEMICAL SEARCHES

DELPHION

Figure - Use The Right Tools For The Search

There are two main criteria for evaluating searches, recall and precision. Recall is the proportion of retrieved documents to relevant documents. A search that missed a large number of relevant documents might have a recall of only 80%. Precision is the proportion of relevant documents to the total number of documents retrieved. A search that includes a large number of "garbage" hits would have a low precision.

30   www.patentlens.net/daisy/patentlens/1558/version/live/part/4/data.

Obviously, a searcher wants a high level of both recall and precision, but increasing one of the metrics tends to decrease the other. It does little good for a search to capture every relevant item if the results set has tens of thousands of entries. The key is to use a search engine that balances recall and precision in an appropriate manner, which means extensive use of Boolean logic, stemming, and user-definable proximity searching. Very sophisticated systems also rank the results using various vector space models, such as latent semantic analysis and Cluster Analysis, and inference models. There are numerous choices, in both free and subscription services, that provide these features.

(6)   Searching For EPO Applications

The EPO (and several other countries and regions) focus allowability decisions on whether the claimed invention recites a novel and non-obvious "technical effect".[31]

What does that mean? Basically, the EPO uses a problem/solution approach to patentability. The examiner will try to identify the key problem(s) that the inventor is trying to overcome (which *are* hopefully set forth in the Specification), and will then search for the *single document* that is the most promising starting point for an obviousness determination leading to the claimed invention. For example, if the claimed invention is a novel composition of steel, the examiner is most likely to focus on the alleged benefit(s) of the new composition, (e.g., greater rust resistance or perhaps greater tensile strength) and search for the closest prior art reference that addresses those characteristics. If the technical effect (benefit) is known in the same or neighboring field for the same component, then that reference is also likely to be used in the patentability analysis.

The bottom line is that searches for EPO patentability need to focus on technical effect. Mere keyword searches for the components or steps of the claims of an application are likely to miss the very references deemed most relevant by the EPO examiner.

C)   Free Patent Databases

- Proximity Searching

All of the widely used Internet search engines, Google ™, Bing™, and Yahoo!™ support *inherent* proximity search using quotes around two or more search terms, (e.g., "black cat"). Unfortunately, while that is an effective good way of narrowing excessively broad searches, it also tends to render the search under-inclusive.

- Google Patents

Google™ Patents[32] provides free text searching for all U.S. patents and published applications, as well as those for Canada, China, European Patent Office (EPO), Germany, Japan, and WIPO.

Google has an excellent pdf of searching tips and tricks

For the most part the service is good, although there are numerous text errors since the text apparently comes from machine optical character recognition of the USPTO images. One big advantage over many other free web sites is that Google Patents allows narrowing of searches using the field codes: priority date,

---

31   Topics relating to "technical effect" are discussed at much greater length in the third Patent Shock book, Tips and Tricks.
32   https://patents.google.com/

assignee, inventor, patent office, language, filing status, citing patent, and Cooperative Patent Classification (CPC) codes.

There are several sites that provide tips and tricks for searching Google.[33] One interesting (but so far not terribly useful) feature is Google's Find Prior Art button, which is accessible from its Google Patents interface.

Perhaps the easiest *explicit* proximity searches use the NEAR and AROUND operators. Yahoo! supports an undocumented NEAR operator (keyword1 NEAR keyword2), and Bing goes one better by permitting user definition of what is meant by NEAR. The syntax is keyword1 near:n keyword2 where n is the number of maximum separating words. Google supports a similar operator, AROUND(#). The World International Patent Office (WIPO) search engine[34] supports both explicit word distances, but uses a different syntax. "electric car"~10 searches for documents where "electric" is within 10 words of "car".

Google and Yahoo! both offer ordered searching using the asterisk character "*" as a wildcard. In Google the asterisk matches one or more words, while in Yahoo! each asterisk matches exactly one word. WIPO supports both single character wildcard search use the "?" symbol, and multiple character wildcard search use the "*" symbol.

- CAMBIA PatentLens

Probably the best free search service is that provided by CAMBIA™ PatentLens™[35]. The system can search U.S. patents and published applications, EPO (European Patent Office) publications, the life sciences portion of WIPO publications, EPO patents, and Australian patents (beginning 2007), all in single search. The system provides ranking, automatic stemming, segment searching, (title, abstract, inventor, applicant, agent, references, description, and claims), and proximity searching using the "near/" connector. Searchers can retrieve documents in full text or as .pdf files. One of the very best features of PatentLens is that it highlights the search terms within the text files. This is extremely useful for quickly ruling in or ruling out the relevance of a particular document.

One of the drawbacks of PatentLens is that it can choke on complex searches, reporting "Wild Card Limit Exceeded". For such searches, one probably has to use Delphion or one of the other paid subscription services.

- USPTO Website

The USPTO website[36] is also a fairly good place to start. The search engine is easy to use, with both the quick-search and the advanced-search interfaces. Unfortunately, the downloading of images on the USPTO website is awkward and unnecessarily time consuming, and patents from 1790 through 1975 are searchable on the USPTO site only by Patent Number and Current U.S. Classification). The website of the U.S. patent office is reasonably convenient for quick searches, and is very convenient for copying full text into a word processing document. One can view and download prosecution history documents through the Public PAIR site.[37]

One of the best ways to use the USPTO database is to combine keyword searching with classification searching. Wikipedia has a decent summary[38] of the Cooperative Patent Classification (CPC) that has been used since January 1, 2013. The patent office provides instructions, but even with the instructions the system is clumsy to use.[39]

---

33   https://www.digitaltrends.com/computing/the-35-best-google-search-tips-and-tricks/

34   https://patentscope.wipo.int/search/en/help/querySyntaxHelp.jsf.

35   www.lens.org/lens/.

36   www.uspto.gov.

37   http://portal.uspto.gov/pair/PublicPair.

38   https://en.wikipedia.org/wiki/United_States_Patent_Classification

39   http://www.uspto.gov/patents-application-process/patent-search/understanding-patent-classifications/help
How to use the Patent Classification (OPC) site

- Espace (European Patent Office)

Another good free source for patent searching is the European patent office.[40] The website includes access to US, European patents and applications, as well as PCT (WIPO) applications, but does not support proximity searching. The site also includes numerous links to Japanese and other government patent sources. One can view and download patents and patent applications through the main search site[41], and publications through the European Publication Server.[42] To download patent prosecution history documents you need to use the Register.[43] Once you find the right application or patent, click on the "All Documents" tab in the left menu to see links to available documents, click the boxes designating the items you want to see, and then click on the "▼ Selected documents" to download.

- WIPO (World Intellectual Property Office)

The WIPO site[44] has a very good search engine that supports proximity searching, wildcards, and so forth. The site is available in many different languages, and includes documents from all of the large patent offices. Also on the plus side, WIPO provides a natural language interface[45], and natural language expansion[46].

- PatentInformatics (Sequence Searching)

PatentInformatics™ provides database sequence searching for nucleic and amino acids.[47] The company also provides a service for producing genealogy trees of patents, and its own general patent searching database derived from USPTO, EPO and other public databases.

- The Dark Web

Although most people don't know it, the portion of the web you can search using Google and other common search engines is only a small fraction of the Internet. Google, for example, is said to have indexed more than 30 trillion web pages, but that is estimated to be much less than 1% of the total web pages available. To search the invisible web you need to use specialty search engines such as the following: Yippy, Librarians' Internet Index, or Direct Search.[48] Historical web pages are available through the WayBack Machine.[49]

D) Subscription Services

- Lexis™ TotalPatent™

TotalPatent™ is probably the best pay service currently available, and the one we use the most at Fish IP Law, LLP. TotalPatent can search the full text databases of more than 25 countries or regions, including machine translations of non-English filings, all in the same search. TotalPatent supports complicated Boolean logic, as well as semantic logic (where, for example, a search for "elephant" could pick up references containing "pachyderm" but not "elephant"). One huge advantage of Total Patent is that the system can show windows of text around the search terms, thus

> **TotalPatent is likely the best subscription patentability search tool**

---

40 www.epo.org.
41 http://worldwide.espacenet.com/?locale=en
42 https://data.epo.org/publication-server/?lg=en
43 https://register.epo.org/advancedSearch?lng=en.
44 www.wipo.int/ipdl/en.
45 https://www3.wipo.int/ipccat/.
46 https://patentscope.wipo.int/search/en/clir/clir.jsf?new=true.
47 http://www.patinformatics.com/
48 http://yippy.com/; www.ipl.org/;
49 www.archive.org/index.php.

obviating the need to open individual documents to see the context. Another huge benefit is that one can download specific segments (patent number, title, date, priority date, claim language, etc) for a large number of patents. The downloaded information can then be searched and manipulated off-line using a word processing program. Still another benefit is that PDF files downloaded from TotalPatent are already optical character recognized. TotalPatent has a no-cost-added alert service.

- Delphion (formerly the IBM Intellectual Property Network)

Delphion™[50] does all the basics, but is not so sophisticated as TotalPatent. Delphion can concurrently search U.S. Patents, European Patents, Patent abstracts of Japan, PCT Patents, and U.K. patents, can access World Patents Index (WPI) titles and other information, can secure patent family listings. Delphion can also graphically summarize large sets of data. Delphion does allow proximity searching, which can be done using the "near" connector. For example, one can find instances of "lipofuscin" within five words of "deanol" by typing "lipofuscin <near/5> deanol". Delphion's ranking program (results scoring) is excellent, and greatly facilitates searching.

- Derwent WPI (General, Chemical & Sequence Searching)

Derwent™ World Patent Index™ is a collection of value-added databases. They have a team of 350 editors that assess, classify and index patents and applications from 41 patent-issuing authorities around the world. Not only is the database huge, (over 31 million patent documents in their databases), but every document is classified according to the Derwent classification system, and the subject matter has been re-abstracted into a standard format that rationalizes the often obscure language used by patent applicants. That method goes a long way towards minimizing differences in terminology employed by different patent drafters.

Other significant benefits are that WPI provides patent family listings, on-going search capability, and even statistics on patent issuances by subject matter, inventor, assignee, and so forth. The biggest drawback is high expense. The service charges a per-record charge for accessed data. There are several strategies for minimizing those charges, and the customer service people are extremely helpful in assisting users to achieve cost-effective searching. But the cost can still be quite high.

Derwent's Merged Markush Service™ (also called Markush DARC) allows chemical structure searches from 1987 onwards. Note that STN and CAS (see below) provide chemical structure searching from the early 1900s. STN/Derwent's GENESEQ provides sequence searching for nucleic and amino acids.

> **Patentability searching of chemical compounds requires special search tools**

Derwent databases are available through Delphion, Dialog™, Orbit™, STN™, and Westlaw™, and possibly other sources, but almost always at an added cost. Delphion does provide free the Derwent titles as part of its standard subscription service.

- STN (General, Chemical & Sequence Searching)

STN™[51] relies upon databases of the Chemical Abstracts Society (CAS) to provide what is probably the most comprehensive chemical searching available. Use of the system, however, does require considerable training, and searches can run many thousands of dollars. Those who want the benefits of STN should run their searches through Science IP,[52] which is run by CAS.

Another CAS option is STNeasy™ (www.stneasy.com). STNeasy focuses on chemistry and related fields, but accommodates keyword searches. The system charges on a transactional basis (about $2 per search), but

---

50   www.delphion.com.

51   www.cas.org/stn.html.

52   https://www.cas.org/solutions/cas-custom-services/ip-services.

viewing the titles of references is free, and viewing the abstracts is only about $4 - $7 each. Full-text articles cost as much as they would elsewhere, about $25 - $40 each.

Still another CAS option is SciFinder™[53]. SciFinder is an extremely powerful tool that provides access to possibly the world's largest collection of biochemical, chemical, chemical engineering, medical, and other related information. The search engine is first rate, there are no extra charges for viewing abstracts, and SciFinder includes marvelous graphical tools for summarizing large sets of references. The only real drawback is that one cannot "pay as you go". Subscribers must purchase a block of "tasks" for several thousand dollars, and then use up those tasks within one year. Fortunately, one can access the SciFinder resources through ScienceIP. That service uses professional, full time researchers to run searches against all available databases.

As noted above, STN and Derwent collectively provide sequence searching for nucleic and amino acids through their GENESEQ databases.

- SureChem™ (Chemical Searching)

SureChem™[54] allows users to find chemical structures in patents, journal articles and other text documents using chemical names (CAS, IUPAC, common, SMILES) to chemical structures. The names are automatically translated into chemical structures using thesauri, and then the chemical structures are used to search structure databases.

SureChem currently gives users access to USPTO full-text patent documents and MEDLINE journal abstracts. The website advises, that additional patent data, including European and Japanese patents, WO applications and New Zealand and Australian patents, will be added in coming months. There is also a version of SureChem (SureChem Enterprise™) that allows users to search their in-house databases.

- NERAC (Patent Databases And Journals)

Searching full text journal articles, newspapers and other publications can be frightfully expensive. One of the most cost-effective ways to do so is NERAC.[55] For a fixed cost of (as low as) a few thousand dollars per year, NERAC provides unlimited access to tens of thousands of publications, as well as worldwide patents and published applications. Searches against the databases cannot be performed directly by NERAC customers, but instead are performed by professionals with particular experience in different technical fields. Thus, a pharmaceutical search may well be performed by someone with an advanced degree in microbiology or biochemistry. Moreover, the person doing the search is available by telephone or email to discuss search strategy, and to fine-tune subsequent searches. Turnaround is usually a day or so, although NERAC is very good at handling emergency searches. NERAC is also wonderful for on-going searches through their on-line TechTrak™ facility.

E) Patent Alerts

The various pay services, (TotalPatent, Delphion, Westlaw, etc) all offer provisions for storing searches, and running them periodically. In most cases, Alerts are included in the monthly subscription fee, but do be careful. Some services charge per Alert.

There don't seem to be any robust, truly free patent alert services, although PatentAlert™[56] does provide alerts in several specific fields of technology.

---

53 https://www.cas.org/solutions/cas-scifinder-discovery-platform/cas-scifinder
54 https://www.surechembl.org/search/
55 www.nerac.com.
56 www.patentalert.com.

Another good choice is Automated PAIR Alerts from Cardinal IP.[57] There is no long term subscription requirement, and the fee is only $10 per month per Alert.

F)   Professional Searching Services

Our office almost never relies on the results of outside searching services for run-of-the-mill prior art searches. For one thing, about 20% of the searches we run from Fish IP Law, LLP result in a critical "hit" within about 10 minutes. In those instances it seems silly to charge the client $750 or more for using an outside service. In other instances, the search justifies the cost, but then we lose out on insights that would have come from doing the search ourselves. Indeed, much of the benefit of searching lies in gaining ideas about how the claims of a new application can be written to take advantage of loopholes in the prior art. Use of an outside searching service eliminates that benefit entirely.

We do use outside services to supplement our own searches, including for example, GreyB Services[58] in India and Cardinal IP in the U.S.[59].

There are several contingency fee searching services, including Research Wire.[60] The typical plan charges several thousand dollars if anticipatory / invalidating prior art is found for independent claims, with the charge reduced to a much smaller base fee if such art is not found.

For an inventor who is drafting and filing his own patent application, perhaps the best thing is to run their own preliminary searches, and then if the invention still seems patentable, take the invention to a patent attorney or agent for further searching. Just remember, that if the attorney saves you money by finding critical prior art, you still need to pay for the searching.

G)   Don't Allow Searching Costs To Get Out Of Hand

Many patent firms and independent searching services charge a standard, fixed fee (usually about $750 - $1500) for patentability searching. That makes sense from a marketing standpoint, but a one-size-fits-all standard fee doesn't work well across completely different technologies. Some inventions are simple to search, while others are notoriously expensive to search. A $750 fee, for example, overcharges for the simple searches

---

57   www.cardinal-ip.com.

58   www.GreyB.com.

59   www.cardinal-ip.com.

60   ResearchWire Knowledge Solutions, New Mumbai-400706, India, www.researchwire.in.

and provides too little funding to adequately run complicated searches. In some instances Fish IP Law, LLP doesn't charge anything for searching, because we find invalidating prior art while we're on the phone with a potential new client.

At the high end, patentability searching can run many thousands of dollars because of the databases used. For example, chemical inventions often require searching of chemical structures (as opposed to merely chemical names). There are only a few such databases available, and they can charge a small fortune. Searches performed according to the USPTO patent search templates[61] require applicants to search non-patent literature, which is often available only through Dialog.[62]

It is counterintuitive, but patentability searches can also be expensive for simple inventions directed to common items. Novel baby bottle designs, improvements to doorknob latches, new pens and pencils, and other very common consumer items can be notoriously difficult to search. Such inventions usually have an enormous amount of prior art, and it is extremely time consuming to sift through that much material. Simple inventions are also usually described with common language, so that a word search on a typical database can yield tens of thousands of hits.

Still further, simple inventions can be difficult to search because the relevant products might never be described in patents or applications. A good search in those cases requires searching of non-patent literature, including for example newspaper and journal articles, and advertising materials. For simple consumer products, we often search catalogs on the Internet. Often an "invention" is already in the Hammacher Schlemmer™ catalog!

Patent Beast   © FISH 2006

H)   U.S. And International Classification Systems

Searching by technology area can be a double-edged sword. On the one hand, such searches can be extremely helpful in gaining a general background on the technology in a field, and in limiting on-going alert searches. On the other hand, the fact that any given technology often spans many classes and subclasses can be extremely misleading.

Admittedly, the USPTO has made a valiant effort to simplify classification, and render it accessible to ordinary users. The best place to start is the USPTO classifications web page,[63] which provides an overview of the

61   https://pdf.usaid.gov/pdf_docs/PA00WFQ8.pdf
62   www.dialog.com/.
63   https://www.uspto.gov/web/patents/classification/selectnumwithtitle.htm.

system as well as detailed instructions. The USPTO also has a page with a list of helpful links about searching, including search strategies and resources.[64] These would likely be the same steps and resources a patent examiner would use.

The classification system is getting better all the time. Back in 2013 the patent office announced the formal launch of the Cooperative Patent Classification (CPC) system, a global classification system for patent documents. According to the press release, "CPC is the product of a joint partnership between the USPTO and the EPO to develop a common, internationally compatible classification system for technical documents used in the patent granting process that incorporates the best classification practices from both offices. It will be used by the USPTO and more than 45 patent offices – a user community totaling more than 20,000 patent examiners – all sharing the same classifications helping to establish the CPC as an international standard."

64   https://www.uspto.gov/patents/search

Chapter III - General Guidelines for Drafting Patent Applications

It is said that only about 60% of U.S. patent applications make it through the patent office to become patents, only about 15% of the issued patents are ever commercialized, and less than 50% of the commercialized patents ever make back the money that went to the patent attorneys or agents. If those statistics are correct, only a few percent of U.S. patent applications are moneymakers for their inventors!

Naturally, patent attorneys give all sorts of excuses for that dismal record. Sometimes the excuses are even valid. Some patent applications have no value because they must be filed well before anyone knows if the technology is worth anything. In the pharmaceutical field, for example, it is commonplace to write patents on drug compounds that have never been tested in clinical trials. In those instances, the patent applications operate as insurance policies, protecting the value of the work done. The applications may also have a defensive value, securing intellectual property before a competitor grabs the same property.

In other instances, however, the time and money spent on patenting is simply *wasted*. We see this all the time. An inventor pays someone ten, twenty or even thirty thousand dollars or more at another firm to obtain a patent, and then comes into our office wanting to sue an alleged infringer. When we look at the patent, we discover that the broadest independent claim (usually claim 1) is 30 - 50 lines long. Right away we suspect there is a problem. Long claims have lots of limitations, and are consequently almost always full of holes. Even if an infringer is blatantly producing a product that falls within the scope of one

> **In patenting, shorter claims are usually much better than longer claims**

of the claims, it is probably impractical to pursue an infringement action through trial on such narrow claims. At the end of the day, the infringer can usually change his product in any of several minor ways to avoid infringement. It's very sad to have to explain to an inventor that all he bought with his hard-earned money was a patent that is little more than a nice wall hanging.

Some of these sad situations occur when patent counsel accepts cases without regard to how broadly the subject matter can be claimed. When I started working as a patent attorney, I was told that patent attorneys have insufficient business knowledge to judge the potential value of a technology. If the search identified problematic prior art, then our job was simply to write the best patent that could be written in view of the prior art, even if I was fairly sure that the coverage would be exceedingly narrow. I disagreed with that approach then, and I disagree with it now. From my perspective, our responsibility as patent counsel is to help our clients decide which technologies to pursue as patent applications, and which to jettison.

A) Get Your Patent Application On File Early

In all or substantially all countries outside the Unites States, priority of invention is determined on a "first to file" basis, i.e. whoever gets to the patent office first gets the patent. That has been the rule for patent applications since 2013.

But previously, the USPTO used a different system based upon a "first to invent" basis. As one might imagine, that system caused all manner of confusion with respect to conception[65], reduction to practice[66], diligence[67], and other issues.

Perhaps surprisingly, the change in law did not completely eliminate issues relating to priority, since one still has to analyze priority in terms of overlapping claims. The first-to-file provision leaves an opening for parties to argue priority because in very limited circumstances (i.e., where an inventor discloses an invention, and another person files on substantially identical subject matter before the inventor files an application). Other issues arise because the first-to-file system maintains a one-year grace period for disclosures made by the inventor or another who obtained the inventive subject matter from the inventor.

The critical point, however, is that now *more than ever*, an inventor should get his application on file as soon

> **The USPTO now uses a first-to-file system, a race to the patent office!**

as possible. If funds are tight, or various technical aspects are still being worked out, that might mean filing one or more provisional applications, discussed below. A utility application can claim priority to any number of provisionals (provisional patent applications) filed within one year of the utility application filing date. If the inventor is worried about disclosing the idea when the application is published at 18 months, then the application can be filed with a petition for non-publication. Just get something on file.

---

65   See 35 U.S.C. § 102(g) (in determining priority "there shall be considered... the reasonable diligence of one who was first to conceive and last to reduce to practice, from a time prior to conception by the other"); *Coleman v, Dines*, 754 F.2d 353 (Fed. Cir. 1985); *Sewall v. Walters*, 21 F.3d 411 (Fed. Cir. 1994)

66   *Medichem, S.A. v. Rolabo, S.L.*, 2006 U.S. App. LEXIS 2653 at 28 (Fed Cir. Feb. 3 2006)

67   *Mahurkar v. C.R. Bard, Inc.*, 79 F.3d 1572, 1578 (Fed. Cir. 1996) (a party that is first to conceive but second to reduce to practice "must demonstrate reasonable diligence toward reduction to practice")

B) Good Versus Bad Patents

Good or bad? Strong or weak? Broad or narrow? What makes a good paten t? The classic definition of a good patent is one that claims an invention as broadly as possible. That definition is fine as far as it goes. But it is deficient because it glosses over both of the fundamental steps in drafting a good patent, namely: (a) identifying what the "invention" is relative to the prior art and the marketplace; and (b) describing the "invention" in a manner that best serves the purposes of the particular client.

Identifying the "invention" in view of the prior art and the marketplace is not necessarily an easy task. Consider, for example, the pop-tops currently found on soda, beer, and other cans. Many years ago, soda and beer cans had pop-tops that actually popped off. The pieces that came off were usually quite sharp at the edges, and tended to cause injuries. The removed pieces also tended to find their way into lakes and streams where they damaged fish and other animals. When the first person came up with the idea of a pop-top that didn't pop off, he almost certainly had a particular mechanism in mind. But the real contribution to the field, the one having commercial significance, was much more than any particular mechanism, or even a set of mechanisms. The "invention" was the *basic idea* of keeping a pop-top on a can, and the invention should have been claimed accordingly.

Instead, *Simpson et al.* (Nov. 1965) claimed their invention with numerous unnecessary limitations, including that the pull-tab had to have a "shallow winged cross section". That was completely unnecessary.

> 1. A sheet metal pull tab particularly adapted for attachment to a tearable container portion, said pull tab being of a ***shallow winged channel cross section*** and including a web having sides and ends....

Harvey et al. (Dec. 1965), unnecessarily claimed pop-tops that had both pouring and vent openings:

> 1. A can and opener for establishing spaced pouring and vent openings therein, and including:
>   (a) a can having an imperforate wall with spaced ***predetermined weakened pouring and vent areas*** thereon;
>   (b) and an opener overlying the ....

Even *Brown et al.* (Oct. 1967), who claimed what became the modern pull-tab, recited their invention with unnecessary limitations as to inner and outer stiffening beads:

> 1. A tab for attachment to a tear strip in a wall of a container..., comprising:
>   a one-piece member of sheet material...,
>   said member having an extending portion for attachment to the tear strip, inner and outer edges of said member being turned to form ***stiffening inner and outer beads extending around at least half of the circumference of the ringlike portion of the member,***

Since the insight that really triggered public acceptance of pop-top cans was the stiffened ringlike pull member, the broadest claim should have read "a pop-top can having a stiffened ringlike pull member". That was the inventive concept.

The difference in approach between claiming embodiments and claiming concepts can be appreciated by comparing the two diagrams immediately below. In both cases, the process of patenting is represented by two opposing funnels. In the "Bad Patent" diagram below, the inventor provides all sorts of ideas (leftmost squiggly lines) on how to solve a particular problem.

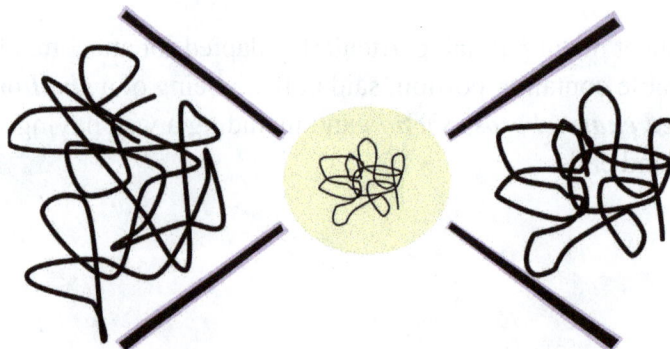

Figure - Symbolic drawing Of A Bad Patent

As represented by the left-hand funnel, a patent attorney or agent reduces the inventor's disclosure to a logical set of instructions and examples. In the right-hand funnel, the patent counsel then fluffs out those instructions and examples to cover multiple options. Sounds good, but in that scenario the counsel is merely charging a lot of money for rewriting the inventor's disclosure.

In the "Good Patent" diagram below, the inventor still provides a disclosure as to how they solved a particular problem. But the patent counsel extracts from that disclosure a critical set of three or four elements that distinguish over the prior art (designated in bold on the left portion of the diagram). Those elements are then expanded into all possible choices. Reduction of the "invention" to its core elements focuses on the concept of the invention, not its implementation. It is precisely this level of reductionist thinking that is so difficult to do, and so important to filing strong patent claims.

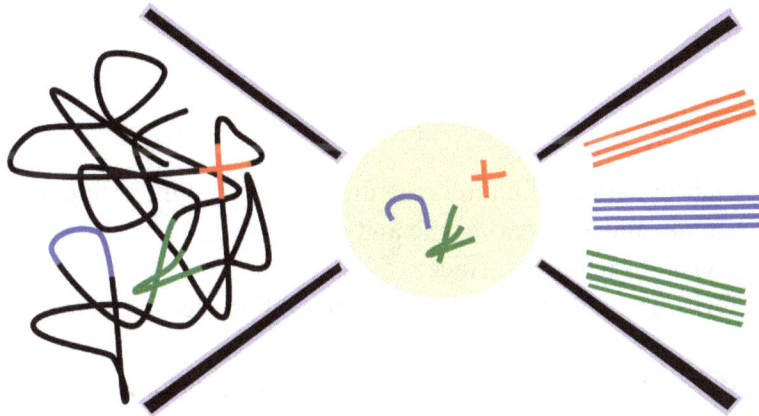

Figure - Symbolic drawing Of A Good Patent

A well-written patent claim also takes into account the needs of the inventor vis-à-vis the marketplace. Among other things, patent counsel should weigh (a) the likely cost of lengthy arguments during the patent prosecution process to achieve the greatest possible coverage against (b) the benefit of narrower claims that might still be "good enough" to keep the competition at bay. Later sections of this book discuss numerous strategies for doing just that, including avoidance of multiple independent claims to preclude restriction requirements (the outgoing funnel in the diagram). At this introductory stage of the book, the main point is that good patenting is a lot more than simply securing the broadest possible coverage on what the inventor thinks is the invention. A good patent means that the patent counsel took the time to see through the applicant's disclosure to the core, commercially relevant, ideas.

Above all, remember that the patent counsel's task is much more than just describing and claiming what the inventor thinks he invented. He should also be describing and claiming all that is inherent in that "invention". To do this, he must thoroughly understand how the invention differs from the prior art, and devise all possible ways of embodying that difference. It often takes several hours to understand where the inventive concept lies, and then to figure out all the alternatives. The bottom line is that the invention is almost always broader than the inventor thinks it is.

> **Patent counsel should claim all that is inherent in that "invention", not just preferred embodiments**

C) Ways To Distinguish Good Patents From Bad Patents

The easiest way to distinguish good patents from bad is to focus on the length and number of claims. Well-drafted patents tend to have claims that are short, and few in number.

(1)   "Bad" Patents Tend To Have Long Claims

Consider the following claim from U.S. 4875144. The invention seems to be a good one, the use of fiber optics to create multiple images in a shirt or other fabric. But the first claim is way too long, and contains numerous unnecessary elements.

> 1. A fabric with an illuminated animated display including a first frame and a second frame and comprising:
>
>   (A) a fabric outer surface;
>   (B) a first plurality of flexible optical fibers each having a first end a second end;
>   (C) a second plurality of flexible optical fibers each having a first end and a second end;
>   (D) said first plurality of optical fibers *gathered into a first bundle*;
>   (E) said second plurality of optical fibers *gathered into a second bundle*;
>   (F) a portion of said second ends of said first bundle of optical fibers secured to said fabric and extending to said fabric outer surface to form at least a portion of said first and second frames of said display;
>   (G) a portion of said second ends of said second bundle of optical fibers secured to said fabric and extending to said fabric outer surface to form at least a portion of said second frame of said display;
>   (H) *a first light source* means adjacent said first ends of said first bundle of optical fibers to emit light to said first ends and through said fibers to sequentially illuminate said second ends forming at least a portion of said first and second frames of said display on said fabric outer surface;

> (I) *a second light source* means adjacent said first ends
> of said second bundle of optical fibers to emit
> light to said first ends and through said fibers
> to sequentially illuminate said second ends forming
> at least a portion of said second frame of said
> display on said fabric outer surface to *create the*
> *appearance of animation* of said display.

Just for starters, why are there limitations as to the fibers being gathered into first and second bundles? A competitor could readily circumvent that claim by merely aligning the fibers in a flat connector rather than in a bundle. Second, the light sources are listed as elements of the fabric. There is no justification for that limitation. The light sources could easily be external to the fabric. Third, as disclosed in the title, the invention relates to a display that "changes". There is no need to limit the invention to displays in which the changes create the appearance of animation.

U.S. 5445073[68] provides another good example of poorly drafted claims. Claim 1 recites:

> 1. An apparatus for cooking potato pieces by heated air
> comprising:
>   a housing; a cooking chamber base within said
> housing, said cooking chamber base being
>   in the shape of an *inverted frustum of a*
>   *cone* with its larger diameter on top, said
>   *chamber being open at the top and bottom*;
>   a removable air permeable *basket in the shape of*
>   *an inverted frustum* of a cone similar in
>   shape to said cooking chamber, with said
>   basket bottom outside diameter almost
>   equal to inside bottom *diameter* of cooking
>   chamber base; said basket having a *screen*
>   *bottom* and a *removable screen cover on*
>   *top*;
>   a *means for heating air, a means for blowing*
>   *heated air* upwardly through said cooking
>   chamber base and said screened basket to
>   fluidize potato pieces in [the] basket.

This claim is very weak. Why limit the cooking chamber to having the shape of an inverted frustum of a cone? A competitor could have a four or five-sided funnel just as well. Further on in that same section the claim recites openings at the top and bottom. Those limitations are completely unnecessary for allowance, and are

---

68   U.S. 5445073 (Aug. 1995) "Apparatus and process for cooking potatoes"

therefore superfluous. The next section goes on to recite that the basket has the same shape as the cooking chamber. So what? Unless that limitation is necessary for allowability, it should be omitted from the claim. The reference to "diameter" is problematic because it once again forces the reader to focus on the funnel as being round. A multi-sided funnel, or even an oblong funnel, would have a perimeter without having a diameter. The references to "screen bottom" and "removable screen top" are also superfluous. The use of means-plus-function language in the third paragraph is just inexcusable. Means-plus-function limitations are so unnecessarily narrowing, that in many instances their use borders on malpractice. Here, the entire third section should have been replaced with the language "a hot air source". The claim should have been worded as follows:

> 1. An apparatus for cooking potato pieces comprising: a housing that contains a plurality of potato pieces, and a hot air source cooperating with the housing to provide an upwardly flowing heated air stream in which air velocities are sufficient to suspend or fluidize the potato pieces and keep them separated from each other during cooking.

Now compare the poorly worded claims of the fabric and potatoes patents (discussed above) with those of U.S. 6681897 (Jan. 2004) "Apparatus for supporting automotive tires" set forth below. In this latter case there are only five claims, and claim 1 is both short and easy to understand. That brevity indicates that the attorney has done the heavy mental lifting required to clearly identify and recite the improvement over the prior art. Such claims tend to be both strong and defensible.

> 1. A method for temporarily retaining a vehicle wheel, comprising the steps of:
>   elevating a vehicle on an automotive hoist so that a
>   support arm disposed on the hoist is at about the
>   same height as a wheel of the vehicle;
>   removing the wheel from the vehicle; placing the wheel
>   on the support arm;
>   removing the wheel from the support arm substantially
>   without bending over; and
>   reinstalling the wheel onto the vehicle.

Patent Beast   © FISH 2010

MY PREVIOUS ATTORNEY WROTE REALLY LONG CLAIMS.

WHY DON'T YOU DO THAT?

YOUR PREVIOUS ATTORNEY IS AN IDIOT.

(2)   "Bad" Patents Tend To Have A Surfeit Of Claims

Well-written patents usually have fewer claims than poorly written patents. The reason is that in order to claim the invention concisely, the attorney needs to do the difficult work of figuring out what the invention really is. It turns out that twenty claims usually suffice, which is, by the way, the number of claims allowed by the USPTO before tacking on excess claim fees. Indeed, even though patent applications often are filed with many claims, they tend to issue with far fewer claims than were originally filed. According to one study, almost 75 percent of patents issued with 20 claims or less, and that almost no patents issued with more than 40 claims.

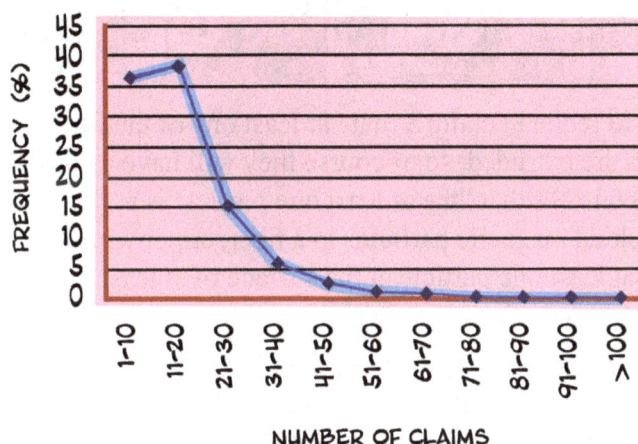

Figure - Number Of Claims In Issued U.S. Patents (2007)

There are innumerable examples of patents with too many claims. For example, U.S. 6669389 (Dec. 2003), "Device for applying a product and method for manufacturing device" for example, has more than 200 claims. Claim 1 is quite succinct, but there are just way too many claims.

1. A device for applying a make-up product, the device comprising:
  an applicator element comprising a plurality of fibers,
  wherein the applicator element is configured to apply
    a make-up product, and
  wherein at least one of the fibers comprises at least one
    particle configured to generate a magnetic field.
3. The device of claim 1, wherein at least one of the fibers has a cross-section that is substantially constant.

11. The device of claim 1, wherein the at least one particle is at the surface of the at least one fiber.

After all, is it really necessary to recite in claim 3 that "at least one of the fibers has a cross-section that is substantially constant"? The fibers are extruded, so of course they will have a constant cross-section. Similarly, is it really necessary to recite in claim 11 that "the at least one particle is at the surface of the at least one fiber"? There are only two ways to include magnetic particles in a fiber, either within the fiber or on the surface of the fiber. Either way there will be at least one particle at the surface of at least one of the fibers. Many of the other 203 claims are similar; just a colossal waste of paper.

Of course, not everyone agrees that patent applications should have a relatively small number of claims. U.S. 6684189 (Jan. 2004) for "apparatus and method using front-end network gateways and search criteria for efficient quoting at a remote location" has 887 claims. U.S. 6708385 (March 2004) for "Flexible manufacturing systems and methods" has 694 claims.

D)　The Structure Of A Patent Application

Patent applications are typically divided into the following sections: title; priority statement; background; summary; brief description of the drawing; detailed description; claims; abstract, and drawing. Each of those sections is discussed below, in the order in which they should be drafted.

Patent attorneys and agent sometimes argue over whether the specification or the claims should be written first. *There can be no reasonable argument on this; the claims should be written first.* The main reason is that whoever is drafting the application needs to understand what the invention is before they can properly describe the preferred embodiments from the most beneficial perspective. From a patent perspective, an "invention" is whatever is claimed as the invention, and often has precious little to do with what the inventor considers to be the invention. Consider the poorly worded claim 1 from U.S. 5509592.[69]

> 1. A new outboard motor carrier for ...comprising:
>   an L-shaped support...;
>   a bolt extending through each of the plurality of bolt
>   holes...;
>   attachment means for an upper safety chain...
>   attachment means for a lower safety chain... ;
>   motor receiving means... ;
>   locking means...
>   an upper safety... ; and
>   a lower safety....

69　U.S. 5509592 (Apr. 1996) "Outboard motor carrier for vehicles"

This claim is just terrible. For starters, the claim is 577 words long, extending more than an entire column in the printed patent. Second, the invention is apparently a bracket for supporting an outboard motor, where the bracket fits into the sleeve of a trailer hitch. Everything else in the claim is irrelevant to the point of novelty, and should have been eliminated during drafting. This application bears all the hallmarks of the specification having been first.

In addition to producing much higher quality work, drafting the claims first saves a lot of money. When the claims are written first, the drafter knows exactly what to focus upon, and merely expounds on the relatively small

> **Claims should be drafted prior to drafting the specification to insure that the claims are properly supported**

number of elements in the claim. If it goes the other way, and the specification is written first, then whoever is drafting the application may have only a poorly developed idea of what is important, and so winds up describing all sorts of irrelevant elements in tremendous detail, out of fear that something critical will be omitted. No wonder the page count in some law offices often rises to 100 pages or more (all of which are usually charged to the patentee on an hourly basis of somewhere between US$ 300 and US$ 700 per hour).

Writing the specification first also tends to result in an excessive number of figures in the drawing. Each sheet of drawing tends to run at least US$ 80, all of which is once again charged to the patentee.

Still further, the number of claims tends to be high when the specification is drafted first. It takes a lot of claims to define the invention because whoever drafted the application never did the difficult mental work of figuring out where the invention really lies. The U.S. patent office charges extra claims fees for both total number of claims greater than twenty, and number of independent claims greater than three.

Of course, all of these unnecessarily high costs are multiplied considerably when the patentee files national phase applications abroad. Foreign filings often require translation at a fixed cost per word, and many foreign countries impose surcharges for excess pages and excess claims. In some instances the countries won't allow anywhere near the number of claims that were filed in the U.S., so that whoever is prosecuting the application has to charge all over again for re-writing the claims to conform to the foreign practice. What a waste of money. Claims should be written before the specification, not the other way around.

Beginning with enactment of the Patent Law Treaties Implementation Act[70] in 2012 (PLT), utility applications need not include any claims. Although that is technically true, it is a really bad idea to file a utility application without at least some claims.

E)   A Patent Application Is Not A Journal Article Or A Project Plan

From time to time an inventor wants to facilitate the drafting process by providing a journal article or business plan that outlines the inventive subject matter. Such documents are of limited use.

Journal articles are usually drafted to show that the author's work is consistent with accepted science, and is merely an extension of what everyone already knew. If an article were drafted otherwise, there is very little chance that it would be published in any respected peer-reviewed journal. Unfortunately, that is exactly the opposite of what is needed in a patent application. In the field of patents, the goal is to point out that the work is completely non-obvious, and even better, is inconsistent with the accepted wisdom.

The focus of a project plan is also entirely wrong for a patent application. A project plan focuses on what will be done, and what results the experimenter or project leader hopes to find. That is all future oriented. In a

---

70   35 USC §§ 381-390.

patent application the focus should be on what has already been accomplished, either in past experiments or at least in mental conception.

Both journal articles and project plans also differ from patent applications in technical respects. Release level, release date and so forth are completely irrelevant to a patent application. Authorship is irrelevant as well, since a patent application needs to identify inventors, not authors. Confidentiality statements in the document are both unnecessary and inappropriate in the patent world, since patent applications are held in confidence automatically until publication, usually 18 months after earliest claimed priority date. Still further, patent applications don't have a table of contents, introduction, purpose and scope, goals, revision history, etc. And although some how-to patenting books suggest using an expressly listed glossary, the better practice in a patent application is to define terms within the body of the specification.

F)   Patent World Records To Avoid

Michael White Engineering & Science Library at Queen's University in Canada publishes annual listings of record breaking patents.[71] Here are a few of the more interesting items:

Longest	3,334 pages	U.S. 6278698 (Aug. 21, 2001) Radio frequency data communications device O'Toole, James E., et al. Micron Technology, Inc. (Boise, ID)
Most drawings	3,654 figures	U.S. 6337634 (Jan. 8, 2002) Radio frequency data communications device O'Toole, James E., et al. Micron Technology, Inc. (Boise, ID)
Most claims	8,958 claims	(reduced to 90 claims in issued patent, U.S. 6991045 (Sept. 18, 2003) Forming openings in a hydrocarbon containing formation using magnetic tracking Vinegar, Harold J., et al. Shell Oil Company (Houston, TX)
Most citing patents	2,373 citing patents	U.S. 4723129 (Feb. 2, 1988) Bubble jet recording method and apparatus in which a heating element generates bubbles in a liquid flow path to project droplets Endo, Ichiro, et al. Canon Kabushiki Kaisha (Tokyo, JP)
Most cited patents	1,719 cited patents	U.S. 7344507 B2 (March 18, 2008) Method and apparatus for lancet actuation Briggs, Barry D., et al., Pelikan Technologies (Palo Alto, CA)

---

71   Global Record Breaking Patents, edited by Rex Yeap, on the PIUG website: http://wiki.piug.org/display/PIUG/Global+Record+Breaking+Patents.

Most classifica- tions	117 IPC classifications	U.S. 5385764 (Jan. 31, 1995) Hydraulically settable containers and other articles for storing, dispensing, and packaging food and beverages and methods for their manufacture Andersen, Per J. and Hodson, Simon K. E. Khashoggi Industries (Santa Barbara, CA)
Longest pendency	67 years (to issue)	U.S. 6097812 (Aug. 1, 2000; filed July 25, 1933) Cryptographic system Friedman, William F. U.S. National Security Agency (Washington, DC), This patent was withheld from issue under an invention secrecy order.
Inventor with the most patents	3,645 U.S. patents	Shunpei Yamazaki Dr. Yamazaki, a scientist at Semiconductor Energy Laboratory of Kanagawa, Japan, is the world's most prolific inventor with more than 8,000 patents and published applications. (updated June 1, 2011)
Inventor with the most patents in a single year	714 in 2010	Kia Silverbrook, Kia Silverbrook is the founder of Silverbrook Research, Ltd., a research firm in Sydney, Australia specializing in inkjet printer technology. He has filed over 8,000 patent applications worldwide.
Most inventors	51	U.S. 7013469 (Mar. 14, 2006), Application program interface for network software platform, Adam W. Smith, et al., Microsoft (Redmond, WA)
Shortest patent application	2 words	U.S. 3164462 (Dec. 15, 1964; filed Feb. 7. 1949) Element 96 and compositions thereof "1. Element 96" U.S. 3156523 (Nov. 10, 1964; filed Aug. 23, 1946) Element 95 and method of producing said element "1. Element 95" Dr. Glenn T. Seaborg U.S. Atomic Energy Commission (Washington, DC)
Simplest Drawing	(image of a tooth-pick)	U.S. 448647 (March 24, 1891) Tooth-Pick Charles C. Freeman (Dixfield, ME)

Chapter IV - Basic Claiming

A)   New, Useful and Non-Obvious

As mentioned above, an "invention" must be new, useful and non-obvious to be patentable. It's usually fairly easy to draft claims so that they satisfy the "new" part of the test (also called "novelty"), because typically no one has invented *exactly* the same thing you did. It's also usually fairly easy to draft claims so that they satisfy the "useful" part of the test. If the invention were not useful you wouldn't have bothered to invent it – although one has to wonder about some of the absurd inventions people come up with![72]

The difficult part is satisfying the "non-obviousness" requirement. But what makes an invention non-obvious? We certainly cannot use the common understanding of the terms "obvious" and "non-obvious" because they are too subjective. What is obvious to one person is often not obvious to another. Indeed, once one learns of an invention, it is all too easy to reach back in one's mind to think, "Oh yes, I would have thought of that if I had put my mind to it." But that "hindsight trap" doesn't make the invention obvious from a patent standpoint.

Patent Beast

© FISH 2008

Panel 1: YOU SAY THE CLAIMS ARE OBVIOUS OVER ....

Panel 2: .... A COMBINATION OF FIVE REFERENCES.

Panel 3: BUT ANY INVENTION IS A COMBINATION OF OLD PARTS.

Panel 4: SORRY, IT'S OBVIOUS.

B)   Past Efforts At Defining Obviousness

Years ago the U.S. patent office and courts required that patentable subject matter reflect an extraordinary mental achievement, a so-called "flash of genius". That standard was quite helpful in the days before computers and automated processes. But a return to the flash of genius standard would be completely unworkable today because a great many inventions result from automated investigation. To give just a single example, pharmaceutical companies regularly screen thousands of compounds to discover those that are most effective for a particular disease. Any "invention" that results may have involved some measure of creativity, but is mostly the result of grinding lab work. In any event, the flash of genius test was rejected long ago when the patent law was expressly amended to state, "Patentability shall not be negatived by the manner in which the invention was made".[73]

---

72 See e.g., http://totallyabsurd.com
73 35 U.S.C. § 103

It is also theoretically possible to devise an obviousness standard that depends upon the amount of effort required during the inventing process. That standard would have the advantage of providing at least some correlation between effort and reward, but it flies in the face of experience. Sometimes the greatest advances are the result of accidents and "flashes of genius", neither of which can necessarily lay claim to having involved much effort at all. Moreover, if an inventor works in a field for ten years before "suddenly" coming up with a great idea, it is difficult to say whether the great idea took ten minutes or ten years to develop. As with the "flash of genius" approach, the "amount of effort" approach has gone the way of the great auk.[74]

(1)   The Graham Factors

The current law is that a patent claim is obvious when the differences between the claimed invention and the prior art "are such that the subject matter as a whole would have been obvious at the time the invention was made to a person having ordinary skill in the art"[75]. While obviousness is ultimately a legal determination, it is based on the so-called Graham Factors, namely: (1) the scope and content of the prior art; (2) the level of skill of a person of ordinary skill in the art; (3) the differences between the claimed invention and the teachings of the prior art; and (4) the extent of any objective indicia of non-obviousness (e.g., commercial success, long-felt but unsolved needs, and failure of others to solve the problems addressed by the invention).[76]

(2)   Teaching, Suggestion or Motivation

Unfortunately, it can be exceedingly difficult to apply the Graham Factors. The test that is most often used is whether there is a teaching, suggestion or motivation ("TSM") in the prior art from which a Person of Ordinary Skill in the Art (a "POSITA") would have derived the claimed subject matter. Under the TSM rule, a patent claim can be properly rejected if invalidating teaching, suggestion, or motivation can be found explicitly or implicitly: 1) in the prior art references themselves; 2) in the knowledge of those of ordinary skill in the art that certain references, or disclosures in those references, are of special interest or importance in the field; or 3) from the nature of the problem to be solved, "leading inventors to look to references relating to possible solutions to that problem".[77]

---

74   *CFMT, supra*, 349 F.3d at 1340

75   35 U.S.C. § 103; see also *Graham v. John Deere Co.*, 383 U.S. 1, 14, 86 S. Ct. 684, 15 L. Ed. 2d 545 (1966); I*n re Dembiczak*, 175 F.3d 994, 998 (Fed. Cir. 1999)

76   See *Graham, Supra*, 383 U.S. at 17-18. Other secondary indicia of non-obviousness include skepticism or disbelief (*Environmental Designs, Ltd. v. Union Oil Co. of Cal.*, 713 F.2d 693, 697-98, 218 USPQ 865, 869 (Fed. Cir. 1983)), and copying, praise, unexpected results, and industry acceptance (*Allen Archery, Inc. v. Browning Mfg. Co.*, 819 F.2d 1087, 1092, 2 USPQ2d 1490, 1493 (Fed. Cir. 1987); *Diversitech Corp. v. Century Steps, Inc.*, 850 F.2d 675, 679, 7 USPQ2d 1315, 1319 (Fed. Cir. 1988)).

77   *Ruiz v. A.B. Chance Co.*, 234 F.3d 654, 665 (Fed. Cir. 2000) (*quoting Pro-Mold*, 75 F.3d at 1572)

Arguments with the Patent Office usually do not occur with respect to the teaching or suggestion part of the test, because those are relatively straightforward. The motivation part of the test, however, is very commonly argued. The reason is that a POSITA must not only have had some motivation to combine the prior art teachings, but some motivation to combine the prior art teachings *in the particular manner claimed*.[78]

For better or for worse, the Patent Office has more or less eviscerated the motivation portion of the teaching-suggestion-motivation test, by focusing on the standard of review in cases appealed to the Patent Trial and Appeal Board.[79] The ultimate determination of obviousness is a legal conclusion based on underlying findings of fact, and the Federal Circuit reviews the Board's ultimate determination of obviousness de novo.[80] However, the Federal Circuit reviews the Board's underlying factual findings, including a finding of a motivation to combine, for substantial evidence.[81] Thus, as long as the Federal Circuit can find any substantial evidence from which the Board could have determined obviousness, it is proper for the Court to uphold that factual determination. And given a factual determination of motivation to combine, the Court can uphold the final determination of obviousness. That is exactly what was done in the *In re Kahn* case.[82] There, the court reiterated, "[s]ubstantial evidence is something less than the weight of the evidence but more than a mere scintilla of evidence" and went on to conclude:

> "We note that the possibility of drawing two inconsistent conclusions from the evidence does not prevent the [Patent Board's] findings from being supported by substantial evidence. Id. Indeed, if a reasonable mind might accept the evidence as adequate to support the factual conclusions drawn by the Board, then we must uphold the Board's determination".[83]

(3)   KSR International Co. V. Teleflex Inc. et al.

One of the most important case on obviousness since the turn of the century is the *KSR* ruling.[84] In that case the U.S. Supreme Court significantly raised the bar on obviousness by holding that a POSITA must be deemed to have an *ordinary* level of creativity. Among other things, this means that a POSITA would think of all permutations where each of the elements has only a small, finite number of choices -- and claims should be rejected where they are directed to inventions that are mere design choices.

---

78 See, e.g., *In re Kotzab*, 217 F.3d 1365, 1371 (Fed. Cir. 2000) ("Particular findings must be made as to the reason the skilled artisan, with no knowledge of the claimed invention, would have selected these components for combination in the manner claimed". (emphasis added)); *In re Rouffet*, 149 F.3d 1350, 1357 (Fed. Cir. 1998) ("In other words, the examiner must show reasons that the skilled artisan, confronted with the same problems as the inventor and with no knowledge of the claimed invention, would select the elements from the cited prior art references for combination in the manner claimed". (emphasis added)).

79 Effective March 16, 2013, the Board of Patent Appeals and Interferences is replaced by the Patent Trial and Appeal Board. Pub L 112–29, §3, 125 Stat 284.

80 *In re Dembiczak, supra*, 175 F.3d at 998

81 *In re Gartside*, 203 F.3d 1305, 1316 (Fed. Cir. 2000)

82 *In re Kahn*, 2006 U.S. App. LEXIS 7070, 15-16 (Fed. Cir. 2006)

83 *Id.* at 1312 (citing *Consol. Edison Co. v. NLRB*, 305 U.S. 197, 229-30, 83 L. Ed. 126 (1938))

84 *KSR International co. V. Teleflex Inc. et al.*, 127 S. Ct. 1727; 167 L. Ed. 2d 705 (2007).

Interestingly, *KSR's* focus on design choices echoed my previous suggestion in *Strategic Patenting*, namely that examiners should still be required to identify a teaching, suggestion or motivation for a claimed combination in the prior art, and they should still consider evidence of non-obviousness, as well as reasoned arguments as to why a POSITA would not have thought of the claimed combination. And absent sufficiently strong contrary evidence and arguments, examiners should still reject claims (and courts should uphold rejections) where the claimed inventions are mere design choices.

Proper application of KSR is absolutely critical to ridding the world of ridiculous patents for "inventions" such as the 1-click placement of Internet orders (U.S. 6149255), peanut butter and jelly sandwiches without crusts (U.S. 6004596), providing reservations for restroom use (U.S. 6329919), printers that print lines with different line spacing (U.S. 4953995), Online Shopping Carts (U.S. 5715314), The Hyperlink (U.S. 4873662), Video Streaming (U.S. 5132992), Internationalizing Domain Names (U.S. 6182148), Pop-Up Windows (U.S. 6389458), Targeted Banner Ads (U.S. 6026368), Paying With A Credit Card Online (U.S. 6289319), Framed Browsing (U.S. 5933841 and 6442574), and Affiliate Linking (U.S. 6029141).

Unfortunately, patents claiming subject matters that are completely obvious are still being issued and upheld. For example, Amazon's original one-click patent U.S. 5960411 (Sept. 1997) has never been invalidated, and was even confirmed on re-examination in July 2010. Claim 1 of that patent recites:

> 1. A method of placing an order...,
>   displaying information identifying the item;
>   and
>   in response to only a single action being performed,
>   sending a request to order the ...;
>   under control of a single-action ordering component of
>   the server system,
>   receiving the request;
>   retrieving additional information previously ...;
>   and
>   generating an order to purchase the requested ...;
>   and
>   fulfilling the generated order to complete purchase of
>   the item
>   whereby the item is ordered without using a shopping
>   cart ordering model.

Similarly, in the peanut butter and jelly sandwich cases, the Federal Circuit killed one of Smuckers'™ patents,[85] but the patent for a sealed crustless sandwich is still on the books. Claim 1 of the U.S. 6004596 patent (December 1999) recites:

> 1. A sealed crustless sandwich, comprising:
>   a first bread layer having a first perimeter surface \
>   coplanar to a contact surface;
>   at least one filling of an edible food juxtaposed to said
>   contact surface;
>   a second bread layer [that] includes a second perimeter
>   surface similar to said first perimeter surface;
>   a crimped edge directly between said first perimeter
>   surface and said second perimeter ...;

There are perhaps hundreds of thousands (if not millions) of parents and children who would have found such a sandwich entirely obvious as of the filing date!

There is hope, however. In a November 2013 appeal of a reexamination case,[86] the Federal Circuit found it was obvious for a trailer to have panels that independently move laterally and vertically. That should have been an easy decision. Panels can only move in so many directions, and such movement can only be either dependent or independent. POSITAs are not complete idiots. Here's claim 1 of U.S. 7214017.

> 1. An apparatus for separating cargo areas in a trailer,
> comprising:
>   first and second panels ... extending in a direction generally
>   perpendicular to a longitudinal axis of the trailer...
>   a mounting system that [allows] each of the first and second
>   panels [to move laterally and vertically] independently
>   of one another [and] the mounting system being
>   attached to at least one of a wall or a ceiling of a cargo
>   space.

(4)   Subject Matter Eligibility

Between 2012 and 2014 the Supreme Court issued three other decisions that rocked the patent world, *Mayo v. Prometheus*[87], and *Ass'n for Mol. Pathology v. Myriad*[88], and *Alice v. CLS Bank*.[89] In 2012 *Mayo* held that claims failed to recite patent eligible subject matter where they were directed to a method of giving a drug to a patient, and using measurement of metabolites of that drug to decide whether to increase or decrease the dosage of the drug. The correlation was deemed to be a natural phenomenon.

---

85   *In re Kretchman et al.*, 125 Fed. Appx. 1012; 2005 U.S. App. LEXIS 6805, (Apr. 2005)

86   *Randall MFG v. Rea* (Fed. Cir. 2013) (Inter Partes Reexamination No. 95/000,326)

87   *Mayo, Supra*, 132 S. Ct. 1289

88   *Myriad, Supra*, 133 S. Ct. 2107

89   *Alice, Supra*, 134 S. Ct. 2347

In 2013 *Myriad* held that tests based on breast cancer mutations are not patentable because the mutations were merely natural phenomena, and creating an assay based on that principal is routine.

Then in 2014, *Alice* held that computer-implemented inventions consisting of (1) methods for exchanging obligations, (2) computer system configured to carry out the methods, and (3) computer-readable medium programmed to perform the methods are not patent-eligible because they merely recite abstract ideas without limitation by a critical "something more." In one bold stroke the Supreme Court subjecting to invalidity challenges hundreds of thousands of software and business patents.

Actually, *Alice* was not decided out of the blue. Focusing back to the U.S. Constitution, the Court pointed out that Art. I, § 8 prescribes a balance; providing a limited monopoly to inventors "[t]o promote the progress of science and useful arts". The problem, of course, is that the patent statute, 35 USC 100 et seq., contains no language of proportionality. If an inventor can somehow broadly patent some minor improvement in a way that can demand tribute from an entire industry, the patent statute would not stand in its way.

The Court had tried to establish that balance in other cases, as well, for example in *KSR v. Teleflex*, using 35 USC § 103 (one of ordinary skill has ordinary level of creativity); in *Bilski v. Kappos* using 35 USC § 101 (machine or transformation is not only test of subject matter eligibility); in *Nautilus v. Biosig* using 35 US § 112 (claims need to inform with reasonable level of certainty); and in *Kimble v. Marvel* using 35 USC § 154 (patent royalties cannot contractually extend past term of license).

> In *Mayo*, *Myriad* and *Alice* the Supreme Court began to seriously enforce proportionality - scope of claims versus contribution to technology

But then in *Alice*, the Court for the first time directly addressed the idea of proportionality. ""[W]e must distinguish between patents that claim the 'building blocks' of human ingenuity and those that integrate the building blocks into something more...thereby 'transforming' them into a patent-eligible invention. The former 'would risk disproportionately tying up the use of the underlying' ideas...and are therefore ineligible for patent protection. The latter pose no comparable risk of pre-emption, and therefore remain eligible for the monopoly granted under our patent laws." (emphasis added).

Now it is true that very few seem to have caught on to the big picture here. Instead of focusing on the fuzzy line of proportionality, both lower courts and commentators have sought a bright line test consisting of two parts:

(1) Is the claim at issue directed to a known judicial exception (an idea of itself, a mathematical relationship or formula, a method of organizing human activity, or a fundamental economic practice); and

(2) If yes, then does the claim recite something significantly more that renders the claim subject matter eligible?

Of course, that test merely raises the question of what is "something significantly more". And that, it turns out boils down to the fuzzy line of proportionality. Although very few commentators (and lower courts) seem to have appreciated it, the *Alice* Court was basically confirming the need to balance the contribution to science/arts against the reward to the patentee.

Now comes the big issue, how should applications be drafted to comply with these cases? The first thing to appreciate is that this new emphasis on subject matter eligibility really only affects the business methods and software groups. Mechanical inventions, physical aspects of electronics, and most other technologies are usually not seriously affected.

For technologies that do fall within business methods and software, claims should include one, or preferably more, of the following limitations:

- A limitation focusing on improving another technology or technical field

- A limitation focusing on improving a function functioning of hardware

- A limitation that requires implementation on a particular machine, not a general purpose process or computer

- A limitation that requires that a process transforms a particular article to a different state or thing

- A limitation reciting an unconventional step, something other than what is well-understood, routine, and conventional in the field

- A limitation that amounts to more than generally linking an abstract idea to a particular technological environment

The USPTO gives specific examples in its June 2020 update to the 2014 interim guidance.[90] Those examples are "must reads" for anyone drafting business method or software related claims. Above all, when drafting claims directed to these technologies, it is critical to consider the concept of proportionality. Practitioners write claims in which the scope of protection is commensurate with the contribution to technology.

> **The USPTO July 2015 guidance on subject matter eligibility is a "must read" when drafting claims directed to business methods or software**

For technologies that involve natural compounds, one really needs to either recite a new use of the compound, or a non-obvious derivative of the compound. *Myriad* invalidated claims that recited assays based on breast cancer mutations, because the mutations were merely natural phenomena, and creating an assay based on that principal is routine. In *Sequenom* the Federal Circuit reluctantly invalided claims that recited assays based on presence of fetal DNA in maternal blood. The Court held that the claimed subject matter was not patent eligible because the DNA in the blood is merely a natural phenomenon, and creating an assay based on that principal is routine.[91]

One other thought. Although the courts have not yet adopted the standard, "something substantially more" should be a sliding scale depending on the scope of the claims. Broad claims should require "something substantially more" than narrow claims to be viewed as more than a mere idea.

(5)　Avoiding Obviousness Rejections

The Patent Office can, and often does, reject a claim as being obvious over a combination of references. For example, if a pending claim recites a combination of elements A, B, and C, the Patent Office might well reject the claim as being obvious over one reference that teaches A and B, and another reference that teaches C.

90　https://www.uspto.gov/patents/laws/examination-policy/subject-matter-eligibility
91　*Ariosa Diagnostics, Inc. v. Sequenom, Inc.*, 788 F.3d 1371, 2015 U.S. App. LEXIS 9855 (Fed. Cir., 2015); petition for rehearing en banc denied, 2015 U.S. App. LEXIS 20842 (Fed. Cir. Dec. 2, 2015)

Patent Beast   © FISH 2008

Panel 1: YOU SAY THE INVENTION IS OBVIOUS BECAUSE ....

Panel 2: .... THE COMBINATION IS REALLY USEFUL.

Panel 3: BUT THEN NOTHING WOULD BE PATENTABLE.

Panel 4: SORRY, IT'S OBVIOUS.

Of course, the goal when drafting claims is to try to avoid obviousness rejections altogether. And the best way to accomplish that is to run a really good prior art search, draft claims that are a little too broad, but not excessively so, and then check for prior art while pretending you are an examiner trying to reject the claims. Try to construe the language of your draft claims in the broadest possible manner consistent with the application. If you include the term "user" in a claim, consider whether the claim would be patentable if a user were a computer or robot, not just a person. If you include the term "hammer" in a claim, consider whether the claim would be patentable if a steel bar or a rock were construed as a hammer. That is what the examiner will do, and it is proper for him/her to interpret the claims in that manner - at least during prosecution. Later on , if the claims are ever litigated, the court will construe the claim more narrowly, as one of ordinary skill in the art would construe them.

Moreover, take into account the fact that prior art references can be cited against your claims even if the references come from a different technical field. The rule is that references can be properly combined if they are in a technical field that a competitor would likely consider in resolving the technical problem at hand, provided the examiner can provide some rationale for combining the references.

And don't worry that your claims will be rejected as being obvious, despite your good faith efforts to avoid obviousness rejections. Among other things the examiners almost have to reject claims in the first substantive office action, citing whatever they can find. The reality is that unless the examiners reject the claims at least once, it's difficult for the supervisor to know if the examiners really looked at the prior art.

Patent Beast   © FISH 2008

Panel 1: BOB TRIES REASONING....
YOU REJECT THE CLAIMS ON THE GROUNDS ....

Panel 2: .... THAT THE INVENTION IS OBVIOUS ....

Panel 3: .... BUT YOU GIVE NO SUPPORT FOR YOUR ARGUMENT.

Panel 4: I KNOW. BUT I DON'T WANT TO ALLOW THESE CLAIMS
OUT TO LUNCH

C)   Structure of Claims

(1)   I or We Claim

The Claims section of a patent application should begin with one of three phrases: "I claim" or "We claim" or "What is claimed is". This is mostly a matter of preference, although the first and second choices depend on the number of inventors, and can become incorrect over time if that number changes through claim amendments.

(2)   Preamble

(a) Structure Of Preamble

Patent claims contain only two sections, a preamble and a body. The preamble usually introduces the subject matter of the claim, defines a work piece, or states a purpose or use for the invention. The body then goes on to list the elements of the apparatus, composition or method of the claimed invention.

Preambles can be of any length. In U.S. 5969204[92] claim 1 begins simply "A method..." and in U.S. 5090759[93] claim 1 begins "An apparatus...." A more typical claim, however, includes somewhat more description in the preamble, such as "A sheet fitting apparatus...", "A tire removing tool...", or "A toaster for toasting bagels...." In the extreme case of a Jepson claim (see below), the preamble includes all the important elements of the device or method that are already known, and the body generally only lists those additional elements that the attorney considers to be new.

(b) Strategic Considerations

There are all sorts of strategic reasons for these widely varying formats. One consideration is that the preamble is often used by the patent office to help decide upon the examining group in which to place an application. By consciously drafting the preamble to focus on one technology or another, a patent drafter can more or less direct his application to one examining group or another.

Examining group 3600, for example, deals with business methods, and is currently behind other groups in their caseload. They are have made significant improvements in recent years, but at one time they were issuing first office actions almost five years after the filing dates! They also have a policy of completely re-examining PCT applications that enter U.S. national phase, even if the International Preliminary Search Report (IPER) was entirely positive. If an inventor wants his application to issue within

> **One can draft claims that specifically target a particular examining group**

a reasonable period of time, it behooves him/her to write the preamble in a manner that targets one of the examining groups that is not generally issuing §101 rejections (rejections for claiming ineligible subject matter). For example, if the invention relates to coupling a refrigerator to the Internet, it may be smart to begin the claim by reciting, "A refrigerator comprising a component that delivers temperature data to a data port..." rather than reciting "A method of delivering temperature date to a data port...."

Where a client contemplates filing multiple applications on a given technology, it can be useful to draft the various preambles to direct the different applications to either the same examining group or to different examining groups. Daughter applications, for example, are sometimes best directed to the same examining group that handled the parent, especially where the previous examiner was helpful in getting previous claims issued. On the other hand, when concurrently filing multiple applications on different aspects of related

---

92   U.S. 5969204 (Oct. 1999) "Process for the production of distyryl-biphenyl compounds".
93   U.S. 5090759 (Feb. 1992) "Apparatus for gripping an object".

technologies, it is probably a better idea to direct them to different examining groups. That way a severe backlog in one group doesn't delay prosecution of the entire portfolio. The strategy also minimizes the possibility that a single poorly trained examiner can hold the entire prosecution hostage. Our office successfully directed three different applications in related technologies to three different examining groups. The main claims were as follows:

1. *A method of transferring data* to a target device across a network via encapsulated packets wherein each of at least some of the packets comprises a split-ID.

1. *A storage device* having a first type of media logically split into a first partition directly addressed by a first IP address and a second partition directly addressed by a second IP address that is distinct from the first IP address.

1. *An electrical device* comprising a plurality of elements that communicate with each other using packets of information addressed to individual ones of the plurality of elements.

Another strategic consideration is elimination of "work pieces" from the body of the claim. Consider a claim directed to a sawhorse for supporting lengths of wood. The wood is the work piece. It is separate from the sawhorse, and is properly excluded from the listing of components of the sawhorse. Thus, it would be wrong to recite the following because the sawhorse is described as comprising the length of wood:

A sawhorse comprising:
   two pairs of legs, each pair coupled in a pivoting relationship;
   a cross beam connecting the two pairs of legs; a vise, pivotally coupled to one of the legs; and *a length of wood* held in the vise.

The proper claim would read:

A sawhorse adapted to secure a *length of wood*,
   comprising:
   two pairs of legs, each pair coupled in a pivoting relationship;
   a cross beam connecting the two pairs of legs;
      and
   a vise, pivotally coupled to one of the legs, and sized and dimensioned to secure the length of wood.

Alternatively, a patent drafter can introduce work pieces in the body of the claim as long as it is clear that the work piece is not an element of the device or method being claimed. For example, it would also be proper to recite the following:

> A sawhorse, comprising:
>   two pairs of legs, each pair coupled in a pivoting
>   relationship;
>   a cross beam connecting the two pairs of legs;
>   and
>   a vise, pivotally coupled to one of the legs, and sized
>   and dimensioned to secure *a length of wood*.

A third consideration in drafting preambles is that the preamble can sometimes be read as a limitation on the scope of the claim. When merely introducing the subject matter of the claim, defining a work piece, or stating a purpose or use for an invention, the language of the preamble has little or no effect on the scope of the claim.[94] But when reciting essential structure or steps, or using language that is "necessary to give life, meaning, and vitality" to the claim, the language of the preamble can be interpreted as limiting the scope of the claim.[95]

(c) Potentially Limiting Nature of Preamble

Unfortunately, there is "no litmus test that defines when a preamble limits claim scope".[96] The general rule is that a preamble "limits the claimed invention if it 'recites essential structure or steps, or if it is necessary to give life, meaning, and vitality to the claim.'"[97] Thus, if the preamble helps to determine the scope of the patent claim, and especially if it appears that "the patent drafter chose to use both the preamble and the body of the claim to define the subject matter of the claimed invention"[98] then the limitations in the preamble are construed as part of the claimed invention. But that general rule cannot be applied slavishly. In another recent case[99] the Federal Circuit held:

Preambles are often limiting in method claims, and sometimes in apparatus claims

> "In general, a claim preamble is limiting if it recites essential structure or steps, or if it is necessary to give life, meaning, and vitality to the claim. However, if the body of the claim describes a structurally complete invention such that deletion of the preamble phrase does not affect the structure or steps of the claimed invention, the preamble is generally not limiting unless there is clear reliance on the preamble during prosecution to distinguish the claimed invention from the prior art".

94 *Rowe v. Dror,* 112 F.3d 473, 478 (Fed. Cir. 1997)

95 *Pitney Bowes, Inc. v. Hewlett-Packard Co.,* 182 F.3d 1298, 1305 (Fed. Cir. 1999)

96 *Catalina Mktg. Int'l, Inc. v. Coolsavings.com, Inc.,* 289 F.3d 801, 808 (Fed. Cir. 2002)

97 *NTP, Inc. v. Research in Motion, Ltd.,* 418 F.3d 1282, 1305 (Fed. Cir. 2005), Rehearing denied by, Rehearing, en banc, *NTP, Inc. v. Research in Motion, Ltd.,* 2005 U.S. App. LEXIS 23112 (Fed. Cir. Oct. 7, 2005)

98 *Bicon, Inc. v. Straumann Co.,* 2006 U.S. App. LEXIS 6813 (Fed. Cir. 2006).

99 *Intirtool Ltd. V. Texar Corp.,* 369 F.3d 1289, 1295 (Fed. Cir. 2004)

- Preambles In Apparatus claims

It is also possible that some elements in the preamble will be considered limiting while others in the same preamble are not considered limiting. This distinction often happens with respect to structural versus intent elements, and plays out as a function of whether the claim is written in apparatus format or method format. The structural elements recited in the preamble of an apparatus (composition or device) claim are often considered to be limiting because the subject matter is being claimed by its structural elements. In the following claim, for example, the Federal Circuit found the elements "blown-film" and "textured liner" to be limitations on the claimed subject matter.

> 1. A blown-film textured liner, comprising:
>   a) a first layer of thermoplastic material having an upper
>   flat surface and a lower flat surface;
>   b) a second layer of thermoplastic material bonded to
>   said upper flat surface of said first layer of
>   thermoplastic material, said second layer of
>   thermoplastic material comprising a random
>   distribution of peaks and …; and
>   c) a third layer of thermoplastic material bonded to said
>   lower flat surface of said first layer of
>   thermoplastic material, said third layer of
>   thermoplastic material comprising a random
>   distribution of peaks and valleys.

Among other things, the Court focused on the fact that the language recites a fundamental characteristic of the claimed invention, and that the specification is replete with references to the invention as a "blown-film" liner, including language in the title of the patent and the summary of the Invention. The court noted that the phrase is used repeatedly to describe the preferred embodiments, and that the entire preamble "blown-film textured liner" is restated in each of the patent's seven claims.[100]

On the other hand, language of intent in a preamble of an apparatus claim is usually considered to be non-limiting.[101] That makes sense because the scope of an apparatus claim depends on structure, and recitation of a purpose or intent imposes no limitation on the structure.[102]

- Preambles In Method claims

The rules regarding interpretation of preamble limitations are the same for method claims, but application of the rule may be a bit easier. In method claims all of the elements recited in a preamble are likely to be deemed limitations on the scope of the claim, regardless of whether they are structural elements or "use" or "intent" elements. The rationale is that a method is performed to accomplish some purpose, and the "use" or "intent" is critical. This difference allows a patent drafter to readily limit the scope of the claim according to the use.

---

100 *Poly-America, L.P. v. GSE Lining Technology, Inc.*, (2004 U.S. App. LEXIS 19234, 15-16 (Fed. Cir. Sept. 2004)
101 *In re Stattmann*, 146 F.2d 290 (C.C.P.A. 1944); *In re Gregg*, 244 F.2d 316 (C.C.P.A. 1957); *In re Sinex*, 309 F.2d 488, 492 (C.C.P.A. 1962)
102 *In re Gardiner,* 171 F.2d 313, 315-16 (C.C.P.A. 1948)

In *Jansen v. Rexall Sundown, Inc.*,[103] for example, the Federal Circuit considered the following claim from U.S. 4945083.[104]

> A *method of treating or preventing macrocytic-megaloblastic anemia* in humans which anemia is caused by either folic acid deficiency or by vitamin B12 deficiency which comprises administering a daily oral dosage of a vitamin preparation to a human in need thereof comprising at least about 0.5 mg. of vitamin B12 and at least about 0.5 mg. of folic acid.

The issue at litigation was whether the purpose recited in the preamble ("treating or preventing macrocytic-megaloblastic anemia") should be considered a limitation on the claim. The Federal Circuit found that the intent language was indeed a limitation on the claim, and that the defendant fell outside the scope of the claims because it sold an over-the-counter product without any intent to treat or prevent anemia.

• Effect Of Prosecution History On Preamble Interpretation

Of course interpretation of a preamble can be significantly affected by the prosecution history. Clear reliance on the preamble during prosecution of a patent to distinguish the claimed invention from the prior art can be a strong indication that the preamble is a claim limitation. In the "broccoli" case,[105] for example, the Federal Circuit considered three patents related to growing and eating sprouts to reduce the level of carcinogens in animals. The relevant claims included:

> (U.S. 5968567 claim 1) A method of preparing a human food product [comprising desirable compounds from sprouts].

> (U.S. 5725895 claim 1) A method of preparing a food product rich in glucosinolates, comprising germinated cruciferous seeds, with the exception of cabbage, cress, mustard and radish seeds, and harvesting sprouts prior to the 2-leaf stage, to form a food product comprising a plurality of sprouts.

> (U.S. 5968505 claim 16) A method of increasing the chemoprotective amount of Phase 2 enzymes in a mammal [by creating a "food product" from sprouts and then "administering said food product" to a mammal].

103 *Jansen v. Rexall Sundown, Inc.*, 342 F.3d 1329, 1333 (Fed. Cir. 2003)
104 U.S. 4945083 (Jul. 1990) "Safe oral folic-acid-containing vitamin preparation"
105 *In re Cruciferous Sprout Litigation*, 301 F.3d 1343, 1347 (Fed. Cir. 2002); (rehearing and rehearing en banc denied)

In interpreting those claims the Federal Circuit found that the preambles did constitute limitation on the scope of the claims, largely based upon the following language from the patent prosecution.[106]

> Claim 1 of the patent, for example, is directed to "[a] method of preparing a food product rich in glucosinolates... and harvesting sprouts prior to the 2-leaf stage, to form a food product comprising a plurality of sprouts".... Although "rich in glucosinolates" is recited in the preamble of the claim, the pertinent case law holds that the preamble is given weight if it breathes life and meaning into the claim....

- Strategic Use Of The Preamble

All of this provides ammunition to the drafter for controlling whether language in the preamble is to be interpreted as a limitation of the claim. Considering the following preamble of an apparatus claim:

> A battery used for hearing aids, comprising:....

If an applicant claims a new type of battery, then the new battery should be compared against previously known batteries. The fact that the inventor intends to use the new battery in a hearing aid is irrelevant. The usage only becomes relevant to patentability if the body of the claim recites a structural element directed to that usage. For example, the attorney could include a limitation to flatness, because hearing aids use flat batteries.

> A flat battery used for hearing aids, comprising:....

But even there, the claim would read on all flat batteries, even if they were also used in other applications. If the person drafting the claims really wants to limit the scope to hearing aid batteries, they must either (a) identify some physical aspect of hearing aid batteries that distinguish them from other types of batteries or (b) claim a combination of battery and hearing aid. The attorney could also format the claim as a method claim. The following claims would achieve those goals:

> A flat battery having a label identifying a use in a hearing aid, comprising:...
>
> A hearing aid having a battery, wherein the battery comprises:....
>
> A method of powering a hearing aid, comprising...
>   holding the hearing aid; and
>   inserting a battery in the hearing aid, said
>   battery having....

Of course, if the attorney definitely wants the language of the preamble to be read as limitations on the scope, they can always use a Jepson format. Jepson format allows a patentee to use the preamble to recite elements or steps of the claimed invention that are conventional or known. When Jepson format is employed, the claim preamble defines the context of the claimed invention, and also provides limitations as to the scope of that

106 *Id.*, at 1437-8

invention. The fact that the patentee has chosen the Jepson format of the claim evidences the intention to use the preamble to define, in part, the structural elements of his claimed invention.[107]

(3)   Body Of A Claim

(a)   Colon/Semicolon Format

The trend in the last few decades has definitely been towards formatting patent claims in a colon/semicolon format. Thus, instead of writing the claim as a single paragraph:

> A chair having: four legs; a seat; and a back held together by magnets.

One might write even this simple claim as follows:

> A chair having:
>   four legs;
>   a seat; and
>   a back held together by magnets.

The claim could also have been drafted without the colon/semicolon format (see below), without changing the meaning. Here, however, one needs to add a comma between "back" and "held". Otherwise the claim could be read as the back being held together by magnets.

> A chair having four legs, a seat, and a back, held together by magnets.

The main advantage of the colon/semicolon format is that it clearly delineates the different components (or steps), and clearly distinguishes between main components and subcomponents. This is somewhat less important for patent practitioners who are used to parsing complex wordings. But when it comes to the courtroom, formatted claims can make a huge difference to the judge and jury. Clear formatting is even useful to patent drafters because it helps them logically write dependent claims, and support the claims in the Specification.

When using colon/semicolon format be sure to include the linker "and" after the last semicolon. Also be sure that the first letter of each "paragraph" remains lower case. Note too that it is possible to have layers of colon/semicolon formats. Thus, it is entirely proper to recite:

> A chair having:
>   four legs, each comprising: a top connector portion; a
>   curved elongated portion; and a bottom foot
>   portion;
>   a seat; and
>   a back held together by magnets.

---

107 *Kegel Co. v. AMF Bowling*, 127 F.3d 1420, 1426 (Fed. Cir. 1997)

(b) Selecting Elements To Include In The Claims

> There *is* a logical process for restricting limitations to the minimum set required for patentability

Regardless of how it is structured, the body of a claim contains all or most of the elements that serve to distinguish the claimed invention over the prior art. Indeed, one of the main goals of patent drafting is to write claims that circumvent the prior art. The secret is to mentally identify four or five elements of the "invention", and then determine which of those elements are absent from each of references in the prior art. The body of the claim should then list the smallest subset of missing elements. In the text below, this principle is first described on an abstract level, and then discussed with the aid of two specific examples, one to a self-evolving marketplace and the other to an internal combustion engine.

On the most abstract level a circumstance might arise in which the invention has five aspects to it, A, B, C, D, and E, and there are three references of concern, R1, R2, and R3, disclosing the following:

R1 discloses A, B;

R2 discloses A, C, and D and

R3 discloses A, B, and D.

It should be immediately apparent that the narrowest possible claim would recite the combination A/B/C/D/E. But there is no need to limit the claim to such an extent. The combinations A/B/D, A/B/E, or A/C/E, are all also viable, and considerably broader than A/B/C/D/E because they contain fewer elements. Indeed the cleanest and broadest claim would simply recite the limitation E, all by itself. This may seem counter-intuitive to some people, but the fact is that the shorter the claim the broader it generally is. Anyone can draft long-winded, narrow claims with lots of elements. The trick is to draft very short claims that still manage to circumvent the prior art, and still be commercially worthwhile.

If in our example another reference, R4, comes to light that discloses A, B and E, the reader should immediately realize that there are still all sorts of viable combinations to consider, including A/B/C/E and A/B/D/E. But here again there are simpler combinations that are probably more desirable, namely C/E, D/E and C/D/E. Those more complicated combinations should probably be included in the patent application as dependent claims.

Of course the analysis is a bit more complicated than that presented so far. A good patents drafter also considers possible obviousness rejections that could be made by the patent office, i.e., which references can be fairly combined together to reject the claims. In our abstract example it might be that R1, R3 and R4 could be fairly combined. That reduces our analytical set to the following:

R1/R3/R4 combination discloses A, B, D, and E

R2 discloses A, C, and D.

Under that scenario the broadest viable combination is likely to be B/E. Now it is true that many patent attorneys and agents are able to make up these combinations in their heads, without recourse to pencil and paper. But beginning patents drafters dealing with all matters, and advanced attorneys and agents dealing with especially complicated matters, would do well to map all this out on paper, or on computer.

(4)   Self-Evolving Marketplace Example

U.S. 6035294 (Mar 2000) "Wide access databases and database systems" teaches a self-evolving generic for storing marketplace information. Information is stored as parameter/value pairs, such as make/Mercedes, model/S500, color/red, year/2003, and so forth. The system is designed to evolve from the bottom up, by allowing users to add new parameters, values and possibly new classifications for use in describing items for sale. When subsequent users add their own items, or search for previously added items, they are presented with parameters and values listed according to frequency of previous use. In that manner the most commonly used terms will float to the top, while the infrequently used terms will sink to the bottom, and eventually be dropped altogether. From that description one can surmise that the available elements from which to draft a patent claim include the following:

> A - storing marketplace information
> B - multiple types of items
> C - in a database
> D - display of item classifications
> E - display of frequency of usage of item classifications
> F - interface to add new item classification
> G - display of parameters
> H - display of frequency of usage of parameters
> I - interface to add new parameter
> J - display of values
> K - display of frequency of usage of values
> L - interface to add new value
> M - nature of item classification (hierarchical, flat, overlapping, etc)

The prior art includes (a) artificial intelligence and expert systems that store data using an ever evolving collection of parameter/value pairs, and (b) U.S. 5799151[108] that teaches an interactive trade network that indexes products using parameter/value pairs. Given that prior art, what is the minimum set of elements needed to recite an allowable claim? The inventor probably needed element D (display of item classifications) to circumvent artificial intelligence and expert systems, and probably also at least some recitation of parameters (element G) and values (element J) so that the claim makes sense. The inventor also needed to recite a mechanism by which a user could add a new item classification, parameter, or value. Including all three of those in the broadest claim is probably unnecessary, so the question is which one or two should be included. An interface to add values probably adds no patentable distinction because there are many systems in which users add dollar amounts, colors, years, and other values. Similarly, an interface to add classifications is a poor choice because it is entirely possible (and even desirable) to prevent users from altering the classification scheme. This leaves an interface to add parameters (element I) as the critical element.

The broadest possible claim is therefore one that recites little more than elements D, G, I, and J, along with an appropriate preamble. Indeed, Claim 1 of the '294 patent properly reads:

---

108 U.S. 5799151 (Aug. 1998) "Interactive electronic trade network and user interface"

> 1. A method of storing marketplace information for multiple types of items in a database, comprising:
>> providing a user with a first data entry interface for selecting an item classification;
>> providing the user with a parameters list that displays a plurality of parameters previously related to the item classification by a plurality of previous users during a process of loading item descriptions;
>> providing a second data entry interface that allows the user to add an additional parameter to the parameters list; and
>> providing a third data entry interface that allows the user to associate individual parameters from the parameters list with individual values from a values list, thereby describing an item falling within the item classification as a set of parameter-value pairs.

The other elements are then properly included in various dependent claims. For example, display of classification usage information (element E) is recited in dependent claim 2, and display of parameter usage information (element H) is recited in dependent claim 3. The hierarchical aspect of the classification scheme (element M) is recited in claim 4, and display of value usage information (element K) is recited in claim 5.

(5) Internal Combustion Engine Example

U.S. 5482015[109] describes an internal combustion engine that has the energy density of a two-stroke engine, but fuel efficiency and reduced pollution at least that of a four-stroke engine. These characteristics are accomplished by carrying the crank pin on a planetary gear such that the crank pin traces out a substantially triangular or other path having a relatively long flattened portion. The net effect is four strokes during a single turn of the crankshaft, with long power and exhaust strokes, but shortened intake and compression strokes. The prior art includes U.S. 5245962[110] teaching variable length connecting rods, U.S. 5170757[111] teaching an engine with traveling gears, and U.S. 5158047[112] that teaches linkages that decrease the piston velocity during the first half of the power stroke. Given that information, a patents drafter would want to address the following elements in the claims:

   A - a combustion chamber
   B - a reciprocating piston
   C - fuel
   D - a first gear carrying a crank pin
   E - a planetary gear traveling around the first gear

---

109 U.S. 5482015 (Jan. 1996) "Device for coupling reciprocating and rotating motions"
110 U.S. 5245962 (Sep. 1993) "Variable length connecting rod for internal combustion engine"
111 U.S. 5170757 (Dec. 1992) "Variable horsepower output gearing for piston engine"
112 U.S. 5158047 (Oct. 1992) "Delayed drop power stroke internal combustion engine"

F - the crank pin tracing out specific paths triangular, quadrilateral and pentagonal, etc
G - the crank pin tracing out a path having a flattened portion
H - a motor vehicle or other application in which the engine is used

The combustion chamber (element A), the reciprocating piston (element B), and the fuel (element C), are all necessary to run the engine, but they are completely commonplace, and add no patentable distinction to the claim. Those elements could be included in the preamble, but are best omitted from the broadest claim as being unnecessary. Circumvention of the prior art does, however, require that the crank pin trace out particular paths, and the only paths that accomplish the desired functions are triangular, quadrilateral and pentagonal paths (element F). The only practical way to accomplish those paths is to provide a first gear carrying a crank pin (element D) and a planetary gear traveling around the first gear (element E). Thus, the minimal set of elements that should be recited in the broadest claim consists of elements E, D, and F. Indeed, that is exactly what was claimed:

A device comprising:
a first gear carrying a crank pin;
a second gear more than twice the size of said first gear
and coupled in a planetary relationship with
respect to said first gear such that said crank pin
travels in one of a substantially triangular,
quadrilateral and pentagonal paths.

Use of the novel crankshaft arrangement in a compound crankshaft, an internal combustion engine, or a motorized vehicle (element H) is recited in dependent claim 2. The flattened path of the crank pin (element G) is recited in dependent claim 3. Other narrower combinations of the various elements are included in independent claims 5 and 6.

D) Claiming Multiple Instances Of An Object

It is often necessary to describe multiple instances of a given component. For example, a bridge may have two cables, or a new type of engine may have 12 cylinders. But avoid getting tongue-tied describing all those different instances.

The best way to do this is to simply claim one instance of the component. If a new type of chair has legs made from some special type of plastic, don't waste energy describing the number of legs. Simply recite "... a chair having "a leg" comprising <<the new type of plastic>>".

For years the rule has been that one could (and should) use the simple term "a" rather than "at least one". For example, a claim reciting "a chair having a leg and <<other components>>" is identical in scope to "a chair having at least one leg and <<other components>>", but the former has the advantage of avoiding the terribly stilted language "the chair of claim 1 *wherein the at least one leg...* " in a dependent claim. Amazingly, this rule is now subject to dispute in view of a recent Federal Circuit decision[113] limiting the term "a sodium phosphate" to a single type of sodium phosphate. The Court advised that if the patentee had intended to cover

113 *Norian Corp. v. Stryker Corp.*, 2005 U.S. App. LEXIS 26528 (Fed. Cir. 2005)

multiple types of sodium phosphate, it should have used "at least one" language. Hopefully, the decision will be limited to the special circumstances of the facts in that case, where: (1) the claim had been amended to recite "consisting of" rather than the open ended "comprising;" and (2) the specification was entirely silent as to examples of multiple types of sodium phosphate.

Where there are two or more instances of the component, one can often still get away with the indefinite term "a", by reciting only one of the components. Thus, one can refer to only a single of the legs of a chair. Similarly, in a claim for an airplane having a new type of wing, the proper claim is to "an airplane having a wing <<with the new feature>>". There is no need to recite "an airplane having two wings, each of the wings having <<the new feature>>".

> ### In claims, try to use "first" and "second" rather than "a plurality of"

Where one does need to claim a plurality of instances of a component, it is acceptable to say "at least two", "at least three", "at least four", etc. It is also acceptable to say "a plurality of", which means the same thing as "at least two" and "more than one".

It is often useful to name the instances by number. Thus, a patents drafter could recite "a chair having a *first leg* and a *second leg* <<having some special relationship to the first leg>>". Details about the first leg would typically be recited in the independent claim, and then details about the second leg would be recited in a dependent claim.

Although it should not be necessary from a patent law perspective, it is easier for clients to understand what is being claims if the practitioner recites "at least" when referring to "first", "second", "third" etc components. "At least a first leg and a second leg" makes is abundantly clear that there are at least two legs, but that there can also be more than two legs.

Note that for terms such as "first" and "second", the usual interpretation is that the terms give no indication of temporal order or position. Thus, in a claim to a chair having "a first leg and a second leg", the first and second legs can be attached or produced in any order, and in any positions with respect to one another. The first leg, for example, might well be in the front or the back of the chair.

It may even be the case that the "first" and "second" items are the same thing! Consider the following two claims in U.S. 6683924 (Jan. 2004) "Apparatus and methods for selective correlation timing in rake receivers":

> 1. A method of processing a communications signal, the method comprising the steps of: generating respective correlation metrics for respective ones of a plurality of multipath components of *a first signal*, a respective one of which has a respective time associated therewith; and generating respective time-offset correlations of *a second signal* with a modulation sequence at respective correlation times ....
>
> 2. A method according to claim 1, wherein the first and second signals comprise the same signal.

In claim 1 there is no limitation as to whether the first and second signals are the same signal, so that claim covers both possibilities. The dependent second claim is expressly limited to situations where the first and second signals are the same signal.

Where there are potentially many instances, it is proper to refer to a "first" instance and a "second" instance. One can also refer to a "first" and "another". See U.S. 6402762 (June 2002) "System for translation of electromagnetic and optical localization systems".

> 1. A system for utilizing and registering at least two surgical navigation systems during stereotactic surgery, the system comprising:
>
> > a first surgical navigation system defining *a first patient space*;
> >
> > at least one additional surgical navigation system defining at least one additional patient space; and
> >
> > at least one translation device....

Of course, this language is still not as clean as it could be. The drafter should have recited "an additional patient space" rather than "at least one additional patient space", and "an additional surgical navigation system" rather than "at least one additional surgical navigation system".

E)   Antecedent Basis

Patent attorneys and agents may be unique in the degree to which they focus on the definite and indefinite articles "the" and "a". If someone asks whether I want to go to "the movies", the patent attorney in me is resistant to answering the question because I don't know which movie they are talking about. Unless there is only a single movie in town, a better phrasing of the question would be whether I want to go to "a movie". Although annoying in social circumstances, and irritating to opponents in deposition situations, that usage comes from years of drafting patent applications. Here's what happened when my wife asked if I wanted to go to "the" movies.

Yes, patent practitioners really do distinguish between "a" or "an" object and "the" object

Patent Beast   © FISH 2009

BOB ON PHONE WITH HIS WIFE, JULIE...

HONEY, DO YOU WANT TO GO TO THE MOVIES?

THAT'S INDEFINITE. WHEN IS IT? WHERE IS IT?

WHAT MOVIE? HOW MUCH DOES IT COST?....

CLICK!

Patent Beast

© FISH 2009

HI HON... LOST YOU ON THE PHONE.

NO, YOU DIDN'T. I HUNG UP.

NORMAL PEOPLE DON'T TALK LIKE THAT!

The rule in patent applications is that the definite term "the" should not be used with respect to an element until the indefinite term "a" is previously used in the same claim, or in a parent claim. The error is called absence or lack of "antecedent basis". This is readily appreciated with a few examples.

- It is improper to say, "A shoe wherein the body is removably attached to the sole". There is no antecedent basis for "the body" and "the sole". One could, however, properly recite: "A shoe having a sole and a body, wherein the body is removably attached to the sole"

- It would also be wrong to recite, "A shoe having a sole and a body, wherein the sole comprises the same material as the body...." The reason is that there is no antecedent basis for "the same material". The correct phrasing would be "A shoe having a sole and a body, each comprising a material…" The claim would even be more clearly worded as, "A shoe having a sole comprising a first material, and a body comprising the first material".

Of course, other areas of law also focus on distinctions between definite and indefinite articles. "[I]t is a rule of law well established that the definite article 'the' particularizes the subject which it precedes. ["the"] is a word of limitation as opposed to the indefinite or generalizing force of 'a' or 'an'"[114]. Patent attorneys and agents just focus on the distinction more than most other people do.

Although the rule requiring antecedent basis is rigorously enforced by the examiners, there are instances in which claims slip through with violations. In federal court, such claims may be deemed invalid for indefiniteness, but only where the defect is "severe". In the *Fisher-Price v. Graco*[115] case the defendant argued that claim 6 was invalid for indefiniteness because it lacked an antecedent basis for "said seating area".

---

114 *Work v. United States*, 262 U.S. 200, 208, 43 S. Ct. 580, 67 L. Ed 949 (1923)
115 *Fisher-Price, Inc. v. Graco Children's Prods.*, 2005 U.S. App. LEXIS 23960 (Fed. Cir. 2005)

> 6. An infant swing comprising:
>
>   an upward extending frame support post;
>
>   a swing arm pivotally coupled to an upper end of said
>   frame support post and extending in a
>   downward direction from said upper end of said
>   frame support post;
>
>   a seat coupled to said swing arm and having an upper
>   seating surface;
>
>   said swing arm and said frame support post defining a
>   reconfigurable swing area therebetween;
>
>   a shield coupled to said seat and extending upwardly
>   from said seat and disposed between said
>   reconfigurable swing area and said seating area.

The Federal Circuit disagreed, noting, "[a] claim is not invalid for indefiniteness if its antecedent basis is present by implication. [citations omitted] It is our conclusion that, in this case, 'upper seating surface' is by implication the antecedent basis for 'seating area.' On that basis, we hold that the second half of the shield limitation of claim 6 is not indefinite.[116]

Other cases reach the same conclusion. In *Energizer Holdings v. ITC*,[117] the Federal Circuit held that lack of antecedent basis for the term "said zinc anode" did not render the claim in which they were recited "insolubly ambiguous" and therefore invalid for indefiniteness. The *Energizer* case reiterated the more general principle, "We have held that a claim is not indefinite merely because it poses a difficult issue of claim construction; if the claim is subject to construction, i.e., it is not insolubly ambiguous, it is not invalid for indefiniteness".[118]

Who knows if these cases would be decided the same way after the *Nautilus* case? *Nautilus*[119] raised the standard for determining whether claim language is sufficiently definite. The prior standard was whether it was "possible" for a court to construe the claim language. The new test is whether the claims "clearly indicate" to a competitor what is the scope of the claim.

> ***Nautilus* raised the standard for indefiniteness from "possible to construe" to "clearly indicate"**

Rigorous attention to antecedent basis can give rise to extremely awkward wording, especially when there is a need to recite "at least one" of a particular element. For example, a patent drafter might claim "an electronic circuit containing at least one transistor operatively coupled to <<some other components>>". Later in the claim, he would then need to refer to "the at least one transistor" to clearly designate that the item being referred to falls within the class the "at least one transistor".

---

116 *Id. at 15-16*
117 *Energizer Holdings v. ITC*, 2006 U.S. App. LEXIS 1760 (Fed. Cir. 2006)
118 *Bancorp Servs., L.L.C. v Hartford Life Ins. Co.*, 359 F.3d 1367, 1371 (Fed. Cir. 2004)
119 *Nautilus, Inc. v. Biosig Instruments, Inc.*, 134 S. Ct. 2120 (U.S. 2014)

F)   Claiming Numbers And Ranges

(1)   Precision And Accuracy

Precision and accuracy are two different things. Precision describes the number of digits that are used to express a value, whereas accuracy describes the extent to which a representation is true. For example, if the true temperature of a liquid is exactly 40°C, it would be more precise to say 40.000°C than to say 40°C, but both would be accurate.

pH 10 is usually taken to include a range of 9.95 to 10.05

In patent law, numbers are usually considered to be approximations, with the amount of wiggle-room governed by the degree of precision. For example, a claimed alkalinity of pH 10 is usually taken to include a range of 9.5 to 10.5, while a claimed alkalinity of pH 10.0 is usually taken to include a range of only 9.95 to 10.05. Of course the same applies to units of length, weight, and so forth.

On the other hand, it is understood that only realistic subsets of the permutations are contemplated. For example, U.S. 4851058,[120] claim 1 recites:

> 1. A magnetically hard alloy composition comprised of at least about 10 to about 40 atomic percent neodymium, praseodymium or mixtures thereof; at least about 50 to about 90 atomic percent iron and from about 0.5 to 10 atomic percent boron.

Obviously, it is impossible for all of the components to be present at the upper ends of the specified ranges, i.e., 40% neodymium, 90% iron, and 10 percent boron.

---

120 U.S. 4851058 (Jul. 1998) "High energy product rare earth-iron magnet alloys"

To avoid confusion, our office currently adds language along the following lines when drafting specifications:

> Unless the context dictates the contrary, all ranges set forth herein should be interpreted as being inclusive of their endpoints and open-ended ranges should be interpreted to include only commercially practical values. Similarly, all lists of values should be considered as inclusive of intermediate values unless the context indicates the contrary.

(2)   Endpoints

Claiming ranges of values presents special problems and opportunities. The most common problem is probably failure to focus on the endpoints of a range. A claim reciting "a temperature from 35 - 45 degrees centigrade" is indefinite unless the attorney specifies whether the endpoints 35° and 45° fall within the range. The better language is to state "a temperature from 35 - 45 degrees centigrade, inclusive". Some attorneys finesse the issue by clarifying in the specification that "unless the meaning is clearly to the contrary, all ranges set forth herein are deemed to be inclusive of the endpoints".

Another problem is that prior art as to any portion of a range can invalidate an entire range.

> An article of manufacture comprising a hydrogel bound to a substrate... comprising: at least one polymer derived from 1 to 99 parts by weight of at least one azlactone-functional monomer and 0 to 99 parts by weight of at least one co-monomer....

In the examples above, the patent office would consider the writer to have suggested all combinations covering the entirety of both ranges (azlactone-functional monomer and co-monomer), even though the inventor may have only consciously contemplated less than 1% of those combinations. As long as the combinations are enabled, (i.e., one of ordinary skill in the art would know how to make and use them by employing at most a reasonable amount of experimentation), all of those combinations are treated as prior art and generally preclude a later inventor from claiming any subset of those combinations.[121] The Federal Circuit has even found obviousness where the prior art merely abutted a previously disclosed range,[122] or were so close to the claimed embodiment that one skilled in the art would have expected them to have the same properties.[123]

Does the term "between x and y" include the endpoints?

---

121 *In Re Lance G. Peterson and Ioannis Vasatis*, 315 F.3d 1325, 1329 (Fed. Cir. 2003); In re Malagari, 499 F.2d at 1303 (C.C.P.A. 1974) (concluding that a claimed invention was rendered prima facie obvious by a prior art reference whose disclosed range (0.020-0.035% carbon) overlapped the claimed range (0.030-0.070% carbon)); In re Geisler, 116 F.3d 1465, 1469 (Fed. Cir. 1997) (acknowledging that a claimed invention was rendered prima facie obvious by a prior art reference whose disclosed range (50-100 Angstroms) overlapped the claimed range (100-600 Angstroms))

122 *In re Woodruff,* 919 F.2d at 1578 (Fed. Cir. 1990, (concluding that a claimed invention was rendered obvious by a prior art reference whose disclosed range ("about 1 5%" carbon monoxide) abutted the claimed range ("more than 5% to about 25%" carbon monoxide)

123 *Titanium Metals Corp. v. Banner*, 778 F.2d 775, 783 (Fed. Cir. 1985) (concluding that a claim directed to an alloy containing "0.8% nickel, 0.3% molybdenum, up to 0.1% maximum iron, balance titanium" would have been prima facie obvious in view of a reference disclosing alloys containing 0.75% nickel, 0.25% molybdenum, balance titanium and 0.94% nickel, 0.31% molybdenum, balance titanium)

(3)   Claiming Inside A Previously Disclosed Range

There are two exceptions to the general rule that a patents drafter cannot claim inside a previously known range. First, it is possible to receive a patent on a subset of a previously disclosed range on the grounds that the subset has an "unexpected result".[124] The applicant must show that the result would have been surprising to a person of ordinary skill in a particular art, and usually only applies to the "less predictable fields" such as chemistry, where minor changes in a product or process may yield substantially different results.

The other theoretically valid exception to the rule is that the reference expressly teaches away from the claimed range. Unfortunately, the only case law directly on point appears to be in a dissent.[125]

(4)   "About"

> **What does the term "about" even mean? It may be indefinite**

The term "about" raises yet another issue with respect to claiming ranges. Should a patents drafter say "about 1-3% chromium" or should they simply say "1-3% chromium"? The answer is that it is probably better to use the qualifier. Both terms should be construed to include slight variations on the specified range, but the former includes those variations within the literal scope of the claim whereas the latter includes those variations (less desirably) only through the doctrine of equivalents.

Although some examiners continue to reject claims containing the term "about" as being indefinite, they are wrong in doing so. Use of the term "about" is entirely acceptable, and should be according its ordinary meaning of "approximately". See *Merck & Co. v. Teva Pharms. USA, Inc.*,[126] "We reverse the District Court's construction of "about" and hold that such term should be given its ordinary meaning of "approximately". See also *In re Harris*,[127] "Application's use of the term 'about' shows that the applicants did not intend to limit the claimed ranges to their exact end-points" and *Jeneric/Pentron, Inc.*,[128] which held that failure to use term "about" limits numeric statements to the exact number recited.

One should, however, be cognizant of what is being qualified by the term "about". In 2005[129] a District Court construed "about 70 mg of alendronate monosodium trihydrate" to mean "exactly 70 mg of alendronic acid when taking into account molecular weight variances for its derivatives that carry accessories". The claim language was as follows:

> A method for treating osteoporosis in human comprising orally administering about 70 mg of alendronate monosodium trihydrate, on an alendronic acid basis, as a unit dosage according to a continuous schedule having a dosing interval of once-weekly.

---

124 *In re Mayne*, 104 F.3d 1339, 1343, (Fed. Cir. 1997)

125 *Para-Ordnance Mfg. v. SGS Importers Int'l*, 73 F.3d 1085, 1088, (Fed. Cir. 1995)

126 *Merck & Co. v. Teva Pharms. USA, Inc.*, 395 F.3d 1364, 1369 (Fed. Cir. 2005), Rehearing, *en banc*, denied *Merck & Co. v. Teva Pharms. USA, Inc.*, 2005 U.S. App. LEXIS 6814 (Fed. Cir. Apr. 21, 2005).

127 *In re Harris*, 409 F.3d 1339, 1343 (Fed. Cir. 2005)

128 *Jeneric/Pentron, Inc. v. Dillon Co.*, 205 F.3d 1377, 1381 (Fed. Cir. 2000)

129 *Merck & Co., Supra*, 395 F.3d 1364

The Federal Circuit did eventually overrule the District Court on that point, and thereby completely changed the outcome of the case. But the Federal Circuit acknowledged that it was a close call.[130]

(5) Claiming Averages

Claiming averages poses significant traps for the unwary. For example, in litigation[131] regarding U.S. Patent No. 6066861, the Federal Circuit considered a claim reciting *inter alia* "pigments having grain sizes ≤ 20 µm and a mean grain diameter $d_{50} \leq 5$ µm. The appeal focused on whether the mean grain diameter should be calculated on a number-based average (average diameter) or a volume basis (diameter of grain with average volume). The analysis is complicated by the fact that the claimed d_{50} term generally indicates a median – not a mean. The majority chose the number-based diameter calculation, although there was a vigorous dissent by Judge Dyk. The lesson here is that if you do recite averages in your claims, you should specify how those averages are to be calculated.

> **Failure to specify what type of "average" can render a claim indefinite**

G) Special Types Of Claims

(1) Structure Versus Method Claims

There are basically only two types of subject matters that can be claimed, things and processes (i.e., methods). Claims to things are variously called device, apparatus, composition, structure, and system claims depending on the nature of what is being claimed. A sample structure claim is as follows:

> 1. A pipe fitting system comprising:
> a body; and
> a collet slidably disposed completely within the body.

Claims to processes are called process or method claims. A sample method claim corresponding to the structure claim is as follows:

> 1. A method of fitting a piece of pipe into a body, comprising:
> providing the body with a collet slidably disposed
> completely within the body; and
> inserting an end of the pipe within the body.

Each type of claim has its advantages and disadvantages. Structure claims are often extremely useful because they deal with recognizable physical objects such as housings, rings, ball bearings, levers, joists, motors, polymers, chemical elements, and so forth. It is therefore relatively easy for a judge or jury to determine infringement. Moreover, a structure claim is infringed as long as the accused product contains the claimed physical

---

130 *Id.*, at 1370-71
131 *OSRAM GmbH v. ITC*, 505 F.3d 1351, 1354 (Fed. Cir. 2007)

elements. Any purpose of the device, and any intention of the user, are generally irrelevant to interpreting either the scope of the claim or infringement. Structure claims are less useful when the structure cannot be determined. For example, computer chips are practically impossible to reverse engineer with current technology. That works well for keeping a chip design as a trade secret, but is likely far less useful when it comes time to accuse someone of patent infringement. The patent holder bears the burden of proving infringement, and it may be impossible to examine an allegedly infringing chip at a sufficient level of detail to ascertain whether the product contains the claimed structure.

Method claims are especially useful where the invention is mostly a process rather than a finished product. In U.S. 6548559 (April 2003) "Thermoplastic compositions and methods", for example, the inventor claimed the following:

> 1. A process for producing a composition comprising the steps of:
>   providing a reduced rubber containing product, a paraffin
>   and a reduced thermoplastic...
>   derived from a waste product;
>   combining the reduced rubber containing product, paraffin
>   and reduced thermoplastic to produce a ....
>   combination...without previously forming and
>   heating an intermediate from the rubber containing
>   product and paraffin; and
>   reducing the rubber/paraffin/thermoplastic combination
>   while the combination is at an elevated temperature
>   of between about 360°F and about 500°F.

There, a major part of the invention was the order in which the ingredients were mixed. It would have been nearly impossible to claim the end product because another patent, U.S. 5114648 (May 1992), had previously taught using the same ingredients to make the same product. Method claims are also useful for claiming use of a product, such as using a drug to treat a new disease, or using a circular saw blade to cut into wet concrete.

Method claims are easier to draft, but often more difficult to enforce

Some attorneys like method claims because they are fairly easy to draft. But method claims can be problematic to enforce. After all, how can a jury decide on infringement of claims to a method of manufacturing if there is no testimony as to the way it was manufactured? Or how can a patent holder sue the thousands of individuals for use of a tool that has other, non-infringing uses. Unless the accused infringer is actively inducing infringement, the patent holder may have a hard time prevailing in court.

There is a loophole with respect to method claims that redounds to the advantage of foreign competitors. In a 2005 case the Federal Circuit held that "a process cannot be used 'within' the United States as required by section 271(a) unless each of the steps is performed within this country".[132]

> "Ordinarily, whether an infringing activity under section 271(a) occurs within the United States can be determined without difficulty. This case presents an added degree of complexity, however, in that: (1) the "patented invention" is not one single device, but rather a system comprising multiple distinct components or a method with multiple distinct steps; and (2) the

---

132 *NTP, supra,* 418 F.3d at 1313 (Fed. Cir. 2005)

nature of those components or steps permits their function and use to be separated from their physical location.

> "**The use of a claimed system under section 271(a) is the place at which the system as a whole is put into service**, i.e., the place where control of the system is exercised and beneficial use of the system obtained. See Decca, 544 F.2d at 1083. Based on this interpretation of section 271(a), it was proper for the jury to have found that use of [the alleged infringer's] asserted system claims occurred within the United States."

(emphasis added). Many attorneys think there is something to be gained by claiming the same subject matter as both a method and an apparatus. It certainly adds to the number of claims, and raises the total cost of prosecution. The reality is, however, that there is no *per se* nonobvious distinction between a method of using a device and the device itself. Thus, claim 1 in U.S. 5562925[133]

> 1. A therapeutic composition comprising a therapeutically effective amount of an inorganic planar dsp2 platinum (II) coordination complex, which complex is protected from light, and which is *suitable for therapeutic administration by injection in solution* therefor, wherein the donor ligands are Cl, Br, CN, NH[3], OS, NO[3], H[2]O, hydroxy, ethylene diamine, or propylene diamine, and wherein the donor ligands of the complex form coordinate covalent bonds with the central platinum ion.

is "not patentably distinct" from claim 1 in U.S. 4339437,[134] despite the inclusion of the new term "suitable for therapeutic administration by injection in solution".

> 1. A method of treating animal malignant tumor cells sensitive to a planar dsp2 platinum(II) coordination compound or an octahedral [sic] d2sp3 platinum (IV) coordination compound wherein the donor ligands are Cl, Br, CN, NO[3], ethylene diamine, propylene diamine, pyridine, H[2]O, OH, OS, in animals which comprises parenterally administering to an animal afflicted with said tumor cells a solution containing one of said compounds in an amount sufficient to cause regression of the animal tumor cells.

(2)   Means-Plus-Function Claims

In 1946 the U.S. Supreme Court struck down a patent claim that recited an invention using purely functional language.[135] In response, Congress added a new section[136] to the patent law, which expressly authorized claims to describe physical elements as a "means" for accomplishing some task. Claims that include one or more such means-plus-function elements are called means-plus-function claims. Here's an example.

---

133 U.S. 5562925 (Oct. 1996) "Anti-tumor method"
134 U.S. 4339437 (Jul. 1982) "Anti-tumor method"
135 *Halliburton Oil Well Cementing Co. v. Walker*, 329 U.S. 1 (1946)
136 35 U.S.C. § 112, para. 6

An apparatus for supporting a baby bottle on an infant carrier
during feeding of an infant comprising:
    means for holding the baby bottle;
    non-obstructing, narrow means, coupled to the means
    for holding, for supporting the baby bottle ....

Means-plus-function claims were very popular until the early 1990s. The idea was that a clever patent drafter

Using means-plus-function language in patent claims is usually a bad idea

could claim an apparatus without expressly limiting the elements by a particular structure. Thus, a doorknob could be broadly claimed as a "means for opening a door", and a bottle could be broadly claimed as a "means for carrying a substance". The problem, of course, is that the essence of a structure claim (apparatus/device/composition/software) is that it defines structure, and means-plus-function claims circumvent structural limitations precisely because they define elements by their function.

Congress resolved that problem by limiting the scope of means-plus-function claims to the embodiments actually disclosed in the specification and drawing, and structural equivalents thereof. For example, if a claim recites "means for opening a door" and the only such means disclosed in the application was a doorknob, the "means" would only include the disclosed doorknob and more or less exact structural equivalents. "means for opening a door" would therefore very likely exclude a latch type opener.

My recommendation is to avoid means-plus-function claims. The scope of equivalents accorded a means-plus-function element is narrower than the scope afforded other elements under the doctrine of equivalents, and it is usually trivial to revise a draft claim to eliminate the means-plus-function language. There is even a risk that failing to clearly link the structure disclosed in the specification with the function recited in the claim can invalidate the claim for failure of the written description.[137] "The duty to link or associate structure in the specification with the function is the *quid pro quo* for the convenience of employing 35 U.S.C. § 112, para. 6".[138]

Our office almost never uses means-plus-function claims, and the practice of others is finally falling into line. In most of the 1980s about 45% of patents contained at least one means-plus-function claim, but according to research done by Patently-O, that number had dropped to only about 6% by 2013, despite a large increase in the average number of claims per patent.

There are still adherents of means-plus-function claims, even among practicing patent attorneys and agents. One argument is that the *Festo* line of cases has all but eliminated the doctrine of equivalents for elements in claims that have been narrowed during prosecution. Since means-plus-function elements are interpreted under 35 U.S.C. § 112 paragraph 6 rather than the doctrine of equivalents, they might escape from the *Festo* limitations. Interesting idea, but it doesn't fly. First, the rationale behind the *Festo* limitations applies just as well to means-plus-function language as to structural language. Second, means-plus-function language unnecessarily narrows the claims. Any element that can be drafted using means-plus-function language can be better drafted using structural language.

Another possible rationale is to use means-plus-function (or step-plus-function) language to narrow the scope sufficiently to avoid §101 invalidity under *Alice* and its progeny. The idea is that the claimed subject matter

---

137 *In re Donaldson Co.*, 16 F.3d 1189, 1195 (Fed. Cir. 1994) (en banc)
138 *Kahn v. GMC*, 135 F.3d 1472, 1476 (Fed. Cir. 1998)

might be found eligible because the claims must be interpreted in a manner that doesn't "preempt the field". That seems to be a valid argument, although failure to preempt the field does not necessarily render the subject matter patent eligible.

There are other, even more obscure rationales for using means-plus-function language. For example, use of means-plus-function language may preclude an interference proceeding,[139] even where the junior applicant copies the claims of the senior applicant verbatim in an effort to trigger an interference. Since the scope of the claims is limited to equivalents of that disclosed in the specification vis-à-vis the means-plus-function terms, claims of different specifications would be according different scopes even though they have identical claims.[140] Of course, since the U.S. has gone from a first-to-invent to a first-to-file system, interference proceedings are almost entirely in the rearview mirror.

> **Means-plus-function claims might be useful to avoid §101 rejections**

In the past, use of a term other than "means" would typically not implicate means-plus-function interpretation under 35 U.S.C. § 112(6).[141] However, in the last few years patent practitioners have become so adept at using nonce words, that the courts have gotten to the point where almost any language that fails to indicate structure is interpreted as a mean-plus-function term.[142]

> **"Connector" and other nonse words, without structure, will trigger a means-plus-function interpretation**

Moreover, almost any use of the term "means" will result in the term being construed as a means-plus-function element. In *Cross Med. Prods., Inc. v. Medtronic Sofamor Danek, Inc.*, the Federal Circuit held that correlation of means-plus-function language with a specific physical structure, as in "securing means … i.e. a nut" is insufficient to disavow the § 112 ¶ 6 equivalents.[143]

(3)   Step-Plus-Function Claims

Step-plus-function claims are simply the method equivalents of means-plus-function apparatus claims. They suffer from all the same drawbacks, and have all the same (tenuous) advantages. The signal for implicating 35 U.S.C. § 112(6) is, however, just a bit subtler. Use of the common method language "comprising the steps of" does not implicate 35 U.S.C. § 112(6), but use of the term "step for" does.[144]

> **Step-plus-function claims generally have the same advantages and disadvantages ads means-plus-function claims**

(4)   Product-By-Process Claims

Product-by-process claims are intended to protect a final product without having to recite the structure of what is being protected. Such claims are appropriate when an inventor processed starting materials in various ways to wind up with a useful product, but doesn't really know what the final product is. All he has to do is recite

---

139 An interference proceeding is a mini-trial internal to the patent office to determine which of two or more competing inventors has priority of invention over a claimed subject matter

140 See MPEP § 2301.03, citing 37 C.F.R. § 41.200(b)

141 *Fonar Corp. v. GE*, 107 F.3d 1543, 1552 (Fed. Cir. 1997), citing *Greenberg v. Ethicon Endo-Surgery, Inc.*, 91 F.3d 1580, 1584 (Fed. Cir. 1996)

142 *Williamson v. Citrix Online, LLC*, 792 F.3d 1339 (Fed. Cir. 2015)

143 *Cross Med. Prods., Inc. v. Medtronic Sofamor Danek, Inc.*, 424 F.3d 1293, 1308 (Fed. Cir. 2005)

144 *Utica Enters. v. Fed. Broach & Mach. Co.*, 109 Fed. Appx. 403, 409-410 (Fed. Cir. 2004)

(a) the starting materials, and (b) the process by which those materials are combined. For example, U.S. 5670671 recites:

> 2. **_Process for the production of_** a [sic] improved form of Ranitidine Hydrochloride having improved filtration and drying characteristics and having:
> (i) a bulk density of not less than about 0.23 gm/ml; and,
> (ii) a tap density of not less than about 0.28 gm/ml, said process comprising adding Ranitidine Hydrochloride to a substantially anhydrous hydroxylic ... and subsequently recovering ....

Although product-by-process claims are almost always chemical inventions, it is possible to write a product-by-process claim for a physical device. U.S. 6047711 (April 2000) "Method and apparatus for converting a power-driven toothbrush into a power-driven flossing device" claims an electric powered tooth-flossing device made by converting an electric toothbrush to vibrate floss rather than bristles.

The attorney who drafted this claim was actually quite clever in using the product-by-process format, since a claim directed to the end device would very likely have been precluded by the prior art. On the other hand, the attorney made other mistakes that render the claim either worthless or nearly so. Among other things he used means-plus-function language (which should have gone the way of the great auk years ago), and he included all sorts of unnecessary limitations, such as the yoke having free ends configured to interact with an anomaly in the floss.

> 1. A tooth flossing device for dental hygiene... comprising:
> A. means for receiving energy from said toothbrush originally provided to move toothbrush bristles; and
> B. **means for converting received energy** into movement of a floss string for dental ....

Here is another example, this time in the field of data processing (U.S. 6089742 July 2000):

> 1. A machine having a memory which contains a data structure which represents the shape of a physical object in a position and/or motion control machine as a hierarchy of bubbles **_generated by a method comprising the steps of_**:
> first locating the medial axis of the object and then creating a hierarchy of bubbles on the medial axis.

Product-by-process claims should be used sparingly. The chief downside is that a competitor can often circumvent the claims by reverse engineering the product, and then using a different method to manufacture the product. Since the claims hinge upon a method of production, the competitor would escape infringement. "[E]ven though product-by-process claims are limited by and defined by the process, determination of patentability is based on the product itself. The patentability of a product does not depend on its method of production. If the product in the product-by-process claim is the same as or obvious from a product of the prior art, the claim is unpatentable even though the prior product was made by a different process".[145] If an inventor does need to file a product-by-process claim, it is probably advisable to follow up with the filing of a structure patent as soon as he determines the chemical or physical structure of the product.

One must also be careful to avoid inadvertently transforming an ordinary claim into a product-by-process claims during prosecution. In an unpublished case,[146] the Federal Circuit held that the following claim had been transformed into a product-by-process claim during prosecution.

> A building construction assembly... comprising:
>   a header having a web and ...;
>   a stud having a ...;and
>   an attachment means passing through said slot and
>   through said hole to **_slideably unite_** said header
>   to said stud....

The cause of the transformation was merely the addition of the italicized language in response to a question as to how the stud 'aligned' with the vertical slot. One could have said:

> A building construction assembly... comprising:
>   a header having a web and ...;
>   a stud having a ...;and
>   an **slidable** attachment means passing through said slot
>   and through said hole **_configured to unite_** said
>   header to said stud....

Still another oddity of product-by-process claims is that the process recited in a product-by-process claim limits the scope of the claim for purposes of validity and infringement, but not for patentability. Thus, the claim is both harder to get, and narrower in scope.[147]

(5)   Markush Groups

Markush groups are simply listings of alternative elements in a peculiar format. The practice began years ago when the patent offices were much stricter than they are today about refusing to allow the disjunctive term "or" in a claim. If someone claimed a chair, for example, he might well want to specify that the chair could be held together "with nails, screws, bolts, dowels, or glue". But claiming the alternatives in that way uses the term "or", which risks rendering the claim indefinite. After all, which of the connectors is being claimed? Markush groups solved that problem by using a stilted format relying exclusively on the injunctive term "and".

---

145 MPEP § 2113; *In re Thorpe*, 777 F.2d 695, 698 (Fed. Cir. 1985) (citations omitted) (Claim was directed to a novolac color developer. The process of making the developer was allowed. The difference between the inventive process and the prior art was the addition of metal oxide and carboxylic acid as separate ingredients instead of adding the more expensive pre-reacted metal carboxylate. The product-by-process claim was rejected because the end product, in both the prior art and the allowed process, ends up containing metal carboxylate. The fact that the metal carboxylate is not directly added, but is instead produced in-situ does not change the end product.)

146 *Slip Track Sys. v. Metal Lite, Inc.*, 113 Fed. Appx. 930, 937 (Fed. Cir. 2004)

147 *Abbott Labs. v. Astellas Pharma, Inc.*, 566 F.3d 1282 (Fed. Cir. 2009)

The chair would be claimed as being held together with "at least one of a nail, a screw, a bolt, a dowel, and glue".

The elements grouped in a Markush claim can be almost anything, from chemical compounds (Jan 2002):

> 4. The deproteinized natural rubber of claim 2, wherein said anionic surfactant is *selected from the group consisting of* carboxylic acid surfactants, sulfonic acid surfactants, sulfate surfactants and phosphate surfactants.

to information processing (U.S. 6892316 May 2005):

> 6. The method of claim 5, wherein *the configuration data is selected from the group consisting of* unique identifier data, architecture map data, field replaceable unit configuration data, and combinations thereof.

to methods of doing business (U.S. 6892145 May 2005):

> 1. A method for collecting power distribution system data, said method comprising: ... receiving at least one input signal sensed by a device *selected from the group consisting of* a current sensor, a voltage sensor, circuit breaker, and any combinations thereof....

More recently the various patent offices are much more receptive to use of the term "or" in the claims. The practice seems to have begun with chemical composition claims that recited R groups in the alternative (... where R1 is H, OH, lower alkyl, lower alkane, methoxy, or ethoxy...), and then expanded to other fields. We still tend to use Markush claiming though, because it is technically more correct, and some day the courts could again determine that claims using "or" are indefinite.

A Markush group is the proper way to claim an alternative list of items

If one is going to use a Markush group, one should at least use it correctly. The proper wording has the format "a ___ consisting of the group selected from the list consisting of ___, ___, ___ and ___". Note that one should use the exact phrase "selected from the group consisting of". Second, the final connecting word is the conjunctive "and" rather than the disjunctive "or". That may seem strange to some, but it actually makes sense. A list consists of elements a, b, c, d, and e, not a, b, c, d, or e".

The following is improper because the Markush groups to claim entirely different inventions.[148]

> 1. ***A system or method selected from the group consisting of***:
> (A) a system for saving a file selected using an email program, the system comprising:
> > (A) an email server...;
> > (B) a system for notifying an email ...; and
> > (D) a method for saving a file ...;
> > (E) a method for notifying an email recipient that a selected file is available for access, the method comprising the steps of....

(6)   Jepson Claims

The Jepson format allows a patentee to use the preamble to recite "elements or steps of the claimed invention which are conventional or known".[149] "When this format is employed, the claim preamble defines not only the context of the claimed invention, but also its scope".[150]

Jepson claims have the general format of a rather lengthy preamble, "A <<device or method>> having <<elements A, B, C, and D>>, wherein the improvement comprises:", followed by a listing of the novel element(s). The following claim from U.S. 6877612 (April 2005) "Filter cartridge for use in severe environments" is a Jepson claim, in which the entire portion preceding "wherein the improvement comprises" constitutes the preamble.

> 6. **An improved filter** cartridge for use in severe environments having a core containing top and bottom ends, a reinforcing band encircling and attached to the core at each of the top and bottom ends, the core surrounded by filtration media and covered at the top and bottom ends by end caps, **wherein the improvement comprises** the end caps and filtration media sealed and secured ....

---

148 U.S. 2005/0086313 (Apr. 2005).
149 37 C.F.R. § 1.75(e) (1996)
150 *Rowe v. Dror,* 112 F.3d 473, 479 (Fed. Cir. 1997)

Note that it is also possible to achieve the same effect as a Jepson claim, without expressly using the Jepson format. Claim 1 of U.S. 6898670 (May 2005) places numerous elements of the prior art in the preamble, but omits the Jepson language, "wherein the improvement comprises":

> 1. A method for storage virtualization in a Storage Area Network (SAN) comprising an array of hosts coupled to an array of storage devices via a Network Switch operative for routing storage I/O operations between the array of hosts and the array of storage devices, the storage devices having a storage capacity, and the array of hosts... comprising the steps of:
> coupling a Storage Virtualization Manager (SVM) ....,
> and
> operating the SVM for ...

Jepson claim format is sometimes used when the invention is only a minor part of something that is already in the prior art, and the person drafting the claims wants to very clearly separate out what is old in the field from what is novel. The format is often a good one, and seems to be appreciated by busy patent examiners. One very strong benefit is that use of Jepson claims forces the patent drafter to figure out just what is the improvement over the prior art. Jepson claims are also relatively easy for jurors and courts to understand during litigation.

The downside, of course, is that when the improvement is so very clearly set forth, its narrowness or invalidity over the prior art may become all too evident. There is also a very real danger in listing too many things in the preamble. The U.S. patent office and several court opinions take the position that the combination of elements set forth in the preamble of a Jepson claim is necessarily old, i.e. recitation of elements in the preamble of a Jepson claim constitutes an implied admission that the combination of those elements is within the prior art.[151] That is mostly true, but not always.

Another potentially serious drawback to the Jepson format is that filing of the claim can be regarded as an implied admission that subject matter in preamble is prior art work of another!!! Even if the Jepson claim is thereafter canceled, the admission can remain.

Use of Jepson claims is dangerous.
A Jepson claim is an implied admission that subject matter in preamble is prior art work of another!!!

Fortunately, not all Jepson claims are deemed to constitute implied admissions. In *In re Ehrreich*[152] the examiner considered material from the preamble of a Jepson claim as prior art when making an obviousness rejection. The *Ehrreich* court found that rather than making an admission about the scope and content of the prior art, the applicant used Jepson language to avoid a double patenting rejection in the applicant's co-pending application. That co-pending application was not available to the public, was not the work of another, and was therefore not prior art under any statutory provision. The court concluded: "We think that a finding of obviousness should not be based on an implied admission erroneously creating imaginary prior art. That is not the intent of § 103.

151 *In re Pfeiffer*, 2000 U.S. App. LEXIS 27336 (Fed. Cir. 2000); Ethicon Endo-Surgery v. United States Surgical Corp., 93 F.3d 1572, 1577 (Fed. Cir. 1996)
152 *In re Ehrreich*, 590 F.2d 902, 909-10 (C.C.P.A. 1979)

H)   Claiming Results Rather Than Structure

A clever patents drafter can sometimes find a way of claiming a result without using either means-plus-function language or product-by-process claims. The following claim was deemed allowable by the PCT examining authority, but never issued.[153]

> 1. A method of imparting an image to a metallic surface comprising:
> providing the surface with a bonding area;
> coating the bonding area with a highly cross-linked polymer having a **hardness great than 80** (Shore D, ASTM D2240) and **a coefficient of elasticity of at least 120%** without breaking;
> curing the polymeric coating; and
> sublimating dyes characterizing the image into the coating.

In that example the applicant recites a minimal amount of structure -- just enough to justify claiming the desired results of hardness, flexibility, and so forth. But one needs to be extra careful with this type of claiming. Patent examiners regularly (and correctly) reject claims that recite results in lieu of structure or specific steps.

I)   Claiming Negatives

It is generally a very bad idea to use the term "not" in a patent claim. The problem is that the term "not" shines as a bright beacon to guide a competitor towards non-infringement. In the claim below, for example, the claim all but tells a competitor to build a non-infringing lamp by including a power source that can be connected to a wall outlet.

> A lamp comprising: a lamp shade; a light bulb having at least has a 100 watt light bulb; and **a power source that is not connected** to a wall outlet.

A much better wording for the claim is as follows:

> A lamp comprising: a lamp shade; a light bulb having at least has a 100 watt light bulb; and a portable power source.

Despite the caveat against using the term "not" in a restrictive sense, it can still be quite advantageous to use the term in an expansive sense. In the following example, the term "not" actually expands the scope of the claim:

> The module of claim 1 wherein the state engine provides a level of intelligence **such that there is not necessarily** a strict one-to-one correspondence between information received from the device, and a signal sent from the state engine.

153 WO/09813147, (Apr. 1998) "Sublimation Dye Transfer Compositions And Methods"

Even so, it's probably best to omit the term "not" in favor of other wording such as "other than".

> The module of claim 1 wherein the state engine provides a level of intelligence *that allows for other than* a strict one-to-one correspondence between information received from the device and a signal sent from the state engine.

J)   Special Considerations For Method Claims

(1)   Software and Business Method Claims

Patent practitioners have used many ways to overly reward patentees relative to their contributions to technology

The patent system is forever trying to balance contributions to technology against benefits (rewards) to patentees. And patent practitioners have forever been trying to game the system by drafting claims that cover more ground than is justified by the contribution.

Until the late '90s, patent practitioners often tried to game the system by drafting claims in means-plus-function format. For example, instead of claiming a door knob having various inventive features, a practitioner might recite a "means for opening a door". The idea was to include within the scope of the claims, all possible combinations of the inventive features with door knobs, latches, and any other "means" that satisfies the function of opening a door. Of course, that strategy seriously upset the balance of contribution vs scope of claim, and was squelched by Congress with passage of 35 U.S.C. 112(6), (now 35 U.S.C. 112(f)).

Undeterred, patent practitioners have more recently come to rely on nonce words, such as "component", "device", "module" and "member" that sound structural, but basically impart no significant structural limitations to the claims. That strategy still upsets the balance of contribution vs reward, and will often trigger a rejection from the examiner. See MPEP § 2181. In addition, the practice has finally started to be seriously curtailed by the Federal Circuit. See for example, *Williamson v. Citrix et al.*[154] addresses interpretation of the language "a distributed learning control module for receiving communications...." The trial court found the claim to be valid by construing the term "control module" to include extraneous limitations related to "a graphical display representative of the classroom". The Federal Circuit, however, construed "distributed learning control module" as being a § 112, ¶ 6 [now § 112(f)] means-plus-function element.

Some practitioners have also tried to game the system by prosecuting claims that go way beyond the scope of the disclosure in the specification and drawing. Interesting strategy, but one that usually doesn't usually work because of the written description and enablement requirements. See for example, *Inphi Corp. v. Netlist, Inc,*[155] and other cases dating back to 1989,[156] and *Univ. of Rochester v. G.D. Searle & Co.*[157]

---

154 *Williamson v. Citrix Online, et al.*, LLC, 603 Fed. Appx. 1010 (Fed. Cir. 2015).

155 *Inphi Corp. v. Netlist, Inc.*, 805 F.3d 1350 (Fed. Cir. 2015)

156 Whether a patent claim satisfies the written description requirement of 35 U.S.C. § 112, paragraph 1 depends on whether the description "clearly allow[s] persons of ordinary skill in the art to recognize that [the inventor] invented what is claimed." Vas-Cath Inc. v. Mahurkar, 935 F.2d 1555, 1562-63 (Fed. Cir. 1991) (internal quotation marks omitted) (quoting In re Gosteli, 872 F.2d 1008, 1012 (Fed. Cir. 1989))

157 *Univ. of Rochester v. G.D. Searle & Co.*, 375 F.3d 1303 (Fed. Cir. 2004)

Patent practitioners also try to game the system using method claims. Because method claims are directed to steps rather than physical structure, they readily lend themselves to drafting claims that overly reward the patent holder. Consider, for example, the invention in *Mayo v. Prometheus*, in which the claimed subject matter was a method of deciding upon a proper drug dosage, by administering the drug to a patient, and then using measurements of metabolites of the drug to either increase or decrease the dosage of the drug. If those claims had been allowed to stand, the patent holder could have extracted royalties from virtually anyone trying to figure out how much drug to give to a patient -- virtually any drug -- any patient -- for any condition. Such claims were ridiculously broad relative to the inventors' trivial contribution to technology.

Another area ripe for abuse are claims reciting software or business methods. Even if the subject matters are recited as system or apparatus claims, the elements of the claims basically involve some sort of hardware that is programmed to implement a set of steps. Since the only claimed structures are well-known electronics, even claims drafted as system or apparatus claims are effectively method claims.

> **Claims reciting software or business methods are especially ripe for abuse**

In *Alice*, the Supreme Court apparently took all of these things into consideration, and basically held that subject matter eligibility doesn't depend on how cleverly the patent drafter worded the claims, and whether the claims are apparatus or methods. The Court instead effectively held that subject matter eligibility depends instead on whether the essence of the inventive, (the "inventive concept"[158]) falls within one of the judicial exceptions, and if it does then whether the claims recite something significantly more.

Patent practitioners and the lower courts should not have been surprised. In *Mayo* the Court rationalized its holding of subject matter ineligibility in part by finding that "... the underlying functional concern here is a relative one: how much future innovation is foreclosed relative to the contribution of the inventor."[159] Similarly in *Myriad*, the Court advised "[p]atent protection strikes a delicate balance between creating 'incentives that lead to creation, invention, and discovery' and 'imped[ing] the flow of information that might permit, indeed spur, invention.'"[160]

And readers should remember that these were unanimous Supreme Court decisions! So the real question is not how to circumvent these decisions, but how to live within them. It is no longer adequate to claim software or business methods (a) merely by reciting that the software resides on a non-transitory memory, (b) by expressly reciting the speed or size of data set with which the electronics can execute the methods, (c) including in the elements a general purpose computer or processor, or (d) focusing on some user interface. Those strategies each worked to some extent in the past, but going forward the courts will look through those smoke screens to find the "inventive concept", and then consider whether there are sufficient limitations narrowing that concept to balance the contribution to technology against rewards to the patentee.

And yes, as many commentators have opined, to some extent the current § 101 analysis does involve conflating subject matter eligibility under § 101 with obviousness under § 103. But this should not be viewed as an error on the part of the Court. Under current statutory law, obviousness is a dichotomy; either a claimed subject matter is obvious or it's not. There is no grey. In the new world under Mayo, Myriad and Alice, the court is viewing obviousness on a sliding scale, weighing the extent of contribution to technology (degree of obviousness), against the reward to the patentee.

---

158 *Alice, supra*, 34 S. Ct. at 2355
159 *Mayo*, 132 S. Ct. at 1303
160 *Myriad*, 133 S. Ct. at 2109

What does this mean from a practical standpoint? It means that when drafting the specification and claims for software or business methods inventions, or even for even chemical compositions extracted from nature, the key is to point out how the claims balance the contribution against the reward.

First, this means writing a strong Background description that clearly points out how numerous prior efforts have been unable to develop a good solution to whatever problem is being addressed. Like a presentation from a good salesman, the emphasis should be on the difficulty of the problem, and the great need for a solution.

Second, this means writing the detailed description in a manner that points out viable alternatives that are not covered by the claims. Patent attorneys and agents are usually fairly good at describing both a preferred embodiment, and all sorts of alternative components, orientations, arrangements and so forth that will also work. But rarely do they ever describe alternatives that fall outside the scope of the invention. That practice leaves the reader (competitor, judge, jury) to understand that the inventive subject matter is extremely broad, but doesn't give a clear picture of the bounds of what was invented.

Third, this means writing claims having scope that is commensurate with the scope of the invention. If the invention is narrow, in a crowded filed, then the corresponding claims should be narrow. If the invention opens up a whole new area of technology (e.g., invention of solid state electronics, or lasers), then yes the claims should be drafted broadly.

All of this, of course, is counterintuitive to a great many inventors. Their goal is to get the broadest possible patent claims, which is completely understandable in a competitive society such as ours. But it doesn't help the society, and indeed it often just puts money in the hands of the patent practitioners and litigators.

In the United States there are four independent categories of inventions or discoveries that are eligible for patent protection: (1) processes, (2) machines, (3) methods of manufacturing and (4) compositions of matter. Since at least 1981 the U.S. Supreme Court has interpreted those categories so broadly that there are really only three categories of exceptions, i.e., subject matter that is not patentable under 35 USC § 101, "laws of nature, physical phenomena, and abstract ideas".[161]

(2)   Claiming Artificial Intelligence (AI) Inventions

Even more than other software inventions, claiming AI inventions runs into serious problems with respect to level of abstraction. At the low end of abstraction, one is very unlikely to secure claims by focusing on formulas or calculations. There is a long-standing rule that algorithms *per se* cannot be patented. At the high end of abstraction, one is unlikely to secure claims by treating AI as black box, i.e., merely reciting that one feeds a set of data into an AI machine, and then the AI figures out what to do. That is just as obvious these days as it is to attach odd types of files to an email message, and let the email client figure out how to send them. The email client is being treated as a black box.

What is still likely to be patentable is to: (1) recite subject matter that is inventive regardless of whether or not AI is involved; (2) recite an invention in the AI itself, for example, how to efficiently model a neural network without using thousands of processing cores; or (3) recite physical structure (e.g., circuitry) that embodies AI processes.

---

161 *Diamond v. Chakrabarty*, 447 U.S. 303, 308–309 (1981)

(3)   Steps Of A Method Claim Are Not Necessarily Sequential

When someone other than a patent attorney or agent reads a method claim, he usually infers that the various recited steps are sequential. For example, in the following claim from U.S. 5114648 (May 1992), an ordinary reader might well assume that the listed steps are to be performed in the order listed.

> 1. A process for producing thermoplastic resin products from an at least partially vulcanized rubber composition, *including the steps of*:
>
> (a) providing said at least partially vulcanized rubber composition;
>
> (b) pre-heating a heavy aromatic ...;
>
> (c) spray coating said heavy aromatic ...;
>
> (d) heating said first intermediate mixture composition;
>
> (e) introducing a thermoplastic composition to said first intermediate mixture...;
>
> (f) masticating said second intermediate composition subsequent to said introduction of said thermoplastic composition; and
>
> (g) extruding said masticated second intermediate composition for producing a final mixture....

> 1. A process for producing a composition comprising the steps of:
>
> providing a reduced rubber containing product, ..;
>
> combining the reduced rubber containing product, paraffin and reduced thermoplastic to produce a rubber/paraffin/thermoplastic combination, *said combination taking place without previously forming and heating an intermediate from the rubber containing product and paraffin*....

Indeed, that was precisely the examiner's argument in rejecting the following claim from a later application to very similar subject matter:

But the examiner was wrong. After several years of arguing, the examiner finally recognized that the earlier claim (and its accompanying disclosure) had no limitation as to order. The later claim did recite a particular order that the original inventor had never contemplated, and on that basis the examiner eventually allowed the claim.[162]

Different patent drafters establish sequence in different ways. Perhaps the most common language for establishing sequence is to use the terms "then", "next", or "thereafter".

162 U.S. 6548559 (April 2003) "Thermoplastic compositions and methods"

> Claim 16. A method for electrolytically treating an aqueous-based solution comprising contaminants, comprising the steps of:
>   (a) contacting said aqueous-based solution with a conductive member having an electric potential…;
>   (b) passing said polarized aqueous-based solution through a first electric field …;
>   (c) *then* passing said aqueous-based solution through a second electric field …; and
>   (d) *then* treating said aqueous-based solution to remove solids therefrom and form a treated solution.

> Claim 1. A method of sampling and analyzing a gas containing volatile organic compounds, comprising the steps of passing the gas through a quantity of liquid…, mixing said tetraglyme with water to form a dispersion, and *thereafter* subjecting the dispersion to gas chromatography/mass spectrometry analysis….

(4)   Hybrid Claims - Combining Method & Structure Limitations

Patent claims are usually either (a) method claims that are primarily directed to steps in a process, or (b) structure claims that are primarily directed to physical limitations such as chemical structures and components -- but not both. The problem is that from time to time an invention is not well described by claims falling into these neat categories. Such inventions must be claimed using hybrid language that combines both method and structure limitations.

The simplest strategy is to claim an apparatus (or chemical structure, etc) in an independent claim, and then recite a method of using the apparatus (or chemical structure). This is often done with pharmaceuticals. In the following example from a withdrawn application,[163] claim 1 recites a pharmaceutical substance, while claim 9 recites use of that substance to treat a disease.

> 9. A method of treating benign prostatic hyperplasia comprising administering an effective dose of a compound of claim 1 or claim 6 to a patient.

---

163 Eventually issued as U.S. 6303594 (Oct 2001) "Arylsubstituted piperizines useful in the treatment of benign prostatic hyperplasia"

Of course, the same technique can be applied to any field (U.S. 6634134 Oct 2003):

> 28. *A method of fishing* ... comprising: a step for *attaching the rod holder of claim 15* to a watercraft or stationary object; a step for attaching a lure or baited hook to a line that is attached to said rod....

Another strategy is to include a step limitation (method) in an otherwise structurally oriented claim. A classic reason to use this strategy is that the product being claimed is substantially indistinguishable from products in the prior art. Even though the real difference is how the product is manufactured, the applicant wants to claim the product rather than the process because product claims are much easier to enforce.

> **A dependent claim is a proper subset of its parent(s), and provides a fallback position in case the parent claim is invalidated**

Here's a sample claim directed to a cured polymer.[164]

> 1. An article of manufacture comprising a hydrogel bound to a substrate, said hydrogel comprising a photocurable and photopatternable composition *which has been photocured*, said composition comprising:
>   a) at least one polymer ...; and
>   b) at least one photocrosslinker....

In that particular case the applicant could have simply recited a cured polymer composition, but specifically chose to circumvent some of the prior art by claiming a photocurable composition that had been photocured.

But it should be noted that some hybrid claims might be declared invalid for indefiniteness. In a November 2005 case,[165] the Federal Circuit held that various claims of Amazon.com's one-click patent[166] were anticipated by the prior art. And interpreting a matter of first impression, the Court further held that claim 25 was invalid for indefiniteness because it attempted to claim both a system and a method.

> 25. *The system of claim 2* wherein the predicted transaction information comprises both a transaction type and transaction parameters associated with that transaction type, and *the user uses the input means* to either change the predicted transaction information or accept the displayed transaction type and transaction parameters.

---

164 U.S. 6156478 (Dec. 2000) "Photocurable and photopatternable hydrogel matrix based on azlactone copolymers"
165 *IPCL Holdings, LLC v. Amazon.com, Inc.*, 2005 U.S. App. LEXIS 25120 (Fed. Cir. 2005)
166 U.S. 6149055 (Nov. 2000) "Electronic fund transfer or transaction system"

In particular, the Court held that claim 25 recited both "the system of claim 2" and a method by which "the user uses the input means…". According to the Court, "it is unclear whether infringement of claim 25 occurs when one creates a system that allows the user to change the predicted transaction information or accept the displayed transaction, or whether infringement occurs when the user actually uses the input means to change transaction information or uses the input means to accept a displayed transaction". In many ways, of course, the rule against hybrid claims set forth in the one-click patent case flies in the face of decades, if not centuries, of patent drafting. Until the rule is clarified by the Supreme Court, or by subsequent Federal Circuit decisions, a patent drafter might do best to avoid relying on hybrid claims.

K)　Design Patents

For several decades at the end of the last century, design patents had become less and less valuable due to the difficulty of establishing infringement. Among other things, the Courts used a complex test that involved both "point of novelty" and an "ordinary observer" perspective.

Beginning in 2008 with the *Egyptian Goddess* case[167], however, the test for design patent infringement was simplified to consist of a single inquiry: whether

> "in the eye of an ordinary observer, giving such attention as a purchaser usually gives, [are the] two designs are substantially the same"

(the "ordinary observer test").[168] In other words, infringement prevails whenever an ordinary observer, familiar with the prior art, would be deceived into thinking that the accused design was the same as the patented design.

Egyptian Goddess opened the floodgates to numerous high profile design patent infringement cases, including Apple's™ establishing infringement over Samsung™ and others regarding cell phone design. And perhaps recognizing the growing importance of design patents, Congress followed up by enacting the Patent Law Treaties Implantation Act of 2012[169], which makes it easier to obtain design patents on shapes and other designs. Among other things, the law harmonizes U.S. practice with most of the rest of the world, increasing the design patent term from 14 to 15 years, and allowing applicants to seek many different design inventions with a single application.

But whether greater emphasis on design patents is a good idea remains to be seen. As the Apple litigations have shown, companies with lots of money can use the most minimal of design "inventions" (e.g. rounded corners on cell phones) to beat down their competition with questionable lawsuits filed in favorable jurisdictions. (Did anyone really expect a verdict against Apple in San Jose, California?)

The tests for determining validity and infringement of a design patent are supposed to be identical to those for a utility patent.[170] This includes subject matter under 35 U.S.C. § 101, originality,[171] statutory bars § 102,[172]

167　*Egyptian Goddess, Inc. v Swisa, Inc.* 543 F3d 665, 678, (Fed Cir 2008), cert denied (2009) 556 US1167 (rejecting "point of novelty" test for proving infringement).

168　*Revision Military, Inc. v. Balboa Mfg. Co.*, 700 F.3d 524 (Fed. Cir. 2012), citing *Gorham Co. v. White*, 81 U.S. 511 (1871) and *Egyptian Goddess, Inc. v. Swisa, Inc.*, 543 F.3d 665 (Fed. Cir. 2008).

169　Patent Law Treaties Implementation Act of 2012, Pub. Law 112-211 (December 19, 2012).

170　*Bernhardt, L.L.C. v. Collezione Europa USA, Inc.*, 386 F.3d 1371, 1378 (Fed. Cir. 2004).

171　35 U.S.C. § 171.

172　*Minn. Mining & Mfg. Co. v. Chemque, Inc.*, 303 F.3d 1294, 1301 (Fed. Cir. 2002).

obviousness under § 103,[173] and so forth. And of course a party challenging patent invalidity must establish invalidity by facts supported by clear and convincing evidence.[174]

The problem, as with utility applications, is that Patent Office grants patents on designs that are mere design choices. A design patent § 103 analysis has only two steps. First, the court must identify a proper primary reference—i.e., a "something in existence" that has "basically the same" appearance as the claimed design. Second, other references can be used (assuming certain conditions are met) to modify the primary reference "to create a design that has the same overall visual appearance of the claimed design." That test does nothing to weed out designs that add little or nothing to the world.

The 2013 decision in *High Point Design LLC v. Buyers Direct, Inc.*[175], illustrates the problem. In that case the Federal Circuit overruled the district court's finding that the claimed slippers were obvious over the prior art. Reproduced below are images of the prior art and patented slipper designs. Do the differences in design really justify a patent?

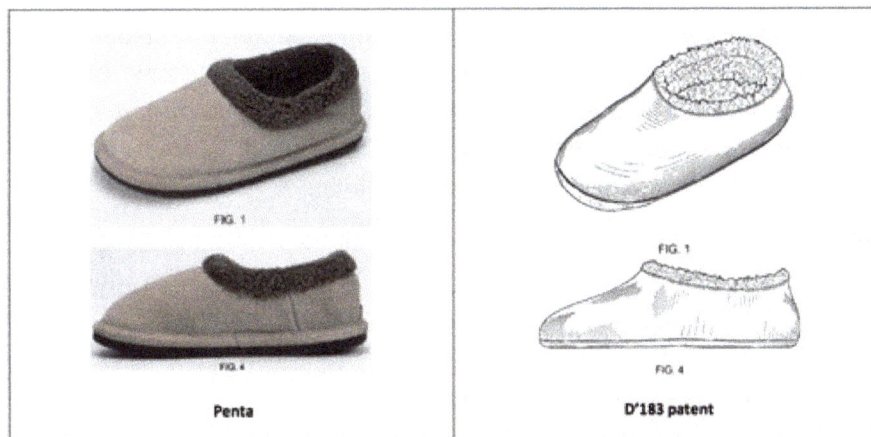

Figure - Prior Art And Patented Slippers Design

Design patents are restricted to claiming ornamental (i.e. nonfunctional) aspects of things.[176] The squiggles at the bottom of silverware, for example, have no function whatsoever except to be decorative. Thus, they would be protected using a design patent. The same goes for designs of sunglasses, automobiles, furniture, and so forth. Similarly, a design for an article of manufacture that is hidden in its end use, and whose ornamental appearance is of no commercial concern prior to reaching its end use, lacks ornamentality and is not proper statutory subject matter. Subject matters that could be considered offensive to any race, religion, sex, ethnic group, or nationality are expressly precluded from patentability.[177]

Many articles, of course, have both a distinctive ornamental appearance and utility, and in such instances they can be protected by both design and utility patents. Thus, the overall shape of a pair of sunglasses might have no functional benefit whatsoever, and therefore could be patented using a design patent. But the chemical composition or the coating of lenses would definitely be functional, and therefore could be patented using a utility patent. In many instances it is extremely difficult to tease out the utilitarian aspects from the ornamental aspects. With respect to sunglasses, for example, the shape of the lenses might be ornamental, functional, or both.

---

173 *Lough v. Brunswick Corp.*, 86 F.3d 1113, 1122 n.5 (Fed. Cir. 1996).

174 *Tone Bros. v. Sysco Corp.*, 28 F.3d 1192, 1197 n.4 (1994).

175 *High Point Design LLC v. Buyers Direct, Inc.*, 2013 U.S. App. LEXIS 18836 (Fed. Cir. Sept. 11, 2013).

176 35 U.S.C. § 171; *Seiko Epson Corp. v. Nu-Kote Int'l, Inc.*, 190 F.3d 1360, 1368 (Fed. Cir. 1999).

177 35 U.S.C. § 171; 37 C.F.R § 1.3.

Design patents have only a single claim, which has substantially the same format for every design patent; "The ornamental design for a _____, as shown". When there is a properly included description of the design in the specification, or a proper showing of modified forms of the design, or other descriptive matter has been included in the specification, the words "and described" should be added to the claim following the term "shown", and the claim should read "The ornamental design for a ____ as shown *and described*".

Design patents also have no specification to speak of, other than the descriptions of the various figures, so that the scope of the claim is determined almost entirely by the drawing. Elements that are considered to be part of the invention are shown in solid lines, and elements that are need to provide context, but are not deemed to be part of the invention, are shown in dotted or broken lines. Design patents are relatively easy to get issued, but usually not worth very much because they are too easy to circumvent. Since the scope of the protection is necessarily limited to ornamental appearance, a competitor need only adopt a different design to circumvent the patent.

A design patent and a product configuration trade dress type of trademark may be obtained on the same subject matter. The underlying purpose and essence of patent rights are separate and distinct from those pertaining to trademarks, and that no right accruing from one is dependent or conditioned by the right concomitant to the other.[178] It is also possible to secure a copyright registration on the same ornamental design as is protected by a design patent.[179] In fact, the Patent Office permits the inclusion of a copyright notice in a design patent, provided *inter alia* that the applicant includes a waiver as follows:

> A portion of the disclosure of this patent document contains material to which a claim for copyright is made. The copyright owner has no objection to the facsimile reproduction by anyone of the patent document or the patent disclosure, as it appears in the Patent and Trademark Office patent file or records, but reserves all other copyright rights whatsoever.

Design patents have always had a place in a patent portfolio for companies such as Oakley™, whose sunglass product lines rely heavily upon ornamental appearance. In light of the recent litigation, it appears that many others could benefit as well.

178 *In re Mogen David Wine Corp.*, 328 F.2d 925 (C.C.P.A. 1964).
179 *In re Yardley*, 493 F.2d 1389 (C.C.P.A. 1974).

Chapter V - Claiming Strategies

A)   Independent Versus Dependent Claims

(1)   What Are Independent And Dependent Claims?

All patent claims are either independent or dependent. Independent claims stand alone, and do not reference any other claim. Dependent claims always reference another claim. Thus, in the following claim set, claim 1 is independent because it does not reference any other claim.

> 1. A chair having only two legs.
>
> 2. The chair of claim 1, further comprising at least one leg made of wood.
>
> 3. The chair of claim 2, wherein at least a portion of the chair is covered with a fabric.

When filing a new patent application, claim 1 should always be independent. During prosecution, of course, claim 1 might be canceled or withdrawn, or it might be amended to recite dependency on a higher numbered claim. No matter. In such cases the examiner will renumber the claims, and place them in logical order, prior to issuance so that the first independent claim is once again numbered claim 1.

Dependent claims reference another claim, and are proper subsets of their parents, i.e. the claim(s) upon which they depend. Continuing with the example above, claim 2 is dependent because it references claim 1 by saying "The chair of claim 1". As proper subsets of their parents, dependent claims include all the limitations of the parent claim. To infringe claim 2, a competitor's chair would not only have to have at least one leg made of wood (the limitation stated in claim 2), but it would also need to have only two legs (the limitation imported by reference to claim 1). Dependent claims can be dependent on either an independent claim, or on another dependent claim. In the example above, claim 3 is dependent on claim 2, and includes all of the limitations of claim 2, plus the limitations of claim 1.

Dependent claims are simply claims that reference another claim, as in "the apparatus of claim 1"

Dependent claims can depend on any other claim, even if that parent claim has a higher number. Thus, claim 2 could be dependent on claim 5 or 7, even though those claims appear later in the listing. Having a claim dependent on a higher number claim often occurs during patent prosecution as a result of cancellation of claims. For example, upon filing claims 2-10 could be dependent on claim 1, and then claim 1 is canceled or withdrawn. The applicant might then add a new claim 18, and amend claims 2-10 to be dependent on claim 18. Even claim 1, which is traditionally an independent claim, could be made dependent on another claim (say claim 15).

Since dependent claims are proper subsets of the claim(s) upon which they depend, people often ask why they are useful. After all, in the example above, a competitor would escape infringement by producing a chair with four legs, i.e. circumventing a limitation from claim 1, regardless of whether the competitor's chair has wood legs or has a fabric covering. The answer is twofold.

A dependent claim is a proper subset of its parent(s), and provides a fallback position in case the parent claim is invalidated

First, dependent claims provide fallback positions during prosecution and enforcement actions. If claim 1 were filed today, for example, it would be anticipated because two-legged chairs have been around for decades. Even if claim 1 somehow made it past the patent office, and issued in a patent, the claim would be invalidated over the prior art during litigation. If claim 1 were the only claim in the patent, the case would be over and the patentee would lose. Claim 2, however, recited the additional limitation that the two-legged chair must have a wooden leg. That claim might well be patentable because the prior art always used metal legs in two-legged chairs. Thus, inclusion of claim 2 in the patent application would have provided a valuable fallback position in case claim 1 was invalidated. The same is true for claim 3. Even if claims 1 and 2 are invalid over the prior art, it might be that the only two legged chairs with wooden legs were made entirely of wood, and had no fabric covering. In that case claims 1 and 2 would be invalid, but claim 3 would still be valid. In short, inclusion of dependent claims in a patent application can provide useful fallback positions during patent prosecution, and then later on during litigation.

The second major benefit of dependent claims is that they help ensure broad interpretation of the claims upon which they are dependent. Consider the following claims:

1. A method of making money for an author, comprising:
    writing a book on patenting that includes at least 90 indexed figures;
    publishing the book through a publisher, and receiving a royalty that provides sufficient income to meet the author's reasonable household expenses without incurring debt.
2. The method of claim 1, further comprising the author having a house that is at least 1500 sq. ft.

3. The method of claim 1, further comprising the author purchasing a house with three acres of land, a 7500 sq. ft. house, a pool, a stable, and a guest house for live-in maintenance help.

4. The method of claim 1, further comprising the author having a spouse and three children in the household.

By itself, claim 1 doesn't establish how much royalty is sufficient to meet the author's reasonable household expenses. Presumably that would be an issue of fact at trial, but it could be argued that "reasonable expenses" are no more than say, $5,000 - $10,000 a month.. However, the fact that the dependent claims are proper subset of independent claim 1 necessarily means that claim 1 is broader in scope than any of the dependent claims. That wouldn't change the scope of claim 1, but it may well help the court to properly interpret claim 1.

This can be shown graphically. The Venn diagram below depicts claims 1 and 2. Since claim 2 is a proper subset of claim 1, the oval for claim 2 is depicted as smaller than, and positioned completely within the circle of claim 2.

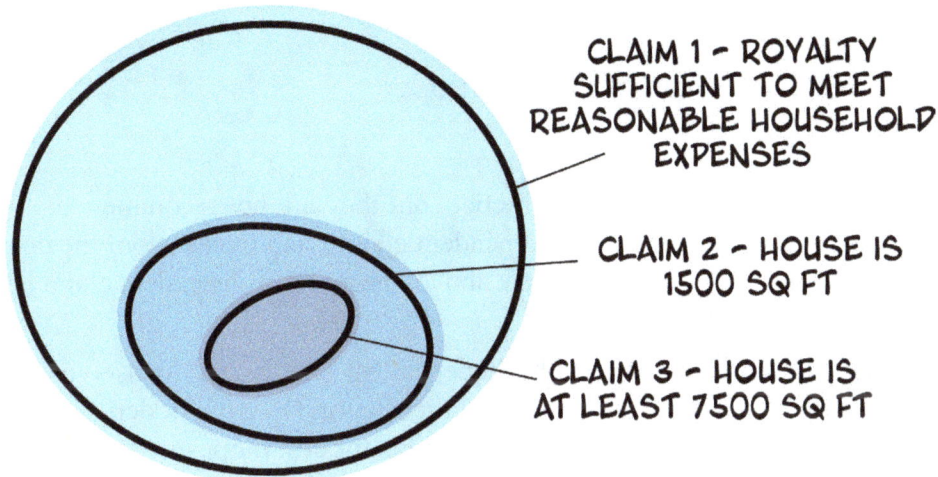

CLAIM 1 - ROYALTY
SUFFICIENT TO MEET
REASONABLE HOUSEHOLD
EXPENSES

CLAIM 2 - HOUSE IS
1500 SQ FT

CLAIM 3 - HOUSE IS
AT LEAST 7500 SQ FT

Figure - Dependent claims Are Proper Subsets Of Their Patents

The inclusion of claim 3, however, requires the term "reasonable household expenses" must be interpreted broadly enough to support a 7500 sq. foot house, not merely a 1500 sq. foot house. Similarly, the inclusion of claims 4 and 5 requires the term "reasonable household expenses" to be interpreted broadly enough to include having a spouse, and sending three children to college at the same time. So to reiterate, adding dependent claims doesn't change the scope of the claims upon which they are dependent. But their inclusion in applications and patents helps the court properly interpret the parent claims in a broad fashion.

The figure below depicts a Venn diagram of dependent claims addressing how different elements of an independent claim can overlap to create a more defensible patent.

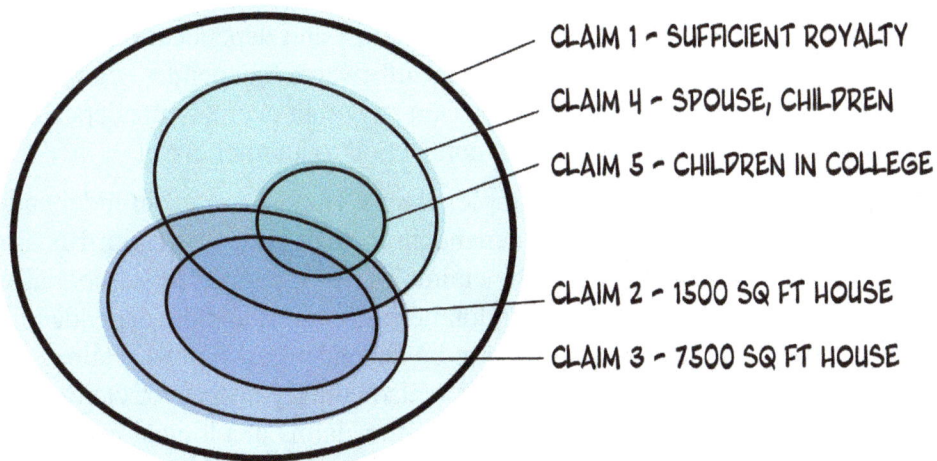

CLAIM 1 - SUFFICIENT ROYALTY

CLAIM 4 - SPOUSE, CHILDREN

CLAIM 5 - CHILDREN IN COLLEGE

CLAIM 2 - 1500 SQ FT HOUSE

CLAIM 3 - 7500 SQ FT HOUSE

Figure - Dependent Claims Help Interpret The Independent claims

(2) Multiple Dependent Claims

Multiple dependent claims are claims that refer to parent claims in the alternative. The following claim is multiply dependent:

> 6. The method of any of claims 1-5....

Multiple dependent claims are allowed in U.S. practice, but they are not recommended. For one thing, the Patent Office charges extra just to have multiple dependent claims, and then each of the dependencies counts as another claim for cost calculations. In the example above, the multiple dependent claim 6 would be counted as five different claims for cost purposes.

It should also be obvious to the reader that multiple dependent claims can themselves have dependencies. Thus, claim 6 may depend upon any of claims 1-5, and then claims 7-10 might depend upon claim 6. In that case each of claims 7-10 would also be counted as five claims for cost purposes.

In U.S. practice it is improper to use multiple-multiple dependent claims; i.e., multiple dependent claims that are themselves children of a multiple dependent claim. Thus, if claim 10 recites "The widget of any of claims 1, 6, or 9, comprising..." claim 11 might properly recite "The widget of any of claims 1, 2, or 3, comprising...." But it would be improper for claim 11 to recite "The widget of any of claims 1, 6, or 10, comprising…" because claim 10 is itself multiply dependent.

(3) Deciding On How Many Independent Claims To Use

Practically every invention can be described in many different ways. The first person to invent a wooden chair, for example, might have focused on the combination of four legs, a seat, and a back, but another person might have focused on the process of using wood and nails to make a seating device. Ideally, one would claim the invention from both perspectives, and possibly others as well.

Most patent applications use a combination of independent and dependent claims

The standard way of claiming an invention from multiple perspectives is to use a combination of independent claims and dependent claims. As discussed above, the distinction is quite straightforward. Independent claims are those that stand alone, without dependence on any other claim, while dependent claims are those that recite some sort of connection to another claim.

In the following example, claims 1 and 6 are all in independent format, while claims 2-6 are all in dependent format. Note that claim 1 is almost always independent. Although the claims must be numbered sequentially during prosecution, there can be gaps caused by withdrawal or abandonment of claims, and the dependencies can be set forth in any order. Thus, it is entirely proper for claims 2-4 to be dependent on claim 1, claim 5 to be dependent on claim 2, and claim 6 to be dependent on claim 3. But is it also entirely proper for claim 6 to be dependent on claim 18! Prior to issuance the patent office will renumber the claims in a logical fashion.

Interestingly, even though it sounds terrible, the wording of "the at least one connector" in claims 3 and 4 is entirely acceptable. The reason is that the drafter is using the definite article "the" to refer to a specific item for which there is antecedent basis, namely "at least one connector". On the other hand it is usually unnecessary to write in such a stilted manner. It would be much better to initially refer to "a connector" and then later refer to "the connector". The term "a connector" means "at least one connector".

> 1. A chair, comprising at least three legs, a seat, and a back, held together with at least one connector.
>
> 2. The chair of claim 1, having a fourth leg.
>
> 3. The chair of claim 1, wherein the at least one connector comprises a nail.
>
> 4. The chair of claim 1 wherein the at least one connector comprises a screw.
>
> 5. The chair of claim 4, in which the screw is at least 1 inch long.
>
> 6. A chair comprising a wooden frame supporting a seat and a back.

A patent can have numerous independent claims. Indeed, some attorneys prefer all their claims to be independent. One advantage is that multiple independent claims make a patent more difficult to analyze when a competitor's attorney is drafting a non-infringement opinion. That result obtains because dependent claims cannot usually be infringed without the independent claim also being infringed. A patent with only one or two independent claims is also much easier to analyze than a patent with 1 independent and 19 dependent claims.

> **There are many potential benefits to using multiple independent claims**

One rather odd advantage of having multiple independent claims is that the claim drafter can call an item by one name in one claim, and the same item by a different name in another claim. For example, the tip of a catheter may be described as "a tip" in one claim, and as "a tapered portion" in another claim. That distinction might turn out to be useful if the term "tip" is ever deemed to be overly vague during litigation.

(4)   Independent Claims Increase Filing & Prosecution Costs

Patent Beast   © FISH 2007

I WOULD LIKE YOU TO DRAFT THE APPLICATION....

....WITH ALL INDEPENDENT CLAIMS.

BUT THE PATENT OFFICE WILL JUST ISSUE A RESTRICTION REQUIREMENT.

THAT'S HOW MY PREVIOUS ATTORNEY DID IT.

There are also serious disadvantages to having so many independent claims. One of the worst problems is that the patent office will often issue restriction requirements, forcing the applicant to prosecute each independent claim (along with its dependencies) in a separate patent application. Such restriction requirements are proper between two independent claims as long as it is possible to practice the combination of one of the independent claims without necessarily practicing the combination in the other independent claim. Another disadvantage is that the examiners typically dislike lots of independent claims. Attorneys sometimes forget that there is a human being examining the patent application, and it does the attorney little good to unnecessarily annoy the examiner.

Another disadvantage is cost. The standard filing fee[180] for a utility application with the U.S. patent office covers up to three independent claims and up to 20 total claims before additional filing fees are incurred. As of June 2022, additional fees for small entities small entity (companies with less than 500 employees) are $240 per independent claim more than three, and $50 for each claim more than twenty. The fees are half that for micro entities under the America Invents Act, and double that for large entities. See Chapter V, section G(1) for a discussion of different entity sizes.

Those additional fees can add up quickly. Let's say a company files a patent application with 20 independent claims. The filing fees (for a small entity filing electronically) are the standard fee of $830,[181] plus the penalty fees for the 17 extra independent claims, which comes to 17 * 240 = $4080, for a total of $4910. Using all those independent claims more than quintuples the filing cost.

It quickly gets worse. The first substantive action of the patent office will be to issue a restriction requirement, forcing the applicant to either abandon, withdraw, or divide out the various independent claims into perhaps five, ten, or even up to twenty separate applications. Let's say the applicant decides to pursue five separate applications. He now has to abandon or at least withdraw several of his originally filed claims with all the attendant prejudice resulting from that action. And in addition he must file another five divisional (i.e. child) patent applications to pursue the withdrawn claims. The out-of-pocket costs on those five divisional applications is 5 * 830 = $4,150, plus paralegal time to file the paperwork. The total cost of filing fees for the twenty original independent claims is now over $8,000 instead of the original $830. If this were a large entity, the unnecessary additional U.S. government filing costs would be over $16,000!

---

180 http://www.uspto.gov/learning-and-resources/fees-and-payment/uspto-fee-schedule.
181 The "filing fees" are comprised of a basic filing fee, a search fee, and an examination fee

Patent Beast   © FISH 2008

Panel 1: BECAUSE YOU INSISTED ON FILING ALL INDEPENDENT CLAIMS...

Panel 2: .... WE WILL HAVE TO ALLOW MANY OF THEM...

Panel 3: ...TO GO ABANDONED.

Panel 4: I HATE THE PATENT SYSTEM!

Even if the examiner doesn't issue a restriction requirement, it is unlikely that all twenty claims will be granted together in the same patent. The more likely result is that after prosecuting all those independent claims for a few years, the patent office will deem three or four of the claims to be allowable. The applicant will pay the issue fee so that the allowed claims can go to issuance. But that leaves seventeen non-issued claims, which must then be filed in a divisional application to continue prosecution.

INDEPENDENT CLAIMS GREATLY INCREASE THE COST OF SECURING US PATENTS

Figure - Too Many Independent Claims Greatly Increase Filing Costs Of U.S. Patent Applications

Worse still, foreign countries will never allow so many independent claims. Thus, after drafting and filing a slew of independent claims for U.S. prosecution, the draftsperson will have to go back and convert some of the independent claims into dependent claims.

All of that is unnecessary. Usually an application containing 20 independent claims could just as well have been drafted with two or three independent claims, and the remainder filed as dependent claims.

(5)   Independent Claims Increase Cost Of Foreign Prosecution

Foreign filing foreign applications can be excruciatingly expensive. Indeed, the problem is much worse where the applicant employs a large number of independent claims. Whereas a single U.S. application with a few independent claims may spawn a family of half a dozen or more foreign applications, the same U.S. application drafted with many independent claims will likely spawn separate families of foreign applications for each of the U.S. divisionals. This is a big reason that a patent family with many foreign filings can easily end up costing the patent holder half a million dollars in prosecution fees!

500,000
400,000
300,000
200,000
100,000
0

■ 1 COUNTRY
■ 5 COUNTRIES
■ 10 COUNTRIES
■ 15 COUNTRIES

3 INDEP   5 INDEP   10 INDEP   20 INDEP
CLAIMS   CLAIMS   CLAIMS   CLAIMS

Figure - Foreign Filing Costs Go Up Even More

In addition, the patent offices of many foreign countries refuse to deal with large numbers of independent claims. The European Patent Office (EPO), for example, allows applications to contain more than one independent claim, but only if the subject matter claimed falls within one or more of the exceptional situations.[182] Otherwise the EPO will usually examine only the first independent claim, and issue a lack of clarity rejection, refusing to examine the remaining claims. The specific rejection will be that "the plurality of claims makes it difficult, if not impossible, to determine the matter for which protection is sought, and places an undue burden on others seeking to establish the extent of the protection".

Having a large number of independent claims is just not practical in foreign countries

Thus, even though the U.S. patent office allows the applicant to keep several independent claims within the same utility application, a foreign patent office may still require the applicant to divide out the foreign application into several divisional applications. Since the expense is often too high to file all those divisionals, the applicant is forced to re-draft his claims to be dependent upon a single independent claim. That additional work is both unnecessary, and expensive. Among other things, all those new claims have to be translated.

As an aside, one wonders why the U.S. Patent Office doesn't adopt a strategy similar to that of foreign countries to reduce the number of claims. As of 2022, the U.S. Patent Office had issued around 11 million patents in the entire history of the country. And yet the Patent Office is currently backlogged with around 684,000 applications.[183]

One solution previously floated by the Patent Office was to severely limit the number of *continuations*. That was a terrible idea. In our many years of experience, Request for Continued Examination (RCE) type continuations are often due to intransigence, inexperience, or illogic on the part of the examiner, and Continuation-In-Part (CIP) type continuations are often the result of the inventor having developed a significant improvement. In both cases the patent office should encourage rather than limit further prosecution. It's a moot point anyway, because rules implementing that idea were deep-sixed by the Federal Circuit.[184]

A better solution is to limit the total number of *claims* of any application to twenty or thirty, and the total number of independent claims to two or three. Yes, that would require those drafting the claims to do the heavy mental lifting of actually figuring out what the "invention" is before filing the application. But we know that can be done. Patent applicants already re-write their claims to meet similar requirements in several foreign countries.

---

182 Article 54 in combination with Rule 29 (2) EPC

183 These and other fascinating facts can be tracked on the USPTO's performance dashboard. https://www.uspto.gov/dashboard/patents/

184 *Tafas v. Kappos*, 586 F. 3d 1369 (Fed. Cir. 2009)

(6)   Use Of Many Independent Claims Is A Smoke Screen

The added out-of-pocket cost of using too many independent claims is only part of the problem. The bigger problem is that filing a great many independent claims is often just a smoke screen for an attorney failing to do the difficult mental work of figuring out what the invention really is. Indeed the "value added" of good patent counsel lies not so much in his knowledge of the field of the invention, or the drafting of application *per se*, but in his conceptualizing of the "invention" at an appropriate level of abstraction. It is that latter skill that allows him/her to clearly identify and claim the inventive subject matter in a commercially valuable manner.

(7)   Recommended Number Of Independent Claims

The patent office recommends that applicants keep their number of independent claims to three or less, and the total number of claims to 20 or less. This is good practice, and in many instances it makes sense to file an application with only a single independent claim. One reason is that multiple independent claims are usually regarded as being directed to multiple inventions, even where they are simply method and apparatus claims directed to the same subject matter. Having several independent claims often triggers a restriction requirement, and ends up forcing the applicant to either prosecute multiple applications or abandon some of the claims. Another reason is that examiners are presently overwhelmed with cases. A case with an unreasonably large number of claims can be viewed unfavorably from the start.

Patent applicants should generally stick to three independent claims

The main exception to filing applications with only a few independent claims is in filing PCT applications. The PCT deals with what they call "disunity" rejections by requiring the applicant to pay an extra fee for each "invention" arising from multiple independent claims. The fee used to be a bargain at only $220 per invention, but as of June 2022, the PCT fee is about $1,330 per invention. While no longer a bargain, that price is still often a good choice when compared to the cost of prosecuting multiple divisionals. When the application goes into national phase, the national phase country or region typically allows the applicant to keep all his claims together.

These suggestions should not be read to imply that only a single inventive subject matter should be disclosed in a given patent application. Quite the contrary. Applications should be filed with several different patentable subject matters, if they can be reasonably combined. The applicant can eventually claim all of those different subject matters in divisionals if need be. It's just more cost-effective to direct the initial set of claims to a single patentable subject matter, and use subsequent divisionals and/or continuations to focus on the other subject matters.

(8)   Claim Differentiation

The doctrine of claim differentiation states that every claim in a patent should be interpreted to have a different scope from every other claim. The effect is to force a parent claim to be read as having broader scope than its "child" dependent claim. This is readily appreciated by example. Consider once again the hypothetical chair claims discussed above:

> 1. A chair, comprising at least three legs, a seat, and a back, held together with at least one connector.
>
> 2. The chair of claim 1, having a fourth leg.
>
> 3. The chair of claim 1, wherein the at least one connector comprises a nail.
>
> 4. The chair of claim 1 wherein the at least one connector comprises a screw.
>
> 5. The chair of claim 4, in which the screw is at least 1" long.
>
> 6. A chair comprising a wooden frame supporting a seat and a back.

In claims 1, 4, and 5, the idea of the connector being a screw was introduced in claim 4. Since claim 4 must have a different scope from claim 1, this necessarily means that claim 1 includes connectors other than screws. That logical conclusion was accomplished without ever claiming what the other choices are, and without ever even including the other choices in the drawing. This can be a significant advantage because for apparatus claims, every claimed element that is susceptible to a drawing should have a drawing. Clever use of the doctrine of claim differentiation allows the person drafting the claims to inherently claim choices without ever having to expressly include them in the drawing figures. To continue with our example, child claim 5 recites that the screw is at least 1 inch long, which necessarily means that claim 4 must be interpreted to include screws having a length less than or equal to 1 inch. Note that claim differentiation only works with dependent claims.

> **Claim differentiation can be a very valuable strategy**

Interestingly, the judicially developed doctrine of claim differentiation cannot be used to trump the statutory limitations on the scope of mean-plus-function and step-plus function claims. As explained by the District Court of NJ in 2001.[185] "A means-plus-function limitation is not made open-ended by the presence of another claim specifically claiming the disclosed structure which underlies the means clause or an equivalent of that structure. Indeed, the doctrine of claim differentiation cannot broaden claims beyond their correct scope, determined in light of the specification and the prosecution history and any relevant extrinsic evidence. Where the meaning of a term is clear based on the relevant intrinsic and extrinsic evidence, pursuant to 35 U.S.C. § 112 P6, the doctrine of claim differentiation cannot alter that meaning."

(9)   Drafting Useful Dependent Claims

Those with less experience tend to draft dependent claims that are technically correct, but that have no real commercial benefit to the patentee. One common problem is trying to list all viable choices in a given dependent claim. For example, if a parent claim recites a mechanical connector, it does little good for the dependent claim to recite that the connector is selected from the list consisting of a nail, a screw, a bolt, a dowel, a tack,

---

185 *Akos Sule et al. v. Kloehn Co.*, 149 F. Supp. 2d 115, 128 (DC NJ 2001); *Retractable Techs., Inc. v. Becton*, 2011 U.S. App. LEXIS 13925 (Fed. Cir. July 8, 2011)

a brad, a clamp..." and so forth. If it turns out that the parent claim is invalid because of prior art relating to the connector being a tack, then both the parent claim and the child claim will be invalidated. If the attorney had listed screws, bolts, and dowels in one dependent claim, and nails, tacks, and brads in another dependent claim, it is entirely possible that one of those dependent claims would still be left standing.

Those with less experience also tend to draft dependent claims that are irrelevant. Remember, the main purpose of most patents is to keep competitors out of the marketplace, or to at least make their entry into the marketplace more difficult. An extreme example of a worthless dependent claim is one directed to an ornamental aspect of a useful device. If the inventor developed a ballpoint pen having a new type of ink, the invention is in the ink, not in the color of the barrel of the pen. The selection of blue, black, or white barrel is merely a design choice having nothing to do with the inventive features. Dependent claims to the color of the barrel would do little more than emphasize that whoever drafted the claims needs to improve his/her drafting skills.

> **Don't waste time and money on obvious dependent claims**

B)   Target Claiming

One of the oldest and best strategies to secure strong patent coverage for an invention is to claim the inventive subject matter using target claiming. In that strategy the applicant drafts a broad claim, and then drafts successively narrower dependent claims relative to a particular parameter. For example, if a manufacturing process is discovered that is effective above pH 8, but works best at around pH 10.3, the broad independent claim might specify a method or apparatus in which the process takes place above pH 8. Dependent claim 1 might specify a pH range of 9.5 - 11.5, with dependent claim 3 specifying pH 10 - 10.5, and dependent claim 4 specifying approximately pH 10.3.

(1)   Simple Target Claiming

The main purpose of target claiming is to retain some measure of protection against infringement, even if prior art comes to the fore that would invalidate the broadest claim. This can be readily appreciated using a Venn diagram. The scope of claim 1 covers the subject matter of the entire target, which includes rings a, b, c, and d. Claim 2 covers rings "a", "b", and "c", while claim 3 covers the inner rings "a" and "b", and claim 1 only covers the innermost ring "a". If invalidating prior art is discovered in ring c, then claims 1 and 2 would fall, but claims 3 and 4 have at least some chance of remaining valid.

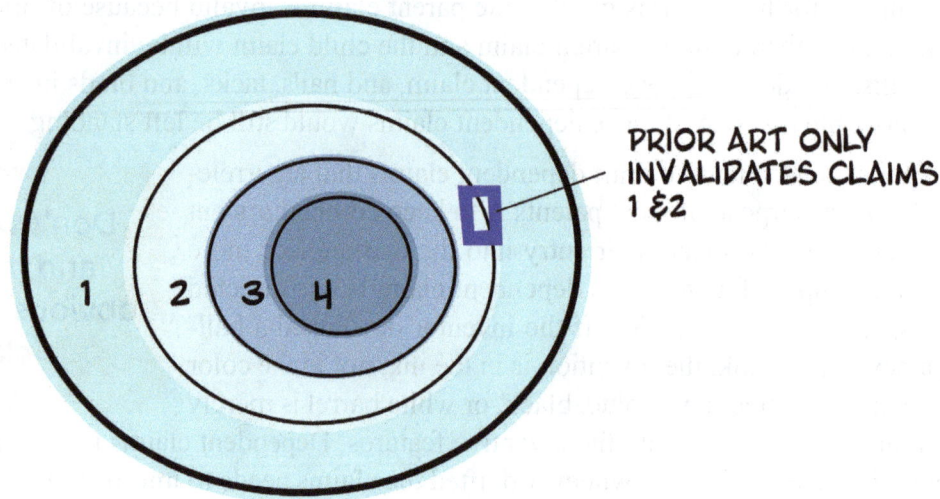

PRIOR ART ONLY
INVALIDATES CLAIMS
1 &2

Figure - Simple Target Claiming

A second purpose of target claiming is to focus whoever is drafting the claims on alternatives to the preferred embodiment. Inventors have often spent a good deal of time and effort optimizing a working model of their invention. It sometimes requires the inventor, or someone else, to step out of that mode and focus on the white space. The proper question is not "what was invented", but "what do we want to stop competitors from doing."

Target claiming is one of the easiest and best strategies

The key to effective target claiming is to choose the targeted parameter wisely. Ideally, the targeted parameter is one that captures the essence of the improvement over the prior art. In the above example the parameter was pH. In other claim sets the targeted parameter might be size, or duration, smoothness, or something else. In some instances it may also be necessary to claim a combination of parameters, especially where those parameters tend to run counter to each other.

For example, it may be that an inventive battery is novel because it has a combination of both higher conductivity and thermal stability. In that instance the targeting would have to recite both elements. Claim 1 might recite "a solid polymer battery having a conductivity of at least [x], and cycle life of at least [y] cycles". (The x and y thresholds are given numbers here because exact numbers are irrelevant to the present discussion). Claims 2 and 3 might recite the same conductivity, but successively higher cycle life. Claims 4 and 5 might recite a higher conductivity, and the same successively higher cycle lives set forth in claims 2 and 3. Note that since a combination of two parameters is employed, a systematic targeting will likely require more claims than targeting of a single variable.

It should be apparent that a patents drafter could also use qualitative parameters to define the target. The only requirement is that the targeted parameter can be split into subsets. In a wine making patent for example, a process may be claimed in which an ingredient is added until the wine turns darker, with dependent claims reciting that the ingredient is added until the wine turns slightly darker, moderately darker, or considerably darker. Of course the terms "slightly", "considerably", and "moderately" should be defined in the specification. By way of further example, a broad claim could be directed to a covering towards the tip of a catheter, with dependent claims reciting that the covering is applied near the tip and at the tip. In those instances the specification needs to define "towards", "near", "at", as well as the term "tip".

Note also that the successively narrower claims can be set forth as independent claims, or as successive dependent claims. However, the use of dependent claiming structure is recommended for the reasons mentioned above.

(2)   Overlapping Target Claiming

Overlapping Target Claiming (OTC) is a more sophisticated version of target claiming. In OTC the patents drafter devises multiple series of claims that independently focus on different parameters. In the example given above it may turn out that in addition to pH, the success of the process is dependent upon adding a large excess of ethanol. Claims 5, 6, and 7 could then be directed to adding at least two times, three times, or four times as much ethanol as some other reagent, respectively.

> **Overlapping target claiming is even better**

The main advantage of OTC is that later identification of invalidating prior art would tend to invalidate a much smaller subset of subject matter. In the drawing below, the added claims 5-7 cover subject matters e, f, and g, such that only the area of the little rectangle is eliminated from patent protection.

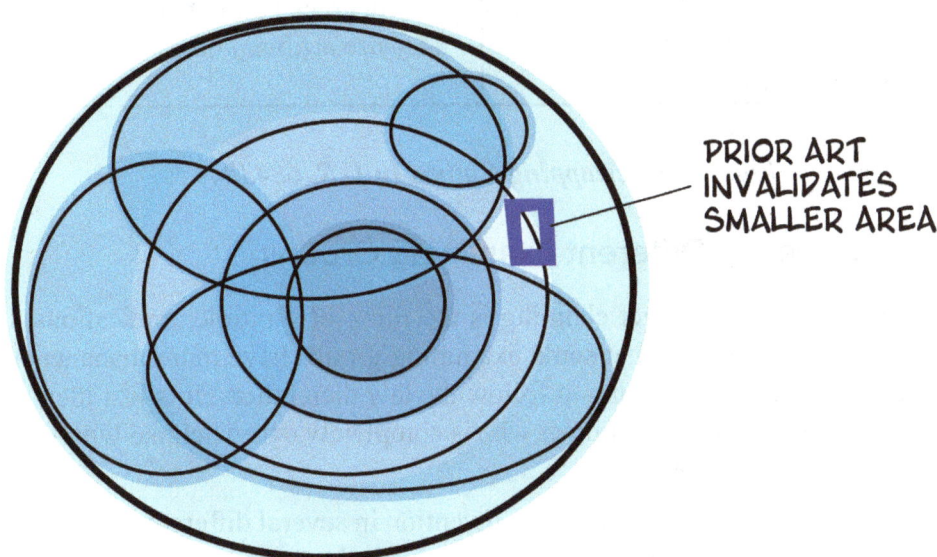

PRIOR ART INVALIDATES SMALLER AREA

Figure - Overlapping Target Claiming

There are many good examples of overlapping target claiming in the patent literature. U.S. 6843844[186] for example, has heavily overlapping claims directed to producing a modified cellulose aggregate. In one series of claims, the independent claim lays out the critical few elements,

> 26. A process for preparing a cellulose modified aggregate while simultaneously reclaiming *submerged land* comprising: *selecting a cellulose* based waste material; ... grinding said treated material ... so as to comminute said materials into fibers; *adding fortifying solution* ...; treating said sun-dried fibers with at least one *activating agent* ....

186 U.S. 6843844 (Jan. 2005) "Modified cellulose aggregate material"

The remaining dependent claims recite alternatives to those features and add new elements.

Cellulose	Activating agent
27 = recycled paper	37 = calcium chloride, calcium hydroxide
28 = industrial waste material	
29 = natural waste material	Modifying aggregate
30 = aquatic vegetation	38 = adding water and cement
Submerged land	39 = adding sand
31 = lake, pond or swamp land	Preventing mold growth
Fortifying solution	40 = treat with an anti-mold
32 = comprises calcium oxide, silica oxide and water	41 = anti-mold solution is ammonium sulfate
34 = comprises fly ash	42 = use artificial heat source
35 = comprises calcium sulfate, calcium carbonate	Curing and drying
36 = comprises calcium silicate, aluminum oxide	43 = cure at approximately 120 degrees Fahrenheit
33 = comprises fly ash	44 = use artificial heat source

Figure - Overlapping Claims In U.S. 6843844[187]

(3)   Targeting Different Examining Groups

A still more sophisticated aspect of target claiming is the filing of multiple applications designed to target different examining groups. The fact is that some examining groups have more manageable workloads than others, and some examiners are more willing to follow the law than others. It is just incredibly frustrating to have an application land in the lap of an examiner who is completely overwhelmed with work, and who keeps rejecting the claims for no good reason.

One way to deal with that problem is to write up the invention in several different claim sets, and then distribute the various claim sets among multiple applications. If this is done correctly, the different applications will be assigned to different examining groups and different attorneys.

> **Directing multiple applications to different examining groups can be a great strategy**

For example, individuals from our office filed three separate applications addressing three different aspects of the basic Zetera™ technology, using Internet Protocol (IP) to directly access different partitions of disk drives.[188] One patent was directed towards communication protocols, systems and methods, the second was directed towards the IP accessible partitions, and the third was directed towards electrical devices with improved communication. The strategy was successful in directing the different applications to five different examining groups, and patents issued from all five applications. This cost a bit more money, but the applicant got some claims allowed early on, and ended up with a much stronger portfolio.

A corresponding strategy can be used in a single application. In that strategy a patent drafter intentionally includes multiple claim sets directed to different inventions in a single application. If the patent office issues a

---

187 U.S. 6843844 (Jan. 2005) "Modified cellulose aggregate material

188 U.S. 7602773 (Oct 2009) "Communication Protocols, Systems And Methods", 7643476 (Jan. 2010) "Data Storage Devices Having IP Capable Partitions", and US7698526 (Apr. 2010) "Electrical Devices With Improved Communication".

restriction requirement, the child applications will likely go to different examiners, and the applicant can then focus on one or another of the different applications depending on his experience (good or bad) with particular examiners. Some examiners are just intractable, and seem to think it is their God given duty to deny all applications, putting the "no" in "innovation". Most examiners, however, are entirely reasonable,[189] and appreciate that allowable claims should be allowed. Obviously, if an application gets split up, one can continue on with favorable examiners, and abandon applicants that were assigned to unreasonable examiners.

C)   Write Short Claims

(1)   Short Claims Are Usually Broader Than Long claims

Many people think of patent claims the way they think of ordinary real estate property claims. They think that a long claim is like a bigger piece of property; it has more "stuff" in it and is more valuable. But exactly the reverse is true. Every word in a patent claim is another limitation, and *the longer the claim is the narrower it is.* A shorter claim is almost always better than a longer one, and is more cost effective because it includes more subject matter. As a first example, consider the first person who invented a two-legged chair. Yes, a two-legged chair does exist.

> **Write short claims**

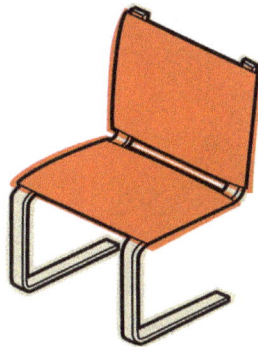

Figure - A Two-Legged Chair Does Exist

Let's assume that the inventor believes metal is the only material strong enough to support a two-legged chair, and he also thinks that metal chairs are only viable if they are covered with fabric. Thus, his broadest claim is "A two-legged chair made of metal and covered with fabric". That might seem like a nice short claim, but it is way too narrow as shown by the following series of diagrams. The set of all two-legged chairs is shown graphically below.

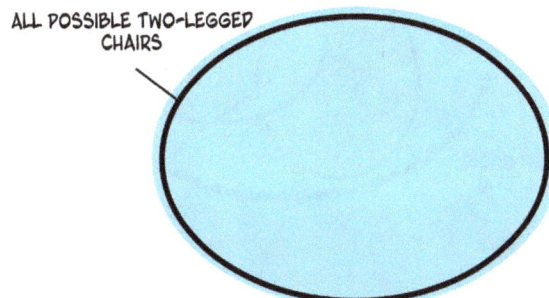

ALL POSSIBLE TWO-LEGGED CHAIRS

189 Actually, a good patent examiner can be an inventor's best friend, by preventing a junk patent from issuing, only to get invalidated during an expensive litigation.

The set of two-legged chairs *made of metal* is smaller than that (a "proper subset"), and includes only the smaller circle in the diagram below.

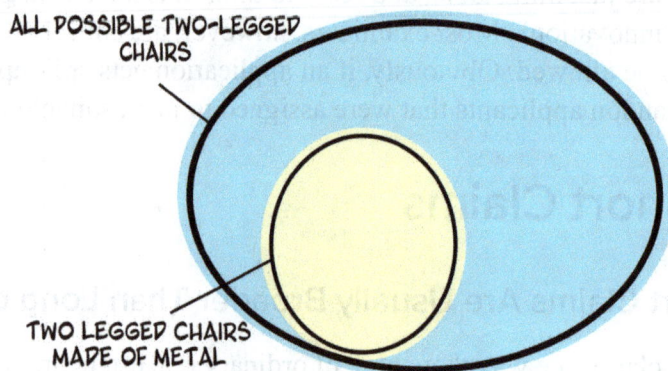

Figure - Two-Legged Chairs Made Of Metal

The set of two-legged chairs *covered with fabric* is also smaller than the set of all two-legged chairs, but in a different manner from two legged chairs made of metal.

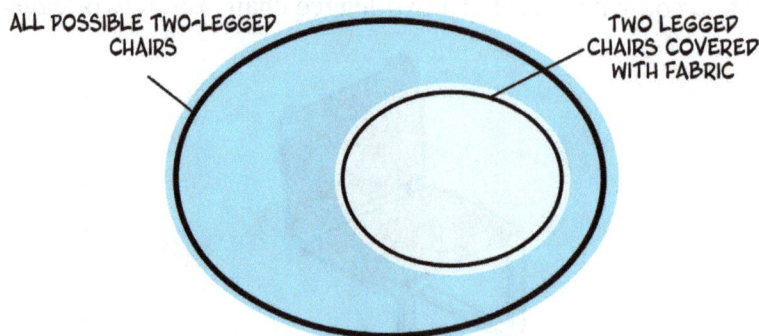

Figure - Two-Legged Chairs Covered With Fabric

Finally, the set of two-legged chairs *made of metal and covered in fabric* is smaller still, because it only includes the overlap of the two subsets. Thus, a claim to a "two-legged chair made of metal and covered with fabric" is too narrow because it contains unnecessary limitations. If the inventor was truly the first person to devise a two-legged chair, the better claim would be to simply state "A chair having two legs".

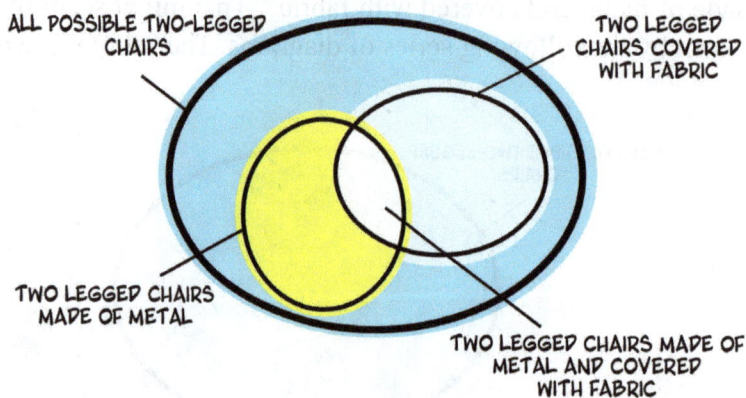

Figure - Two-Legged Chairs Made Of Metal And Covered With Fabric

As an aside, there is no statute requiring that patent claims be written as a single sentence. That, however, is the tradition, and the USPTO enforces that tradition.[190]

(2)   Omit Unnecessary Elements

Omitting unnecessary elements is critical to drafting short claims. Consider the very first person to invent a chair of any type. He claims "a chair having four legs, a vertical back, held together with nails, screws, bolts or dowels". That claim is way too narrow! The seat doesn't have to be flat, the back doesn't have to be vertical, the chair could be built with some other number of legs, and the seat, back, and legs could be held together with connectors other than those listed. The following chart shows how the original claim should be reworded to omit unnecessary elements.

ALL UNNECESSARY ELEMENTS SHOULD BE OMITTED

EXAMPLE: WORLD'S FIRST CHAIR

A CHAIR COMPRISING:
- A FLAT SEAT;
- A VERTICAL BACK;
- FOUR LEGS; AND
- THE SEAT, BACK, AND LEGS HELD TOGETHER BY NAILS, SCREWS, BOLTS OR DOWELS.

→

A CHAIR COMPRISING:
- A SEAT;
- A BACK;
- AT LEAST TWO LEGS; AND
- THE SEAT, BACK, AND LEGS HELD TOGETHER BY CONNECTORS.

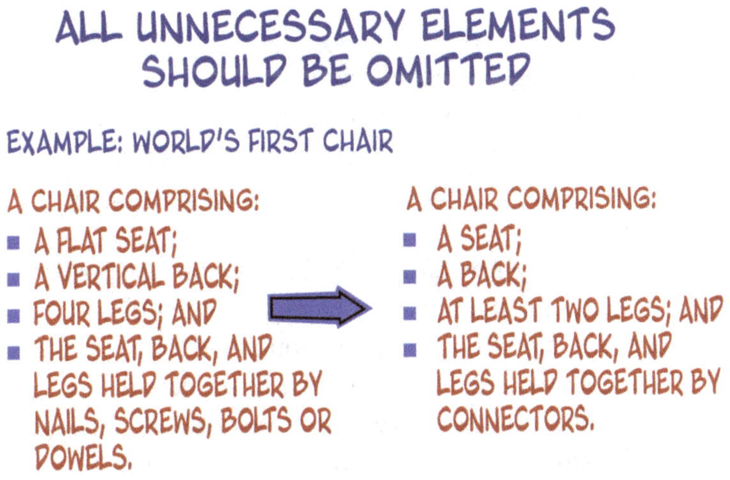

Figure - All Unnecessary Elements Should Be Omitted

Most patent attorneys and agents are adamant in saying that they eliminate all of the unnecessary elements in their patent claims. But the facts belie their words. One can pick almost any patent, in almost any field, and find claims that are bloated with unnecessary elements. Consider the following claim in U.S. 4958145[191] for a sensor that detects improper posture while lifting an object:

> 1. A back incline indicator for indicating whenever the back of a user is bent beyond an acceptable limit, comprising:
>   (a) a *hollow casing* having a side plate,
>   (b) attaching means on the casing *for securing the casing to the back of a shirt collar* of a user with the side plate resting against the back of the user,
>   (c) electric audio signal ...
>   (d) electric tilt switch .....

---

190 *In re application of Alfred A. Fressola,* (PTO Feb. 19. 1992), decision at www.ipmall. info/hosted_resources/commissioner decisions/cd_90.pdf; *affirmed,* 17 F.3d 1442, (Fed. Cir. 1993); *Petition for Rehearing Denied,* 1994 U.S. App. LEXIS 1489 (Fed. Cir. 1994)
191 U.S. 4958145 (Sep. 1990) "Back incline indicator"

That claim is just terrible. Why recite that the casing is hollow? For that matter why recite a casing at all? It is perfectly possible to produce the device as a solid electronic device without a hollow casing, similar to an RF (radio frequency) tags. In that embodiment there would be no casing at all, let alone a hollow casing. The point

Eliminating unnecessary elements is critical to claim drafting

is that the housing has nothing whatever to do with the invention. Recitation of "a housing" would therefore have no effect on patentability. The same analysis, of course, applies to several other elements in the claim. There is absolutely no reason that the claim should recite an attaching means for attaching the casing to the back of a shirt collar. The device could just as readily be worn on the front of the user. If the element is not needed for patentability, it should be eliminated (at least from the broadest claim).

U.S. 5749838[192] provides another good example:

> 1. A posture training device, comprising:
> *a rigid frame* positionable against the back of a person at the intersection of a backbone curve defined by the person's backbone and a transverse curve thereof;
> a *rigid generally box-shaped hollow module* disposed in the frame and movably engaged therewith between a good posture position ...and a poor posture position, corresponding to ... second convexities of the curves, *each second convexity being greater than the respective first convexity*....

This claim is also a waste of good paper. It makes no sense to require the device to be attached to a rigid frame. Why not just say a frame? Indeed, why recite the frame at all? The rest of the claim is also replete with unnecessary elements, including the rigid, box-shaped, hollow module, and the business about one convexity being greater than another. The invention is providing a posture sensor with tactile signal generator. Why not just claim this as "A posture sensor with a tactile signal generator?" Unless there is some special reason to the contrary, claim limitations in independent claims should be rigorously limited to those needed to circumvent the prior art.

(3)   But Sometimes It Is Useful To Add More Words

Of course, there are occasions in which unnecessary elements can properly be added to a patent claim. The primary use is when an invention involves so few elements that the simplest claim would be rejected out of hand by the patent office, just by virtue of its simplicity. In that case it can be a very good idea to include a few other elements to make allowance more palatable to the examiner.

The U.S. patent office's distaste for very short claims is true of all types of claims, but especially method claims. Indeed, the patent office seems to have an unspoken rule against allowing method claims with only a single step. The remedy is to simply add another step, even if the added step is merely introduce an element.

192 U.S. 5749838 (Feb. 1992) "Posture training device"

For example, if the claim involves a single processing step relating to a chemical, one can always avoid a "single step" patenting rejection by adding the limitation "providing the chemical".

Additional verbiage can also be added to apparatus claims in an innocuous manner. For example, in a patent directed to a new gearing mechanism for a bicycle, one could add limitations to the claims that define the bicycle as having a seat, handlebars, wheels, and so forth. Those limitations lengthen the claim, but very likely have no significant impact on the scope.

Another strategy for making a claim more palatable to the patent office is to recite optional elements. Look at the following claim from U.S. 6356546.[193] The claim is very broad, but includes plenty of extra text to hide the (possibly overbroad) scope. For example, the italicized portion is a necessary corollary from element (d), and therefore adds nothing besides bulk to the claim.

> 1. A Universal-Transfer-Mode network (UTM network), comprising a plurality of Universal-Transfer-Mode modules (UTM modules) interconnected by a passive core, said passive core consisting of a plurality of optical cross connectors through which routes are established among said UTM modules...comprising:
> (a) STM ports;
> (b) ATM ports;
> (c) Frame relay ports; and
> (d) IP ports; protocol), and each of said UTM ports includes
> (a) a hysteresis control...; and
> (b) a scheduler of data packets of variable ....

Careful review of this claim establishes that all of the important limitations occur in the italicized text of the preamble. All of the subsequent text is merely surplusage, and fails to limit the scope of the claim in any significant manner!

Here's another doozy.[194] What verbosity.

> 10. A method of diagnosing if a tissue has been exposed to BoNT/A enzymatic activity comprising contacting a tissue sample suspected of having been exposed to BoNT/A enzymatic activity with an anti-SNAP25 antibody wherein the antibody binds preferentially to BoNT/A cleaved SNAP25; and detecting whether the anti-SNAP25 antibody bound to the tissue sample, wherein the presence of the anti-SNAP25 antibody binding to the tissue sample indicates that the tissue sample has been exposed to BoNT/A activity.

193 U.S. 6356546 (Mar. 2002) "Universal transfer method and network with distributed switch"
194 U.S. 2016/0003824 (Jan. 2016).

D)   Write Claims That Can Be Realistically Enforced

Market-oriented claiming by itself, of course, is not the whole story. One should also focus on securing claims that are realistically enforceable. Method of manufacture claims, for example, can be very difficult to enforce. Once a computer chip is manufactured, who can tell whether one of the polymer layers was cured at 100° F or 120 °F? Enforcement of such claims requires discovery as to the exact manufacturing process of the defendant, and such discovery is exceedingly problematic unless opposing counsel is particularly generous. In the case of overseas manufacturing such discovery can be downright impossible to obtain.

If the invention does lie in the method of manufacture of the product rather than the end product itself, the goal is to identify some relevant difference between products produced by the inventive method versus other methods. Perhaps the novel manufacturing process produces materials that are harder or softer than the previous methods, or is slightly smoother, or have some superior electrical property. In that case the claims should be directed to a product having the material with the claimed property.

Method of use claims can also be difficult to enforce. In the pharmaceutical field, for example, physicians and medical staff administer the drugs, not the manufacturers. The manufacturers merely provide drugs for others to administer, and can often escape infringement of method of use claims by asserting that they are selling the drugs solely for some non-infringing purpose. Indeed, the only way to establish infringement of a method of use claim may be to show that the manufacturer purposefully put his product into the marketplace to cause people to infringe the patent (inducement to infringe), or to establish that there are no substantial non-infringing uses of the product (contributory infringement). Those proofs can easily increase the cost of litigation by hundreds of thousands of dollars.

The excuses wear pretty thin when it comes time to justify using method claims for certain fields. As shown below, apparatus claims and method claims are often readily converted one into the other. But the apparatus claim is often enforceable against a manufacturer, while the corresponding method claim may only be enforceable against a consumer.

Apparatus Claim	Method Claim Method Claims
A bath soap dispenser, comprising: a container sized and dimensioned such that the bath soap is applied to at least part of a body surface by movement of the container along the body surface; wherein at least part of the bath soap is retained within the container during the movement; and wherein the soap is advanced by pressure of a finger on the base plate.	A method of dispensing a bath soap onto a body surface, comprising: providing a dispenser containing a base plate and a bath soap, wherein at least part of the soap is retained within the container during the movement; advancing the soap by pressure of a finger on the base plate; and moving the container along the body surface

Figure - Apparatus claims Can Be Easier To Enforce

One should also focus on who or what entity can be sued. For example, in countries where claims to methods of treating diseases in humans are unenforceable (as is the case in many foreign countries), it is better to claim a new chemical entity or a method of manufacturing than trying to claim a method of treating. Generally, physicians (and their staffs) cannot be sued for treating patients even if the drugs they are using infringe a patent,[195] but a manufacturer of the drug can be sued for producing and/or marketing an infringing drug.

> **Direct claims against a manufacturer, or other entity against which they can be realistically enforced**

Similarly, where an invention is a new use for an old machine, it is much better to claim (a) a controller, software or other new aspect that allows the old machine to perform its new function, and (b) to focus on the new purpose of the machine. Even if a patent attorney is successful in securing allowance of method claims, a litigating attorney might well have a terrible time enforcing those claims.

A third example of why it's important to draft more easily enforceable claims is somewhat subtler. A composition claim is usually the Holy Grail in chemical applications. But in the field of polymers it is often the worst type of claim because polymer composition claims tend to be extremely narrow, and readily circumvented. From a litigation perspective it is much better to focus on claiming a class of polymers according to their characteristics, rather than claiming specific compositions.

More Enforceable	Less Enforceable
A computer chip comprising a dielectric layer having xyz properties....	A computer chip manufactured by laying down a first layer comprising…, a second layer comprising….
A method of shampooing hair using an anti-psoriasis compound....	A method of treating psoriasis using a shampoo having an anti-psoriasis compound....
A controller that cooperates with an xyz machine, using a protocol intended to treat a cancer in an organism.	A method of treating cancer, comprising using an xyz machine to irradiate the cancer....
A method of imparting an image to a metallic surface comprising: …coating the bonding area with a highly cross-linked polymer having a hardness greater than 80 and a coefficient of elasticity of at least 120% without breaking …	A coating comprising 80–99.5 wt% of a polymerizable acrylate selected from mono-, di-, and triacrylates, urethane-modified acrylates, and polyester-modified acrylates, and 0.5 – 15 wt% of a photointiator…

Figure - Claim Wording Greatly Affects Enforceability

Yet a fourth example shows that even seasoned patent attorneys and agents can write claims that have little chance of being enforced. U.S. patent application no. 2004/0093307 claims a banking system in which a transaction takes place at least in part in a foreign country. Unless enforcement can take place against SWIFT (Society of Worldwide Interbank Financial Telecommunication), the system cannot be enforced because U.S. patent law has very limited international reach.

---

195 35 U.S.C. 287(c).

> 1. A banking system comprising:
>   a first bank account directly owned by an first emerging
>   local bank chartered in a first emerging market
>   country;
>   a second bank account which is owned by a trust entity,
>   wherein the emerging market bank is the
>   beneficiary of the trust entity; and wherein the
>   first bank account and the second bank account
>   are bank accounts at a first international
>   correspondent bank.

E)   Sequence Of Claims

The usual practice is to list the broadest claims first, followed by successively narrower claims. This may seem obvious because the first claim is always independent, and the dependent claims are always listed after the parent independent claim. The issue arises, however, when an application contains multiple independent claims. Should the person drafting the claims put the broader independent claims near the front of the application or near the back? Actually, it probably doesn't matter. Some examiners say that they don't care about the ordering of the claims, but others feel that a broad claim in the middle or end of the list may be an attempt to sneak one by. My preference is to list the broader independent claims ahead of the narrower ones.

F)   Creative Claiming

Having discussed the basic structure of a patent application, and having reviewed the basic claim types, we can now move on to more creative aspects of claiming.

(1)   Business Methods

One of the most important developments in patenting in the last decade is the widespread use of business method claims. Such claims have now been used to protect almost any method imaginable, including methods of advertising, accounting, distributing goods and services, teaching courses, tax avoidance strategies, and most notoriously, selling goods on the Internet. It is even possible, for example, to claim a method of writing a book or a method of drafting a patent application.

> Claim 2. A method of authoring a talking book with a memory...
>
> Claim 10. A method by computer for drafting a patent application having at least sections including claims, a summary of the invention, an abstract of the disclosure, and a detailed description of a preferred embodiment of the invention....

The Federal Circuit first *formally* authorized business method claims in the famous *State Street* case of 1998.[196] Prior to that time the received wisdom was that business methods were unpatentable.[197] The truth is a bit different, however, because patent attorneys and agents had been drafting business method claims for years. In the early 1990s, for example, I filed claims directed to the selling of annuities by a banking institution. Ordinarily that combination would violate the Glass-Steagall Act of 1933, which was in force at the time, and which mandated separation of banking and insurance activities. But the inventor recognized a loophole in the Act, and our job was to secure a patent on that loophole. A business method claim seemed the best way to proceed. Here was one of the independent claims.

> 1. A method of providing an annuity through a bank, comprising:
>   providing a deposit account at the bank;
>   depositing funds into the deposit account;
>   obligating the bank to make at least one future payment as
>   a function of the amount of funds in the deposit
>   account;
>   qualifying the method to provide a tax benefit under
>   26 U.S.C. § 72; and
>   utilizing a computer based architecture to implement
>   the method.

There are even business method patents dating back into the 1800s, including what may be the first patent[198] on a method of storing data using punched cards. Note use of the method term, "preparing":

> 1. The improvement in the art of compiling statistics, which consists in first ***preparing*** a series of separate record-cards, each card representing an individual or subject; second, applying to each card at predetermined intervals circuit-controlling index-points ....

196 *State Street Bank & Trust Co. v. Signature Financial Group*, 149 F.3d 1368 (Fed. Cir. 1998).
197 *Hotel Security Checking Co. v. Lorraine Co.*, 160 F. 467 (2d Cir. 1908); *In re Howards*, 394 F.2d 869, 872 (C.C.P.A. 1968); and *In re Schrader*, 22 F.3d 290, 296 & n.14, 297-98 (Fed. Cir. 1994).
198 U.S. 395781 (Jan. 1889) "Art of COMPILING STATISTICS"

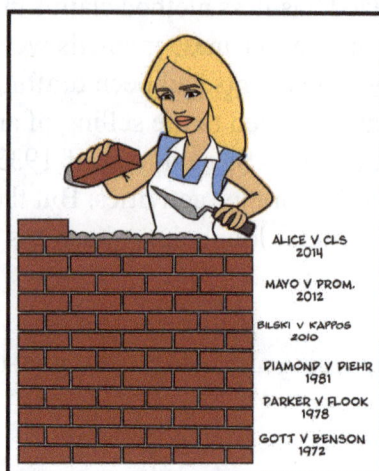

Figure - Pursuing Business Method Claims Is Like Fighting Against A Brick Wall

On the other hand, patent filers need to appreciate that securing broad business method claims can be a decidedly uphill battle, a bit like fighting against a brick wall that the courts have been constructing over the years. The allowance rate for business method claims is very low, reported to be only 5 - 6 %, and the time to allowance can easily be five years or more.

But despite *Alice* and other Supreme Court cases that restrict availability of business method claims, it is still a good idea to at least consider filing business method claims for difficult-to-patent technologies. For example, where a bioactive compound is already known, and its use to treat a particular condition is already known, an applicant might still be able to secure a patent by claiming a method of marketing the compound by placing certain claims on the packaging. The patent office will almost certainly issue a § 101 (*Alice*) rejection against such claims, but as long as the claims are sufficiently circumscribed, they can eventually be allowed.

> **Despite *Mayo*, *Myriad* and *Alice*, it is still a good idea to at least consider filing business method claims**

Similarly, if there is nothing particularly novel about the operation of a computer program, an applicant might still be able to secure a patent for the use of that type of program to increase productivity of workers.

There is also the argument that the pendulum might shift over the next few years. Many patent practitioners have put their applications into "sleep" mode by filing appeals to final office actions. Since decisions on appeal are usually at least a couple years out, that strategy keeps the applications pending until perhaps there is a change in the law.

Note that even though it might make sense to pursue business methods claims in the U.S., that is not necessarily the case for filing in foreign countries. Regardless of novelty and non-obviousness, such claims are routinely rejected in Japan and most or all of Europe on the grounds that there is no "technical contribution" to the field. In those countries it is much better to write the claims in the format of an apparatus, a computer-readable media, a system, and so forth. Interestingly, South Korea does allow business method claims, provided they are stated as being implemented in hardware.

(2)   Other Creative Method Claims

Method claims can be very creative indeed. For example, in the pharmaceutical field, an applicant often needs to claim a new use of an old compound. The typical claim has the format "A method of treating <<a disease>>, comprising administering <<a drug>> according to a protocol sufficient to treat <<the disease>>".

Such a format can be problematic, however, in that infringement occurs by the treating physicians rather than the manufacturers. Physicians are largely immune from patent infringement lawsuits when treating patients,[199] and infringement suits against manufacturers must be based on indirect infringement (contributory infringement or inducement to infringe). One way to allow filing of an infringement action directly against the manufacturer is to file a claim directed to "A method of marketing <<a drug>>, comprising packaging <<the drug>> along with labeling that identifies <<the drug>> as being useful to treat <<the new indication>>".

Creative patenting methods are really only limited by one's own imagination. There was once a claim pending before the USPTO that recites a method of improving domestic harmony! Instead of focusing on interpersonal relationships, the claim recites use of a landscape sprinkler that automatically reverts to a run position after an adjustment is made. The specification supports the claim by pointing out that considerable marital disharmony can be caused by one spouse blaming the other for modifying the watering times, and then burning out the lawn because the controller was left in the adjustment position!

(3)   Information Processing By Humans Or Machines

Quite a few patents have issued that recite "appreciating", "recognizing", "analyzing" or otherwise processing information. Even though the strategy was successful at the time, it would very likely be rejected under current law as being directed to a mental step (no real-world effect). The history, however, is interesting.

In the late 1990s, our office successfully used that very strategy with respect to U.S. 6063772[200] to a pharmaceutical.

> 1. A method of treating a disease responsive to ribavirin, comprising:
> *recognizing progression of the disease* as being mediated at least in part by Th1 lymphocytes;
> *recognizing ribavirin as being effective* to promote a Th1 response and suppress a Th2 response...;
> and
> administering ribavirin to a patient having the disease within the dosage range.

U.S. 4683195[201] employed a similar mental step strategy, but instead of reciting "recognizing", the claims use the term "suspected of containing".

> 1. A process for detecting the presence or absence of at least one specific nucleic acid sequence in a sample containing a nucleic acid or mixture of nucleic acids, or distinguishing between two different sequences in said sample, wherein the sample is *suspected of containing* said sequence or sequences, which process comprises....

---

199 35 U.S.C. 287(c).
200 U.S. 6063772 (May 2000) "Specific modulation of Th1/Th2 cytokine expression by ribavirin in activated T-lymphocytes".
201 U.S. 4683195 (Jul. 1987) "Process for amplifying, detecting, and/or-cloning nucleic acid sequences".

U.S. 6541267[202] employed a similar strategy, this time relying on the mental step of "correlating".

> 1. A method of determining oxidative stress in a subject, comprising:
>   **correlating a presence of an aldehyde** in urine of a subject with an oxidative stress in the subject;
>   providing a test reagent comprising a pH regulator...;
>   combining the test reagent with the urine... and
>   **correlating a color** of the aldehyde-modified chromogen with the oxidative stress.

Throughout the 2000s this seemed like a very good strategy. In *Metabolite Labs., Inc. v. Lab. Corp. of Am. Holdings*, the Federal Circuit upheld claims directed to correlating levels of homocysteine and vitamins B6 and B12 in claim 13 of U.S. 4940658 against challenges to indefiniteness, sufficiency of written description, enablement, anticipation, and obviousness.

> 13. A method for detecting a deficiency of cobalamin or folate in warm- blooded animals comprising the steps of:
> assaying a body fluid for an elevated level of total homocysteine; and
> correlating an elevated level of total homocysteine in said body fluid with a deficiency of cobalamin or folate.

The U.S. Supreme Court had a chance to put a stop to such claiming in 2005. But after first granting certiorari, the court later denied certiorari, which opened the floodgates. As of January 2006, the USPTO database listed 11,717 patents that include the term "correlating" in the claims. By June 2022 that number had risen to 122,893. Perhaps recognizing their mistake, the Supreme Court has since handed down several decisions that seek to limit claims to multiple types of information processing.

In the field of computer software, for example, the Supreme Court handed down the *Bilski* decision,[203] which invalidated claims that it said did not "add" anything to the otherwise abstract idea of minimizing economic risk. The Court found that the claimed method failed to meet 35 U.S.C. § 101's eligibility requirements because it simply described the idea of hedging against economic risk and applied it using "familiar statistical approaches" and "well-known random analysis techniques."

At the present time, claims that rely on "recognizing" as a patentable feature are likely invalid over *Alice*. Nevertheless, there are examples of information processing that have passed muster under *Alice*. These include constructing and serving a new, hybrid web page (*DDR Holdings, LLC v. Hotels.com*[204]), removing malicious code from email messages (2014 Guidance), creating a task node and inserting it under an associated task (*ex parte Kogan*[205]), directed to a physical edge device (*ex parte Emmendorfer*[206]), and creating a hybrid model with a normal and reduced dimensionality (*Ex parte Wegman*[207]).

---

202 U.S. 6541267 (Apr. 2003) "Methods for testing oxidative stress".
203 *In re Bilski*, 545 F.3d 943, 88 U.S.P.Q.2d 1385 (Fed. Cir. 2008)
204 *DDR Holdings, LLC v. Hotels.com, L.P.*, 773 F.3d 1245 (Fed. Cir. 2014)
205 *Ex Parte Kogan*, 2015 Pat. App. LEXIS 1908 (Pat. App. 2015)
206 *Ex Parte Emmendorfer*, 2015 Pat. App. LEXIS 2622 (Pat. App. 2015)
207 *Ex Parte Wegman*, 2015 Pat. App. LEXIS 12350 (Pat. App. 2015)

(4) Purification

Another way of circumventing close prior art is to draft claims that expressly recite purification. For example, U.S. 6896910[208] claims a concentrated water extract of a combination of herbs.

> 9. The agent according to claim 8, wherein said agent is formulated into powder, granules, tablets, capsules, a solution, suspension, solution for injection, jam, syrup, essence or *a concentrated solution.*

Prior to *Myriad*, it was also possible to distinguish over the prior art by reciting a purified compound from an old product, even a product of nature such as a tomato. Claim 1 of U.S. 6890574[209], however, would likely be invalid under current law, first because the compounds derived from purification are merely products of nature, and second because the claim recites a mental step of adding the concentrate "as a taste enhancer".

> 1. An *isolated nucleic acid* consisting of the sequence of SEQ ID NO: 5.

(5) Kit, Labeling, Or Packaging

Still another way of circumventing close prior art is to draft the claims to expressly recite a kit, labeling, or packaging. For example, U.S. 6811038[210] recites a kit of components, where the components by themselves might not be patentable:

> 18. *An automotive door storage kit*, comprising:
> a bracket adapted to be mounted to a surface;
> and a door retaining device adapted to be used
> in conjunction with the bracket to stabilize an
> automotive door having gins adapted to be
> connected to an automobile….

Similarly, U.S. 6726899[211] recites:

> 24. A *commercial package* comprising a composition of 1)
> a composition comprising a polymerizable acrylate resin, an
> antimicrobial agent of Formula (I) according to claim 1 and
> at least one component selected from the group consisting of:
> glutaraldehyde and a chelating agent and 2) *labeling having
> printed instructions indicating the use thereof as a dental
> facing preparation.*

---

208 U.S. 6896910 (May 2005) "Anti-fatigue and tonic agent containing wild ginseng".
209 U.S. 6890574 (May 2005) "Clear tomato concentrate as a taste enhancer".
210 U.S. 6811038 (Nov. 2004) "Bracket for vehicle door storage"
211 U.S. 6726899 (Apr. 2004) "Calcified tissue facing preparation containing antimicrobial agent".

(6)   Combined Method and Apparatus claims

It is proper to combine method claims with apparatus or composition claims. The answer is yes. If claim 1 recites some new type of chair, then claim 2 could recite a method of sitting on a lawn, comprising "providing a chair as in claim 1, placing it on the lawn, and sitting in the chair".

Similarly, if claim 1 recites a method of producing ethanol using a specific process, a dependent claim 22 might well recite "a processing plant having a distilling column and heat exchanger arranged to utilize the method of claim 1 inch".

(7)   Chemical Claims

Polymers present a special problem for patents drafters. Among other things, a claim to a specific formulation is way too narrow, and can almost always be circumvented by simply changing the formula. Fortunately there are two very good strategies for claiming polymers.

> A method of imparting an image to a metallic surface, comprising:
>   providing the surface with a bonding area;
>   coating the bonding area with a highly cross-linked polymer having a **hardness greater than 80** (Shore D, ASTM D2240) and a coefficient of **elasticity of at least 120%** without breaking;
>   curing the polymeric coating; and
>   sublimating dyes characterizing the image into the coating.

The first strategy is to claim the polymer by its properties. This is most readily done in a method claim that recites a polymer having the desired characteristics. The following claim was deemed allowable by the PCT (WO 98/13147, "Sublimation Dye Transfer Compositions and Methods", (1998)), but was never pursued in national phase.

The other strategy is to claim the structure of the polymer as opposed to its chemical composition.

> **Polymers can be claims by their functions or their structures**

Pharmaceutical and other chemical inventions are quite easy to claim, so long as the chemical entities are novel. In that case an applicant can simply claim the structure and its variants. Problems arise, however, when the compound is old. In that case there are several alternative claiming strategies, including claiming a new use, a precursor, a manufacturing intermediate, a new dosage form or regimen, a new route of administration, or a combination with some other drug, excipients and so forth. Note that claiming a metabolite of a drug doesn't usually work because the metabolite is deemed to be inherent in the previously known compound.[212]

---

212 *Schering Corp. v. Geneva Pharms., Inc.*, 339 F.3d 1373, 1380 (Fed. Cir. 2003)

1. A method of fabricating a nanoporous material, comprising:
   providing a first polymeric strand and a second
      polymeric strand, wherein each of the first
      polymeric strand and the second polymeric
      **strand independently comprises a
      crosslinking functionality and a thermostable
      portion** ...;
   crosslinking the first and second polymeric strands by
      reacting the crosslinking functionality....

It is even possible to claim a pharmaceutical where (a) the compound is old, (b) the use of the drug for the disease is old, and (c) the formulation is old.

1. A method of producing a nanoporous composition
comprising:
   providing a **template strand having a plurality of
      repeating units and a plurality of reactive
      groups**...;
   *wherein at least one of the modifying molecule and
      the polymeric strand has a thermolabile group*.

1. *A method of modulating Th1 and Th2 response* in activated T cells of a human patient comprising administering Ribavirin to the T cells in a dosage which promotes the Th1 response and suppresses the Th2 response.

1. *A method of inversely modulating Type 1 and Type 2 responses* of lymphocytes contained within an environment by adding ribavirin to the lymphocytes in a concentration which increases the Type 1 response and suppresses the Type 2 response.

17. A composition comprising interferon gamma or an interferon gamma-inducing compound in *an amount that is determined to be effective* to increase activity of at least one component of a proteasome or guanylate binding protein and to thereby elicit a non-cytolytic reduction of viral propagation in a hepatocyte infected with HCV.

Now, one might argue that such claims are worthless because they would never issue. But as the footnotes show, the patent office did grant patents that include these three claims. The claims were challenged in federal court, but the case settled before there was a ruling on validity. The bottom line is that the claims were never invalidated

In difficult cases one should consider claiming upstream or downstream aspects of a combination. For example, when claiming an old drug for a new use, it is not possible to claim the drug as a chemical composition. Yes, one could try claiming a different dosage regimen or dosage form, but those may already be known as well, or be obvious. For example, if a drug is already known in 25 mg tablets, and prescribed at 75 mg/day (tid), the patent office will not be particularly happy about granting a claim to a dosing of only 25 mg/day. And claiming a new use *per se* might be patentable, but would be very difficult to enforce. The current manufacturers would simply say that they are producing the drug for the old off-patent uses, and the physicians can't be sued for simply prescribing the medication.

The answer may be to determine whether the lower dosage results in a new metabolite profile (a downstream aspect). In that case one could claim giving a drug (any drug) that produces the new metabolite profile. Since the higher (known) dose would produce another profile, and presumably no one in the prior art ever saw the new profile, the claim might well be both patentable and enforceable. Similarly, from a manufacturing standpoint, one can sometimes claim slightly different strategies or components (upstream aspects) required when shifting from low volume to high volume production.

(8)   Mechanical Claims

Claims in the mechanical arts can sometimes be creatively drafted using semi-functional language and mental steps. One trick is to claim some physical characteristic (e.g., length, weight) as being "sufficient" to achieve a particular goal. For example:

> 1. A dispenser for powder or granular material comprising:
>   a. a hopper for containing powder or granular material having a bottom member of **substantially arcuate configuration**, said bottom member including a plurality of openings therethrough and throughout the length thereof;
>   b. a wiper ... including at least one blade having a **length sufficient for contacting the bottom member** at said openings and offset from a contiguous wiper blade.....

Mechanical inventions are best claimed from multiple different perspectives

Another trick is to claim the invention from several different perspectives. The claims below[213] address the same substantive invention, but do so from the different perspectives of the length of the compression and power strokes, (claim 1) movement of the crank pin, (claim 7) the use of planetary gears, (claim 11) and in another patent the noncircular shape of the path traveled by the crankpin.[214]

213 U.S. 5799636 (Sep. 1998) Split cycle engines"
214 U.S. 5482015 (Jan. 1996) "Device for coupling reciprocating and rotating motions"

--or--

1. A device comprising:
    a first gear carrying a crank pin;
    a second gear more than twice the size of said first gear
        and coupled in a planetary relationship with
        respect to said first gear such that said crank pin
        travels in one of and pentagonal paths.

--or--

7. A method of increasing the efficiency of a device producing usable power from internal combustion, the method comprising:
    providing the device with a piston, a cylinder, a
        connecting rod, a crank pin ...; and
    moving the crank pin in a manner that the piston has
        two top dead center points and two bottom dead
        center points during each 360 degree rotation of
        the crankshaft.

Still another trick is to claim minor distinctions that are added to a product solely for the purpose of providing patentable subject matter. For example, in desktop computer printers the profit lies in the cartridges rather than the printers, but the cartridges are easy for competitors to knock off. A powerful strategy is to design a cartridge that relies upon some completely unnecessary feature, and then patent that feature. The following claim[215] appears to follow that strategy by claiming a mechanism that is completely unnecessary to the basic functioning of the printer, but merely couples operation of the cartridge with movement of the paper advance.

(9)   Incorporate Classification Definitions To Achieve Fast Allowance

1. An ink-jet printer comprising: an ink cartridge; a recording head; an ink supply passage connecting the ink cartridge to the recording head; a valve opening/closing mechanism ... ***operable to open the ink supply passage as a result of a rotation of the paper feed driving mechanism***.

It happens far too often nowadays that a patent application becomes "lost" in a patent examining group with very long average time to issuance. Many examining groups have delays of two to four years before issuing the first office action, and there were years in which the business methods groups had delays of four to seven years.

---

215 U.S. 6234616 (May 2001) "Mechanism for opening or closing ink supply passage in ink-jet printer"; Brother apparently did the same thing with a design patent, U.S. Des. 383743 (Sep. 1997) "Ink ribbon cartridge for facsimile transmitter-receiver"

One can try to circumvent such delays in several other ways, by (1) filing an application with a Petition to Make Special, (2) filing an application with a request for Prioritized Examination, (3) using one of the Patent Prosecution Highway countries; (4) using a PCT First filing strategy, and (5) filing with a petition for Accelerated Examination. These strategies are all detailed in the *Green Fields Patenting* book.

(10)   Add Orthogonal Limitations To Circumvent Prior Art

Adding orthogonal limitations can circumvent prior art

Yet another filing strategy that can be used in difficult cases is to include limitations in a claim that have little or nothing to do with the underlying invention. Consider, for example, a case in which an applicant is trying to claim subject matter that was disclosed many years ago, but never really commercialized. Simply claiming the apparatus or method in a straightforward manner is not a viable option because the prior art anticipates the invention. Thus, a method of whitening teeth with a peroxide solution could not currently be claimed as follows because the method has been practiced for decades.

> 1. A method of whitening teeth, comprising:
>   providing a polymeric material for use in conforming a
>   tray to a set of teeth;
>   providing a solution containing peroxide to a user; and
>   providing instructions to the user to apply the solution
>   to the tray, and then juxtapose the tray against
>   the teeth to effect whitening of the teeth.

But one can still add a novel step that would preclude competitors from entering the space. In a silly example, the combination of steps in the following claim may not have been done before, and might be allowable since carbamide peroxide is known for tooth whitening, but is also known to be a skin irritant.

> 1. A method of whitening teeth, comprising:
>   **receiving information that a solution containing**
>   **carbamide peroxide is effective to both**
>   **whiten teeth and treat fungal skin infections**;
>   providing a polymeric material for use in conforming a
>   tray to a set of teeth;
>   providing the solution to a user; and
>   providing instructions to the user to apply the solution
>   to the tray, and then juxtapose the tray against
>   the teeth to effect whitening of the teeth.

Of course the patent office might reject the claim as containing irrelevant information.[216] But assuming one could secure issuance of the claim, one could send letters to competitors advising them of the dual use. Upon

---

216 *Tate Access Floors, Inc. v. Interface Architectural Res., Inc.*, 279 F.3d 1357, 1371 (Fed. Cir. 2002), citing *Toro Co. v. White Consol. Indus., Inc.*, 266 F.3d 1367, 1371 (Fed. Cir. 2000) and *E.I. du Pont de Nemours & Co. v. Phillips Petroleum*, 849 F.2d 1430, 1433 (Fed. Cir. 1988))

receipt of that letter the competitor is suddenly infringing. Of course this is exactly the sort of "sharp" practice that gives attorneys a bad name.

The strategy can be expanded in all sorts of ways, including claiming undesirable activities of competitors in challenging a patent. For example, one could make competitors think twice with the following sort of claim:

> 1. A method of whitening teeth, comprising:
>   (a) providing a polymeric material for use in conforming a tray to a set of teeth;
>   (b) providing a solution containing peroxide to a user;
>   (c) providing instructions to the user to apply the solution to the tray, and then juxtapose the tray against the teeth to effect whitening of the teeth;
>   and
>   (d) filing a pleading with a court that challenges validity of a patent claiming steps (a) - (c).

The claim is clearly novel because no one has yet practiced step (d). Moreover, the patent office will have a terrible time establish *prima facie* obviousness because the absence of this sort of claim in the prior art necessarily means that there was no teaching, suggestion or motivation in the prior art for practicing step (d).

One reader commented that a competitor could avoid infringement simply by not doing (d)" - filing a pleading with a court that challenges validity of a patent claiming steps (A) TO (C). But that argument is not valid. The fact is that counterclaiming for invalidity is a compulsory counterclaim, so that that failure to assert the counterclaim could be malpractice. The fascinating part is that a defendant's assertion of invalidity would help the patent holder establish infringement, thus placing the defendant between a rock and hard place.

Should Congress allow this sort of claiming strategy? Probably not, and indeed the Patent Office has begun rejecting claims with such limitations. But adding minor or even completely obvious limitations to claims is still a very common, and sometimes necessary strategy. It's not at all uncommon for a primary examiner to reject a claim even though he can't find any invalidating prior art. In fact, the primary examiner will often tell us so, and admit that the claim is simply "too short" to get supervisor approval. In such instances we add obvious limitations to the claims to make them longer, and indeed sometime the examiners even suggest such limitations.

Patent Beast © FISH 2008

I CAN'T FIND ANY REASON TO REJECT THE CLAIMS ....

.... SO I'M SAYING THEY ARE OBVIOUS.

BUT THAT ISN'T PROPER!

I KNOW. BUT I DON'T WANT TO ALLOW THESE CLAIMS.

The problem here is that under our current system, an attorney or agent must resolve two sometimes irreconcilable goals. On the one hand attorneys and agents have a legal obligation to so whatever he/she can in the client's interest, as long as those efforts are legal. And adding orthogonal limitations can be a very successful strategy. On the other hand, attorneys and agents are members of society too, and may well want to avoid socially offensive results. We see this in the criminal area all the time, where for example, a defense attorney has a duty to get his client off the hook, even though the client clearly did the crime. The result is bad for society in that the client did not have to pay for the crime, but it would have been malpractice for the attorney to act otherwise.

Chapter VI - Drafting The Specification

As set forth in the Manual of Patent Examining Procedure (MPEP)[217], a patent specification application should include a title, a priority statement, a background, a summary, a brief description of the drawing, a detail description, and an abstract. Although these items are listed here in the order in which they usually appear in the specification, that is not the order in which they should be drafted. After the claims are written, the best order for drafting a specification is summary of the invention, followed by abstract, title, background, and then brief description of the drawing, and finally detail description.

There is a method to the madness. The Summary of The Invention should be drafted immediately after drafting the claims because the summary is basically just a rewording of the claims in ordinary English (as opposed to the stylized claim language). The abstract should be written next because it is just a short recitation of the summary. The title is an even further distillation of the abstract, and should probably be drafted next, even though almost everyone has a working title in mind long before the claims are even written.

> **Draft the claims first**

It is only after writing the claims, the summary, and the abstract that a patent drafter should begin drafting the background. This is because a well-crafted background section is a sales pitch. It forces the reader to conclude that a problem exists for which there are no good solutions, and that any solution would therefore be non-obvious. A patent drafter cannot effectively write that storyline unless he knows where it is going to end up, which will of course turn out to be the utter brilliance of the invention being claimed. In short, the background section should only discuss issues that create a straw man problem for which the invention is the solution. And the most effective way to do that is to write the background after writing the claims, summary, and abstract.

The brief description of the drawing and the detailed description sections are written last because they are focused on the particular embodiments of the claimed subject matter shown in the Drawing figures. By having previously written the claims, summary and background, the attorney avoids falling into the trap of describing the preferred embodiments as "the invention". The invention is whatever is *claimed* to be the invention.

A) Title

The title of the patent application should be broader than the abstract. The abstract should in turn be broader than the summary section, and the summary should be broader than the all of the independent claims put together. Thus, if a patent drafter has claims directed to methods and compositions, he should be careful to word the title so that it is broad enough to encompass both methods and compositions. For practical reasons, titles should also be short, usually containing no more than about five to ten words. It seems that inexperienced patent drafters sometimes want to describe the entire invention in the title!

Although the title alludes to the claimed invention, but it is not supposed to describe the invention. Thus, if the claims recite use of a novel class of polymers in automobile tires, the title may be properly worded as "Polymers Containing...", "Polymers Containing... and Their Use in Automobile Tires", or "Automobile Tire Methods and Compositions", depending on the focus

> **Use a meaningful title, which is broader than the broadest claim**

217 MPEP § 608.01(a), see also 37 C.F.R. § 1.77

of the claims. One should almost never set forth a preferred formulation in the title because it would be too limiting.

The U.S. patent office will object to titles that it considers to be mis-descriptive or insufficiently descriptive. That situation arises from time to time when an application is originally filed claiming one aspect of an invention, but then a divisional or other continuation focuses primarily on another aspect. In that instance the child application should usually have a different title from the parent.

Steer clear of using trademarks in the title. A trademark identifies the source or origin of a particular class of products or services, whereas a patent application is directed to the underlying inventive products or services. Thus, when athletic shoes began using Velcro™ type fasteners, an appropriate title may have been "Athletic Shoes With Interlocking Clothing Fasteners", not "Athletic Shoes With Velcro™ Fasteners".

A patent drafter should also avoid using words in the title that merely identify the fact that the invention is novel. The patent office regularly rejects use of the words "novel" and "improved" in the title as being redundant. If the subject matter of the patent application were old (i.e., not novel or improved), it should not have been filed in the first place.

A final point is that numeration is important in the title as elsewhere in the application. Even if the inventor is only contemplating one method and one apparatus, it is better to say "Methods And Apparatus For Cleaning Teeth" because it leaves the door open for arguing that the inventor contemplated multiple methods and apparatus.

B)   Priority Statements

When a patent application claims priority to a parent, grandparent, or other more distant application, a description of that priority claim is placed between the title and the background. Examples can be found in thousands upon thousands of issued patents. For example, U.S. 6893641[218] recites the following priority claim:

> The present application is a continuation-in-part (CIP) of U.S. patent application Ser. No. 09/802,862, filed on Mar. 12, 2001 now U. S. Pat. No. 6,468,542, which is a divisional application of U.S. patent application Ser. No. 09/524,508, filed on Mar. 13, 2000 and issued as U.S. Pat. No. 6,316,002, which in turn claims the priority of U.S. provisional application No. 60/158,377, filed on Oct. 12, 1999, wherein all of the U.S. priority applications are herein incorporated by reference.

Some priority claims are quite long and complicated. U.S. 6881822[219] claims priority to one divisional, five CIP (continuations in part) and six provisionals. It is very common to claim priority to both U.S. and foreign patent applications.

Priority claims are only proper where (a) the child application has at least one inventor in common with the priority parent, (b) the parent was co-pending with the child when the child was filed, and (c) the subject matter being claimed in the child was disclosed in the parent in an enabling manner.[220] An "enabling" disclosure

218 U.S. 6893641 (May 2005) "*Ganoderma lucidum* spores for treatment of autoimmune diseases"
219 U.S. 6881822 (Apr. 2005) "PSCA: prostate stem cell antigen and uses thereof"
220 MPEP § 201.06(d)

is one that provides sufficient teaching to allow (in the physical sense, not the permissive sense) a person of ordinary skill in the art to make and use the claimed invention with relatively little experimentation.

The patent office usually only addresses the first two issues (common inventor and co-pending), and ignores the issues of enabling disclosure. As a result many patent applications are often with priority claims that are partially invalid.

> It is possible to fix a badly worded priority claim

Priority claims can also be valid when a child application is filed, only to become invalid later on. That can occur because the patent drafter considered filing claims to the earlier disclosed subject matter, only to later decide to limit the claims to the newly disclosed subject matter. In such instances an honest attorney will withdraw the relevant priority claims.

The main advantage of a priority claim is that the child application (the one claiming priority) is treated as if it had been filed on the filing date of the parent. Of course, priority treatment is only accorded as to subject matter disclosed in the parent application. As to later filed, new, subject matter, the child application only has priority back to the filing date of the child application. Thus, even though patent attorneys, agents, courts, and others talk about a patent having an early priority date, many such patents actually have two, three, or even more priority dates for the different claimed subject matters.

Although applicants are usually quite careful to expressly include all the many generations for their claimed ancestry, it is not strictly necessary to do so. In a 2005 case,[221] the Federal Circuit held that the priority date of a continuing (divisional) application went back to a PCT application, even though the divisional did not expressly recite the priority. In that case the priority arose from the continuation claiming priority to a parent, which itself claimed priority to the PCT.

A few more items of interest. Provisional patent applications are not allowed to claim priority to anything. PCT patent applications can claim priority to patents and applications, but only insofar as they were filed within a year of the PCT filing date.[222]

It is entirely proper to remove priority claims, and indeed, doing so may be advisable under some circumstances. First of all, it is appropriate to remove priority claims where the subject matter recited in the pending claims was not set forth in the documents to which priority was claimed. Indeed, retaining the priority claims in those circumstances adds nothing whatever to the priority of the currently claimed subject matter. Such applications have multiple priority dates, one for the previously disclosed subject matter, and another for the currently disclosed subject matter. If the current claims are only directed to the new subject matter, then retaining the priority claim is misleading at best. In any event there is probably no harm in withdrawing the priority claims under such circumstances.

It may also be proper to remove priority claims to gain additional time to file national regional phase applications. That situation arises because PCT applications never issue as granted patents. They are only place-keepers for national and regional phase applications. If the PCT application claims priority to a provisional application that was filed almost a year earlier, then the applicant only has a maximum of 18 or 19 months from the filing date of the PCT application to file the national/regional phase applications. That usually means a further out-of-pocket expense to the applicant of about US$ 5,000 per country or region. But that expense can be pushed back another 12 months (for a total of 30 or 31 months, or longer depending on the country or region)[223] simply by removing the claim to the priority date.

> Priority claims can be canceled to allow more time to file a PCT application

---

221 *Broad. Innovation, L.L.C. v. Charter Communs., Inc.*, 420 F.3d 1364, 1368 (Fed. Cir. 2005)
222 MPEP § 1893.03(c).
223 National/Regional filing deadlines are 31 months in Australia and the European Patent Office. The deadline is 32 months in

Of course there is some danger that removing a priority claim will allow intervening prior art to preclude patentability. But where the applicant doesn't have the money to pursue foreign filing with the priority claim in place, and might later have the necessary funding if the priority claim is withdrawn, then it may make sense to withdraw the priority claim. A still further potential benefit of withdrawing priority claims is that any resulting patent will issue with a longer patent term (i.e., 20 years from the PCT filing date rather than 20 years from the withdrawn priority date). A patent drafter should weigh all of these considerations.

C)   Field of The Invention

The Field of the Invention (or simply "Field") should be carefully chosen to balance among competing considerations. On the one hand the Field should be sufficiently broad to encompass all contemplated embodiments of the claimed invention. For example, if it has been discovered that a particular ceramic is useful for filling dental caries, the Field may properly be worded as "dentistry". But if the inventors contemplate that the ceramic may also be used for filling voids in bone elsewhere in the body, the Field should probably be worded more broadly as "bone repair, including orthopedics and dentistry". Still further, if the ceramic itself comprises the principal novelty, the Field is more properly worded as "medical ceramics" or merely "ceramics".

One competing consideration is that designation of the Field can be viewed as an admission on the part of the patentee that one of ordinary skill in the art would look in that entire field for guidance in solving the problem addressed by the invention. A patentee may therefore want to describe the Field narrowly enough to support a future argument for excluding prior art. Consider, for example, a novel software approach for attacking viruses in computer systems. If the Field is described as "antiviral systems and methods", there is a substantial possibility that a patent examiner will cite references from the biological world against the claims. In that instance it is probably better to limit the Field to "antiviral software".

> **Drafting the Field of the Invention balances among competing considerations**

Some patent drafters try to satisfy these competing needs by describing the Field from a hierarchical perspective. Typical language along those lines might be "The field of the invention is athletics, more particularly sporting goods, more particularly basketballs, and more particularly methods of inflating basketballs". That sounds nice, and possibly even sophisticated. But any justification for such verbosity is dubious. It is better to invest the effort to develop simpler language. In the example just cited, the person drafting the application could far more simply have stated, "The field of the invention is basketballs" or "The field of the invention is inflatable devices".

A key reason for drafting the field (and indeed the entire specification) in simple terms is that it prevents the attorney from hiding sloppy thinking among a morass of words. Consider a draft application that claims methods for increasing the water absorbency of polymers. The specification disclosed some applications with respect to filtration of fluids, and the draft recited the Field of the Invention as a hierarchy of uses, culminating in use of the modified polymers for water treatment. But that wasn't the invention. The water treatment aspect was merely a particularly interesting application of the invention. The Field was more properly characterized as "absorbent materials". Use of hierarchical listings is not necessarily wrong. But it does beg the question of whether the drafting attorney adequately thought through all the considerations.

Canada, China (PRC), Malawi, Korea and Singapore, however China requires notification by the 30 month, with 2 months additional to submit a translation.

In some instances the deadline can be extended even further. For example, in Canada the deadline can be extended to 42 months with payment of a penalty. The complete list can be found at the WIPO Internet site: http://www.wipo.int/pct/en/texts/time_limits.html. The two letter country codes are listed at www.uspto.gov.

Another consideration in delineating the Field is the potential for licensing to different companies. It is not at all unusual for inventors, managers, or major shareholders to have interests in related but distinct companies. In those instances it may be important to separate out related technologies by filing overlapping patents in different fields. Thus, in the example above it might be advantageous to draft one patent application for one company that focuses on the absorbent materials, and to draft another applica0tion for a second company that focuses on the equipment needed to modify the materials. Making the Field too broad can result in unnecessary conflict.

D) Background

The background section has historically been used to describe the "state of the art" at the time the application is filed. Most patents appear to follow that practice, and examples abound of very lengthy summaries of the field.

Such tedious passages can be a waste of time. Indeed, I often wonder about patent attorneys and agents who insist on drafting long-winded background sections trying to establish their great knowledge of the subject matter, and thereby impress their clients or colleagues? If so, the attempt usually falls short, degenerating instead into pedantry. It does nothing to get the claims allowed.

But just as a tour-de-force of the prior art is not very helpful in getting the application allowed, the reverse is also true. Some attorneys write only a sentence or two for the background, providing little more than a restatement of the Field Of The Invention. In doing so they miss out on a marvelous opportunity to instruct the reader, whether patent examiner, judge, jury, or competitor, to understand where the current invention fits into the evolution of the technology, and why it is inventive relative to the prior art. Laziness should not be mistaken for cleverness.

(1)   Write The Background As A Sales Pitch

For those familiar with form logic, the background section involves inductive reasoning. It tells a story to the reader. We start with what we know, and build up to the conclusion that the world needs something. In contrast, the summary and detailed description sections involve deductive reasoning. We start with the general concept of the invention, and work our way down into the details.

Another way of looking at this is to consider a patent application as a sales / marketing document; the background should be written as a lead-in to the sales pitch. Indeed, the background is a perfect opportunity to show the patent examiner (and later on a judge or jury) that the claimed invention really is a significant advancement over the prior art. And just as any good sales pitch begins with a problem to be solved, a patent background should identify a problem, demonstrate how difficult it is to solve that problem, and then show how brilliant (or clever, diligent, observant, or whatever) the current inventor was in solving that problem. That approach automatically places the claimed subject matter in the most favorable light to secure a patent, and yields all sorts of support that can be used later on during prosecution to argue against obviousness rejections. It also helps later on during litigation, because many of the key arguments that the attorneys will use to support novelty and non-obviousness are right there, in black and white, in the Background.

> A strong Background section is important for many reasons

The sales aspect of the background can be achieved most effectively by clearly identifying a problem, describing the various ways that others tried to solve the problem, and then discussing why those previous solutions were inadequate. That process is shown below.

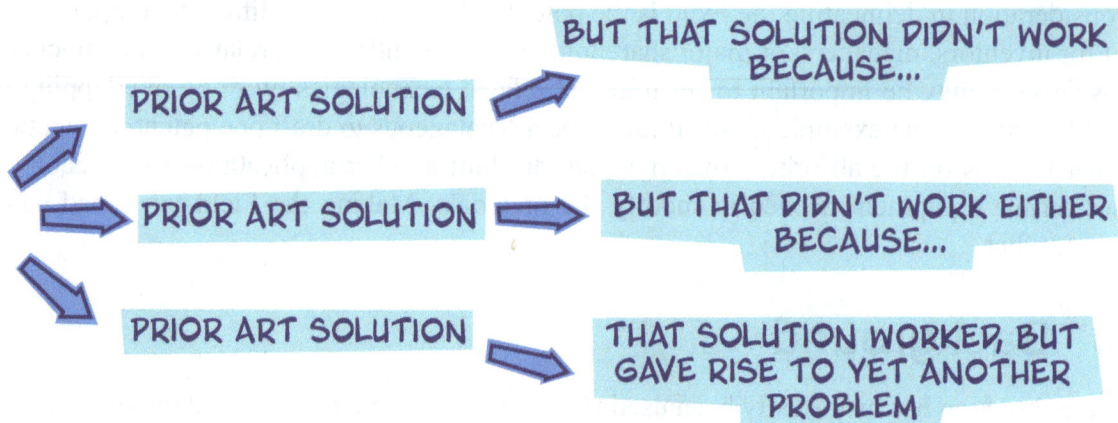

Figure - The Background Should Show The Problem Is Intractable

The "problem to be solved" is best framed in such a way that either no one else clearly identified the problem before, or if the problem had been previously identified, no one else was able to solve it. That task is not so difficult as it may seem. The framing step is just a rearrangement of the wording of the first paragraph of the summary. In U.S. 6272727,[224] for example, the summary section begins:

> It has recently been discovered that the above-mentioned problems can be resolved by biasing the upper portion of files in a file drawer or other file holder towards the rear of the file holder.

Rearranging that sentence, one can recite the problem as a "need for devices and methods that can conveniently position file folders...." Some readers will recognize this approach as being analogous to that popularized by the Jeopardy™ television show; use the answer to define the question.

Once we have a statement of the problem to be solved, we can then go back and build a case for why that problem has been so difficult to solve. A general overview focuses the reader on the environment in which the problem occurs.

> Folders are ubiquitous in modern offices. In most cases folders comprise little more than a folded piece of paper or plastic, with the "fold" ranging anywhere from the hard, creased fold of a standard "manila" folder, to a soft "fold" or bend of a hanging folder. Folders generally also have a tab or other extended portion at one of the sides for including identification information.
>
> In most instances office folders are used to contain papers, and where the papers comprise a file of information, the folder is properly called a file folder. But it is widely accepted that items sold as file folders may also contain computer disks, writing implements, and a host of other items, and the terms file folders and folders are used synonymously herein in a broad generic sense.

---

224 U.S. 6272727 (Aug 2001) "File biasing methods and apparatus"

Next, we describe how the problem manifests.

> Folders are generally intended to be kept upright in a file drawer, file box or other file holder so that the file identification information is viewable on all of the files at the same time, and so that each of the files are more or less accessible without significantly disturbing the other files. It is not always feasible, however, to maintain folders in an upright position, and this is largely due to the fact that smaller and heavier items tend to fall to the bottom (folded portion) of a folder, where they increase the thickness of the folder. Where this occurs in multiple files within the same file drawer or other holder, all of the folders tend to fall forward or backward in the file holder. While this problem is often only a minor nuisance, it does create difficulty in viewing the folder identification information, and in accessing individual folders and their contents.
>
> Where this occurs in multiple files within the same file drawer or other holder, all of the folders tend to fall forward or backward in the file holder. While this problem is often only a minor nuisance, it does create difficulty in viewing the folder identification information, and in accessing individual folders and their contents.

We then follow up with descriptions of the various ways others have failed to solve the problem.

> The problem has been addressed in part by providing a moveable partition. Such partitions can effectively reduce the volume of space available to the files, thus tending to keep them upright. Alternatively, a partition can be made to pivot against the floor of the file holder. This biases the bottom portions of the files forward and allows the top portions of the files to fall backward.
>
> While such partitions are of some use, the relatively free pivoting tends to tilt the files much farther than is necessary. Previously known such partitions are also limited to file drawers, such as those found in metal cabinets, which are strong enough and otherwise adapted to securing such partitions.

In general, this is the template for a Specification background.

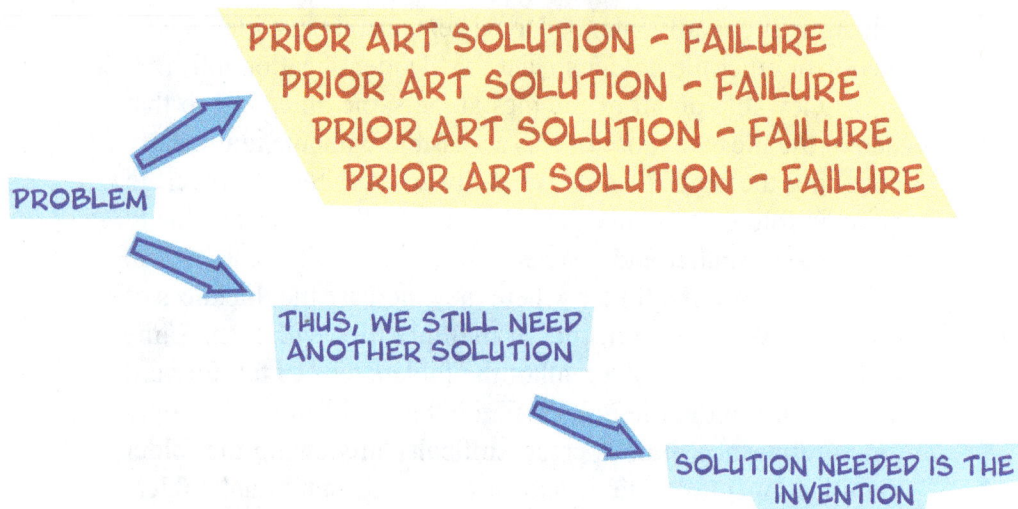

Figure - The Background Ends With Need For The Invention

(2)   Use Boilerplate Format To Conclude The Background

The final step is to restate the problem such that the claimed invention exactly fits the bill. In the example above, the background section ends with the following statement: "Thus, there remains a considerable need for devices and methods that can conveniently position file folders in substantially any file holder".

(3)   Soap Dispenser Example

Here's another example. The summary section states that the invention is "directed to a personal soap dispenser in which a bath soap is applied to a body surface by movement of the dispenser along the body surface, and wherein at least part of the bath soap is retained within the dispenser during the movement". Viewing the invention as a solution to a problem, we then characterize the problem as a need "to provide methods and apparatus for improved containers for bath soaps". That description of the problem forms the final sentence of the background section, and is preceded by a general overview that focuses the reader on the environment in which the problem occurs, and a description of the difficulties encountered by others in solving that problem. The entire background section is as follows:

Bath soaps have been known for centuries, and are typically produced from saponified fat, however, in more recent years, synthetic detergents began to replace the crude soap preparations. Regardless of the method of preparation, a bath soap generally comprises one or more detergents that reduce the surface tension of water. Depending on the particular detergents in a soap, soaps may exhibit more or less strong emulsifying power. For example, soap gels for laboratory cleaning purposes may include relatively aggressive detergents, while personal bath soap may be especially mild and scented.

Many people enjoy personal hygiene (i.e. taking a bath or shower) in a home environment because of an esthetically pleasing scent or rich formulation of their bath soap. Unfortunately, personal hygiene may become less enjoyable, when a person is on a trip and needs to stay overnight in a hotel.

Many hotels provide their guests with a miniature soap bar or a miniature bottle of shower gel. However, depending on the class of the accommodation, the quality of these bath soaps may be less than desirable. Furthermore, even when a higher quality bath soap is provided, the formulation or fragrance may or may not meet with the traveler's approval. Thus, it is a common practice among travelers to include a personal bath soap in their luggage.

Some travelers prefer liquid soap as their bath soap of choice, and there are many liquid soaps with various formulations and fragrances available. The liquid soap is typically stored in a bottle-type dispenser with a snap-top cap or a pump-action pump to dispense the liquid soap. Unfortunately, both types of dispensers are prone to accidental release of the liquid soap, thereby potentially rendering other travel utensils and objects at least temporarily unusable.

To avoid some of the problems associated with liquid soap, many people prefer a soap bar as their bath soap. Soap bars are also available in many formulations and fragrances, and can easily be taken along with the traveler. However, soap bars usually retain a considerable amount of moisture after use, and therefore need to be covered in some way to avoid accidental contamination of other travel utensils with soap scum.

Some travelers wrap the soap bar in a paper towel to absorb the excess liquid. However, when the paper towel becomes saturated with water, the traveler is left with the rather unpleasant task of removing and disposing of the sticky wrapping before the next use. Other travelers store the wet soap in a dedicated soap box. Storage of wet soap in a box presents a different problem, because due to the lubricating effect of soap scum, soap boxes tend to accidentally open or leak during the travel. Using a sealed, or otherwise hermetically locked box may prevent accidental opening or leakage, and sealed and locked boxes generally protect the remaining travel utensils relatively well, however, the soap typically softens or dissolves in the soap box when the wet soap is tumbled around in a watery environment.

> Even without considering traveling, soap bars are typically placed onto a soap dish, or in a recess in a sink or shower, and therefore often share the same fate as soap bars in a sealed and locked soap box. This is especially unpleasant when more than one person uses the same soap bar, and one person is forced to handle the pulped remainder of the soap left behind from a previous person.
>
> Although various containers for bath soaps are known to the art, all, or almost all of them suffer from one or more than one disadvantage. Therefore, there is a need to provide methods and apparatus for improved containers for bath soaps.

Note that in both of these examples, the Background section *never* discusses the claimed invention. It just discusses the background to the claimed invention. In that manner the reader can clearly distinguish that which is new (the claimed invention) from that which is old (the Background).

(4)   Incorporation By Reference

Drafting the Background as suggested in this chapter will almost certainly entail referencing other patents and patent applications. Such references should be expressly incorporated by reference: (a) to provide a source for experimental data and other information that might be needed during prosecution; and (b) to provide express enablement for prior art details of the currently claimed invention, without wasting a lot of space in the current application describing the details. It is a good idea to insert the following language shortly after discussing the first reference.

> This and all other referenced patents and applications are incorporated herein by reference in their entirety. Furthermore, where a definition or use of a term in a reference, which is incorporated by reference herein is inconsistent or contrary to the definition of that term provided herein, the definition of that term provided herein applies and the definition of that term in the reference does not apply.

Some countries, notably Japan, do not allow incorporation by reference. Thus, if one files a formal PCT or U.S. utility application claiming priority provisional application, and incorporating figures or other information by reference without actually inserting the information into the formal application, a subsequent filing in Japan will omit all of that referenced information. European practice does allow incorporation by reference, but the EPO will sometimes require the applicant to remove the incorporation statement, and instead, literally add into the application whatever material is supposed to be incorporated. Thus, if one tried to incorporate by reference an entire textbook on pharmaceutical development, the EPO might well require that the applicant copy into the application all material that he is actually incorporating.

In U.S. practice, applicants are not allowed to incorporate material by reference using a hyperlink.[225]

(5)   Avoid Saying Too Much

In the Background, as in other sections of the patent application, it is all too easy to say too much. Perhaps the most common mistake in that regard is to discuss the claimed invention in the Background section. Don't do that. Keep the background directed to the prior art. The first hint of the claimed invention should come at the very end of the background section, where the applicant states what problems still remain in the field.

Another blunder is to refer to prior uses, patents, and other disclosures as prior art. The term "prior art" is a "term of art" in patent law, and use of that term is effectively an admission that the references are relevant to patentability of the presently claimed inventions. There is no need to go down that road. The references are either prior art or they are not. In either instance there is no advantage to admitting that they are prior art in the Background.

Keep the Background focused on the prior art, not the claimed invention

Note also that "[P]atent documents need not include subject matter that is known in the field of the invention and is in the prior art, for patents are written for persons experienced in the field of the invention."[226]

E)   Summary Of The Invention

The summary section of the specification can be efficiently drafted using the text of the claims. Working on a word processor such as Word™ we usually block and copy the entire set of claims into the summary using the "paste special" function and then change the style from preamble and body to paragraph text.

(1)   First Paragraph Of The Summary Section

The first sentence or paragraph of the summary section should be a very short recap of the independent claim(s). This can be accomplished very simply by rewriting the independent claims from a slightly broader perspective, but omitting as much of the jargon as possible. U.S. 6547965,[227] for example, contains only a single independent claim set forth below.

> 1. A filtration system comprising:
>   at least two production modules mechanically coupled
>   in series and fluidly coupled in parallel to form a
>   production chain;
>   each production module having a common feed fluid
>   flowpath, a common waste fluid flowpath...;
>   an energy recovery device fluidly coupled to the at least
>   two production modules...; and
>   a pressure pump coupled to the production chain to
>   provide pressurized fluid to the production
>   modules.

---

225 37 C.F.R. § 1.57(d) and MPEP § 608.01(p)
226 *Ergo Licensing, LLC v. CareFusion 303, Inc.*, 673 F.3d 1361, 1369 (Fed. Cir. 2012), citing S3 Inc. v. NVIDIA Corp., 259
    F.3d 1364, 1371 (Fed. Cir. 2001)
227 U.S. 6547965 (Apr. 2003) "Large tube assemblies for reverse osmosis"

The claimed idea is basically to provide modularized filtration systems having an energy recovery device. So the summary section begins with the phrase:

> The present invention is directed to modularized filtration systems having an energy recovery device.

Note that the text does not read "the invention is a device that..." or "the present invention is a method in which...." First of all, such wordings are entirely too narrow. Any invention can probably be described as either a thing (device, chemical, etc) or a method of using the new thing. The opening sentence in the summary needs to leave open those other possibilities. The broader language also helps prevent opposing counsel from trying to read limitations from the summary into the claims. Such importation of extraneous limitations into the claims is, of course, entirely inappropriate, and would normally be overturned on appeal by the Federal Circuit.[228] But why take the chance? There are plenty of good ways to be constructively vague. In addition to the language suggested above, a patent attorney might also state, "aspects of the present invention further reside in constructions and arrangements of parts and uses in which...."

Another example by the same inventor is U.S. 6521127.[229] Here the patent again contains only one independent claim, which is reproduced below.

> 1. A modular filtration system, comprising:
> a feed fluid flowpath, a waste fluid flowpath, and a
> product flowpath, wherein the feed fluid
> flowpath, the waste fluid flowpath and the
> product flowpath comprise a channel or conduit;
> a plurality of production modules... disposed within
> an outer casing... ***mechanically coupled in***
> ***series and fluidly coupled in parallel*** relative to
> the waste fluid and product flowpaths;
> ***the [three flowpaths] substantially parallel*** to one
> another throughout the length of each of the
> production modules; and
> a substantial amount of the feed fluid bypassing at least
> one of the production modules.

The claimed idea is a bit more complicated, but is basically that the filter contains production modules are mechanically coupled in series, but fluidly coupled in parallel. So just say that. The first paragraph of the summary reads:

> In the present invention apparatus and methods are provided in which filter containing production modules are mechanically coupled in series, while the filters contained in the production modules are fluidly coupled with the feed, filtered and waste fluid flowpaths in parallel.

---

228 *Tate Access Floors, Inc. v. Interface Architectural Res., Inc.*, 279 F.3d 1357, 1371 (Fed. Cir. 2002), citing *Toro Co. v. White Consol. Indus., Inc.*, 266 F.3d 1367, 1371 (Fed. Cir. 2000) and *E.I. du Pont de Nemours & Co. v. Phillips Petroleum*, 849 F.2d 1430, 1433 (Fed. Cir. 1988))
229 U.S. 6521127 (Feb. 2003) "Modular filtration systems and methods"

Such a short, clean, ultra-summary is often used by the judge and jury to fashion their understanding of the scope of the invention. It has credibility because it tracks the independent claim, but it is written to be easier for non-patent people to understand.

All the dependent claims are listed below:

> 2. The system of claim 1 wherein the production modules each contain a section of each of the feed fluid, waste fluid, and product flowpaths.
>
> 3. The system of claim 1 wherein the production modules each contain a section of at least two of the feed fluid, waste fluid, and product flowpaths.
>
> 4. The system of claim 1 wherein the production modules each contain a section of at least one of the feed fluid, waste fluid, and product flowpaths.
>
> 5. The system of claim 1, wherein the outer casing is supported by a support above ground level.
>
> 6. The system of claim 1, wherein the casing is at least partially disposed in a well.
>
> 7. The system of claim 1 wherein the filters are reverse osmosis membranes.
>
> > 8. The system of any of claims 1-7 further comprising a pump which pressurizes the feed fluid flowpath.
> >
> > 9. The system of any of claims 1-7 further comprising a work exchange unit which pressurizes the feed fluid flow path.
> >
> > 10. The system of any of claims 1-7 further comprising a fluid column which pressurizes the feed fluid flowpath.
>
> 11. The system of claim 1, wherein the substantial a
>
> mount of the feed fluid bypasses between an outer wall of the production module and a well casing.
>
> 12. The system of claim 1, wherein at least one of the production modules is not sealed at the outer casing.

These dependent claims are then rolled into more or less separate sentences in the remainder of the summary.

> Among the many different possibilities contemplated, each production module may advantageously contain not only a filter, but all three flowpaths, so that a series of coupled modules can be installed, accessed, and removed as a single unit. It is further contemplated that coupled modules may be deployed in space efficient manner, such as by insertion into a deep or shall well, a tower, along the ground, into the side of a hill or mountain, or even under a road or parking lot. It is still ether contemplated that adjacent production modules may be designed to mate with one another using a slip fit joint, and that the production modules may be maintained in mating relationship through connections to supporting cables or rods.

If there are multiple independent claims, the patent attorney should try to combine them together into an intelligible whole. This is important because a patent is supposed to have a one to one correspondence with an invention.[230] An inventor is entitled to one patent for one invention; not two patents for one invention or one patent for two inventions. It is quite embarrassing for the patent office to use an applicant's own language to buttress its restriction requirement. A useful construct for combining relatively independent inventive concepts is to describe them as "aspects" of the invention.

This was done effectively in U.S. 5546849[231] in which substantially the entire summary section reads:

> A first aspect of the present invention is a hydrostatic heating apparatus for heating a particulate product in a liquid....
>
> A second aspect of the present invention is a combination heating and packaging apparatus comprising a hydrostatic heating apparatus as given above and with an aseptic packager connected to the enclosed chamber product outlet opening for aseptically packaging the particulate product.
>
> A third aspect of the invention is a method for the continuous heat-treatment of a particulate product. The method comprises the steps of: (a) providing a liquid column which is open to atmospheric pressure, where the liquid column has an upper portion and a lower portion, the upper portion having a volume sufficient to increase the boiling point of the liquid in the lower portion by a predetermined amount; (b) heating the liquid in the liquid column lower portion to a temperature sufficient to heat the particulate product; and (c) continuously passing the particulate product through the liquid column lower portion with the particulate product directly contacting the liquid.

---

230 35 U.S.C. § 101, "Whoever invents or discovers any new and useful process, machine, manufacture, or composition of matter, or any new and useful improvement thereof, may obtain a patent therefor, subject to the conditions and requirements of this title".

231 U.S. 5546849 (Aug. 1996) "Hydrostatic heating apparatus"

Be careful not to overly limit the summary section to just apparatus, just methods, or some other overly narrow characterization of the invention. The courts are not supposed to read limitations from the summary section into the claims, but the reality is that they tend to do that either expressly or subconsciously.

For example, one should not say, "The present invention is a method of...." Such language is excessively limiting for at least three reasons. First, it arguably implies that the inventor(s) contemplated only inventive methods, and failed to contemplate inventive apparatus. Second, the word "is" implies that the language being used to definitively set forth the scope of the invention. Third, the term "a method" in this particular context implies that there is only one method. In fact, it is better to eliminate the term "is" altogether. Thus, it is better to say, "the invention *is directed to*..." rather than "the invention *is*...."

It is also important to clarify that the inventor is contemplating multiple embodiments. Thus, it is better to say that "the invention *is directed to methods and apparatus* for..." than "the invention *is directed to a method or apparatus* for...." In U.S. 5913384[232] there are three sets of claims, directed to: a "method for lubricating a surface of an exercise treadmill (claims 1- 7), a "manual applicator for applying a lubricant to an apparatus" (claims 8-14), and a "treadmill maintenance kit for use with a treadmill" (claims 15-19). These are all properly circumscribed by the summary section that begins "The present invention provides apparatus and methods for lubricating the friction bearing surfaces of an assembled treadmill, using an elongated applicator". The language combines multiple characterizations, but eliminates use of the term "is", and cannot reasonably be read to imply that the invention is limited to only one embodiment.

(2)   Subsequent Paragraphs

The subsequent paragraphs of the summary section should be devoted to listing the various elements recited in the dependent claims. A good approach is to combine all the alternatives for a given subset in a given summary section paragraph. In the example above regarding the filter patent, the remainder of the summary section reads:

> In preferred embodiments the filtration system is arranged so that multiple production modules mechanically are coupled in series to form a production chain, and each of a common feed fluid flowpath, a common waste fluid flowpath, and a common product flowpath carried along the production chain.

Now it is true that some degree of accuracy will be lost during the conversion of claim text into summary section text. In the example above, the jargon terms "flowpath" and "production module" were eliminated entirely. But there is actually a benefit in that the specific terminology does not limit what the inventor may later decide to claim as the invention. In the above example, the second portion of the summary section no longer slavishly conforms to the requirements for antecedent basis that are needed in the claims.

> In yet another aspect of preferred embodiments the energy recovery device comprises a turbine positioned to extract energy from a flow-by or "waste" fluid. Still more preferred embodiments additionally include a modularized pressurization device for pressurizing a feed fluid, and provide a common drive shaft for the energy recovery and pressurization devices.

232 U.S. 5913384 (June 1999) "Treadmill Lubricating Devices And Methods"

Here's another example. In U.S. 6895987[233] the summary section captures the gist of the invention in the first sentence, and then goes on to summarize each of the dependent claims (identified in the superscript parentheses).

> The present invention provides an irrigation control system in which a device (irrigation scheduler) automatically modifies irrigation schedules of installed irrigation controllers. The inventive subject matter considers water requirements of the landscape plants, and generally comprises the following steps: providing an irrigation controller programmed to execute irrigations on watering days by closing an electrical circuit connecting the controller and at least one irrigation valve; providing an irrigation programmed to execute irrigations on substantially the same (i.e. substantially equivalent) watering days as the irrigation controller; and the irrigation scheduler selectively interrupting the electrical circuit to control the execution of irrigations on watering days. (Claim 5)

> In a preferred embodiment of the present invention, the irrigation scheduler is not an integral part of the irrigation controller. (Claims 2, 6) This means that the irrigation controller generally operates absent an irrigation scheduler. In this preferred embodiment, irrigations on watering days are at least partially determined by a microprocessor that is disposed in the irrigation scheduler.
>
> The microprocessor uses a switching circuit to cause interference with the valve reception of the control signals output by the irrigation controller. (claim 7) The output is an electrical signal that controls the opening and closing of at least one irrigation valve.

> Preferably, the microprocessor, disposed in the irrigation scheduler, uses at least one of an ETo value and a weather data in calculating the ETo value to at least partially derive the days, of the watering days, the irrigations will be executed on. (claim 3) Furthermore, the weather data is at least one of temperature, humidity, solar radiation, and wind. (claims 4, 8)
>
> The ETo value may be a current ETo value, (claim 9) an estimated ETo value (claim 10) or an historical ETo value. (claim 11).
>
> In a preferred embodiment of the present invention, the microprocessor is programmed to receive inputs that control when the microprocessor is able to interrupt the electrical circuit to prevent or enable the execution of irrigations by the irrigation controller. (claim 12)

---

233 U.S. 6895987 (May 2005) "Device That Modifies Irrigation Schedules Of Existing Irrigation Controllers"

(3)   Transition From Summary To Detail

The last paragraph of the summary section is traditionally a transition to the brief description of the drawing. The preferred language is "Various objects, features, aspects, and advantages of the present invention will become more apparent from the following detailed description of preferred embodiments of the invention, along with the accompanying drawings in which like numerals represent like components". That language helps distinguish the summary from the preferred embodiments, without limiting either. That language also specifies that like numerals represent like components, a clarification that can easily be overlooked, and come back to haunt the patent attorney many years later.

Some attorneys still list specific objects and advantages in the summary section. The main rationale favoring the approach is that listing objects and advantages can assist some readers in understanding what the inventor was trying to accomplish. That can be helpful, especially in European litigation, where the scope of the claims is often interpreted in light of the advancement the inventor made over the prior art.

One problem is that the objects and advantages are almost always limiting to the inventive concept. Consider a patent that claims data retrieval software, in which the patent specification recites faster access and lower retrieval costs as objects and advantages. The courts are not supposed to read those objects and advantages as limitations in the claims, but they can properly use them under some circumstances to interpret some of the terms of the claims. For example, if the claims specify a "user-friendly" interface, a court might conclude that the term "user-friendly" excludes interfaces that slow down overall access times, or fail to reduce retrieval costs. This is especially true if all of the examples tout both advantages.

Another problem is that a statement of objects and advantages offers little or no offsetting benefit. The same information can (and should) be worked into the detailed description section during discussions of why some variations are preferred over others. Moreover, the typical listing of objects and advantages offers little by way of distinguishing prior art references. The sorts of things that are listed, (faster, better, cheaper, more efficient, and the like), are almost always fuzzy characteristics that offer no patentable distinction over the prior art.

(4)   Should A Patent Have A Summary Section At All?

There has been a trend in recent years to minimize the summary section, and in some cases to even go so far as to eliminate the summary section altogether, or relegate it to a single sentence. The rationale arises from a worry that the inventor's view of what he considers to be the inventive subject matter will change during prosecution, and some District Court judge will improperly read limitations from the summary section into the subsequently revised claims.

However, eliminating the background is problematic. The patent attorney who follows that approach is merely trying to give himself a fallback position in case he didn't understand what should have been claimed in the first place. It's a bit like a high school student using overly complicated sentences to prevent his teacher from realizing that he didn't know what he was talking about. The better approach is for the patent attorney, and the inventor, to do the heavy lifting of figuring out what the invention is *before* starting to write the specification. When that is done correctly, the summary section provides an extremely useful starting point for a judge or juror to understand how the invention is an advancement over the prior art. If the invention should be invalidated because it is not novel, then it should be invalidated. If the claims should be read narrowly, then they should be written narrowly. Sloppiness and laziness are poor substitutes for doing the job right in the first place.

F)   Brief Description of the Drawing

The brief description of the Drawing section provides an overview of the Drawing. In that sense it can replace or supplement the Titles or captions of the Figures. By convention patent attorneys usually use separate, single sentence paragraphs for each figure. The usual format is as follows: "Figure ___ is a ___ view of _____" as in "Figure 1 is a side view of an antenna".

Proper designation of the view is important because it orients the reader. Commonly used views are top, bottom, left side, right side, perspective, horizontal, cross-sectional, and so forth. Instead of specifying a specific view, it is acceptable in some instances to replace the view description with another word. For example, it is acceptable to state that a figure is "a schematic of..." or that a figure is "a table showing... " or "a chart of...."

Sometimes the figures of a given drawing represent different views or aspects of the same object or method. In such instances the patent drafter should state the relationship in the brief description of the Drawing. For example, when figure 2 is another view of the object shown in figure 1, one might write, "Figure 2 is a top view of the motor of Figure 1".

Another commonly used phrase in dealing with drawings of physical objects is that a figure is a horizontal or vertical cross-section of the object of another figure at 1-1 or 2-2. The dashed numerals in that instance are designations that identify where in the referenced drawing the cross-section is taken. There are many good examples of such is usage in the patent literature. U.S. 5658723,[234] for example, contains the following brief description of figure 6:

> FIG. 6 is an elevational longitudinal cross-section of a first embodiment of a reaction slide according to the current invention, the cover, overlay and base being sectioned along line VI--VI of FIG. 5.

Brief descriptions of the drawing can be relatively long. For example, U.S. 6015902[235] includes a relatively long, but entirely appropriate description:

> FIG. 11 is a graphical representation of the efficiency of 32P radiolabeled, restriction enzyme-nicked plasmid DNA capture onto phenathridinium activated polystyrene microparticles prepared as described in Example 6.
>
> Each point on the graph represents the peak response (highest concentration of intracellular calcium achieved) to the addition of the indicated concentration of the indicated compound. In FIG. 28 a , NPS 457 is a racemic mixture containing compound IB (see FIG. 36 a) and the corresponding isomer; NPS 447 is R-fendiline; and NPS 448 is S-fendiline.

234 U.S. 5658723 (Aug. 1997) "Immunoassay system using forced convection currents"
235 U.S. 6015902 (Jan. 2000) "Intercalators having affinity for DNA and methods of use"

U.S. 6313146[236] includes many longer examples, including this whopper:

> FIGS. 28a and 28b are graphical representations showing that the ability of molecules to mobilize intracellular Ca (2+) in cells expressing a calcium receptor is stereospecific. Different cells were 'tested for response to pure stereoisomers and racemic mixtures. HEK 293 cells stably transfected with a cDNA clone corresponding to pHuPCaR4.0 (top panel, FIG. 28 b), the rat C-cell line 44-2 isolated from a medullary thyroid carcinoma (middle panel, FIG. 28 b) and bovine parathyroid cells (FIG. 28 a and bottom panel FIG. 28 b) were loaded with fura-2 and suspended in buffer containing 1.0 mM (top and middle panels FIG. 2 8b) or 0.5 mM extracellular Ca (2+) (FIG. 28a and bottom panel FIG. 28b). Intracellular Ca (2+) was monitored using a fluorimeter.

Many good patent drafters specify that the object being shown is an embodiment of the invention. Commonly used phrases are that a figure is a particular view of something "according to an aspect of the invention" or "according to an aspect of the inventive subject matter". Those phrases may sound a bit stilted, but they help to distinguish the embodiment shown in the Drawing from the more general concept of "the invention".

If a figure shows an embodiment that is admittedly old (i.e., the embodiment is not considered to be novel), the figure should be labeled with the designation "prior art".

G) Drawing

Patent drawings are used in interpreting the claims. Indeed, every apparatus claim that is amenable to a drawing is supposed to have a drawing, and every element that can be shown in a drawing is supposed to be shown in a drawing.[237] This applies to both independent and dependent claims.

Patent drawings usually depict aspects of preferred embodiments of the invention. To that end, drawings should be extremely simplistic, and should include *only* those elements that show differences over the prior art, and that are needed to give proper context to those differences. Unless special allowance is made, drawing figures in a utility application are always two-dimensional (2D) and in black and white. Some countries do allow 3D figures, including for example S. Korea.

In a well-written patent the Drawing depicts little else but: (a) the novel feature(s) of the invention; and (b) enough of the surrounding structure so that a reader can understand what the invention is. Most of the time this can be accomplished using somewhere between 1 and perhaps 10 sheets of drawing. Of course, some patents require more sheets of drawing due to the complexity of the invention. U.S. patent application no. 2005/0114906,[238] for example, has 41 sheets of drawing, all of which may indeed all be appropriate to properly describe the inventive subject

> **Every element in an apparatus claim that is amenable to a drawing is supposed to have a drawing**

236 U.S. 6313146 (Nov. 2001) "Calcium receptor-active molecules"
237 MPEP § 608.02
238 U.S. 2005/0114906 (May 2005) "System for interactive television"

matter. Other patents have a ridiculous number of drawing sheets. U.S. 6316975,[239] for example, appears to have 3,273 sheets of drawing!

There is a counter-argument that the Drawing and corresponding detailed description should be extremely detailed. One rationale is that a detailed drawing and description ensure that (a) the invention is enabled, and (b) that the best mode is disclosed.[240] However, a long, drawn-out specification with many drawing figures sometimes means that the drafter didn't take the time to figure out how the "invention" differs from the prior art.

Enablement and best mode refer to the claimed subject matter, not to the "invention" *per se*. If an invention lies in using glue rather than a mechanical fastener to hold together particular parts in an automobile, it is quite sufficient to describe the pieces and the glue. Indeed, the disclosure should focus on the types, amounts, and placement of the glue, and possibly different configurations of the pieces being glued. The Drawing should depict the parts, the glue, and surrounding elements, not the thousands of others parts in the automobile.

Another rationale for using complicated drawings and descriptions is that the patent attorney may someday want to claim an aspect that was disclosed in the detail, but not appreciated and claimed early on in prosecution. Here again the argument is an indictment of the patent attorney. It is the patent attorney's job to figure out what is inventive, and claim that the first time around. Yes, there should be an appropriate amount of back-up detail in both the Drawing and the Detailed Description to support limitations that may later be added into the claim language. But the best way to include back-up detail is to figure out what the "invention" is up front, i.e., how the invention conceptually differs from the prior art. In addition, the strategy of disclosing in great detail to facilitate later claiming very often fails because the disclosure only sets forth one or two alternatives. To rely on the Drawing figures to support the writing of broad claims downstream, the patent attorney would have had to disclose substantially all commercially feasible embodiments of the elements being claimed.

> **Steps in a method claims *should* be depicted in a figure, but a figure is not required**

A third rationale for extensive Drawing is that the detail can serve as a defense against patent claims of others. By describing every aspect of the preferred embodiments in an application, publication of the application or resulting patent may someday bar a competitor from claiming a particular element. True enough. But a patent attorney should not go too far along those lines. Disclosure of that much detail is likely to spur competitors to find substitutes for the disclosed elements. Some of those details are better kept as trade secrets, so that the patentee has more time to develop the alternatives himself. The bottom line is that describing everything one can think of is just poor patent drafting.

Methods should be depicted in Drawings, including method of synthesis or other manufacturing. This can be accomplished readily by drawing text boxes in Microsoft Word™ or other word processing program, inserting short descriptions of the steps of the methods (one step per box), and then connecting the boxes with lines. The boxes should be labeled in the same manner as any other component in a figure of a physical object. It is usually a good idea to include at least some of the steps set forth in dependent claims

Those new to drafting patent applications often don't realize the tremendous number of rules and regulations involved. For example, a line connecting a component with an element number should touch the edge of the component, but not extend beyond the edge. Arrow heads are prohibited, except when designating a group of components, and in that case it should not touch any of the components. Solid lines should be used on objects or edges in the foreground, and dotted lines on object or edges in the background. Stippling, shading, and so forth have special meanings, and may indicate a particular type of material such as glass, wood, or concrete.

---

239 U.S. 6316975 (Nov. 2001) "Radio Frequency Data Communications Device"
240 Under the America Invents Act of 2011, the best mode requirement continues to exist during prosecution, but failure to include best mode is no longer a defense to infringement during litigation.

Figures cannot be too "crowded on a page". The designation numerals must be more than 0.1 inch tall in U.S. patents. The paper must have at least one-inch margins all around. Multiple items in a single drawing must either be connected with lines, or expressly shown as being connected through being connected using brackets. The patent office requires 1" margins on the page, with numerals at least 1/4" high. Lead lines should be short, and should avoid crossing one another. Lead lines should connect only to the edge of the referenced elements, and have no arrows. When referencing a collection of elements (such as the brace as a whole), the lead line should have an arrow, and should be appropriately distanced from the collection.

It is strongly recommended that anyone creating patent drawings read through the drawings section of the MPEP,[241] but then still rely upon a professional draftspersons to create their formal drawings.

The number of figures in a patent drawing is up to the discretion of the patent attorney. An appropriate number of figures is usually less than ten or twelve. One main exception is that in design patents the subject matter is described in the figures, rather than with words. It is commonplace in that circumstance to have a minimum set of six figures, for top, bottom, four sides, and a perspective view. That set of views must be repeated for each embodiment being claimed, so that the number of figures in a drawing for a design patent can easily rise to ten or twenty.

Inventors tend to provide patent drafters with orthogonal views (front, back, side, and bottom). Such views are acceptable in most cases, but it is much better to use perspective drawings (e.g., from lower right front, upper left back, etc), whatever best shows the inventive features. To the extent necessary to clearly delineate the invention, it is often a good idea to include one or more exploded views and cross-sections.

Patent attorneys should be thoughtful and consistent in their use of numbering schemes. Components should generally be grouped in logical fashion, with subcomponents sharing a digit. Thus, in an electronic schematic, an RF stage may be designated 20, and individual components in the RF stage may be designated 22, 24, 26, and 28. Similarly, a power section may be designated 30, and individual components of the power section may be designated 32, 34, and 36. Where there are several different objects in the Drawing, it is probably best to separate the numbering by hundreds. Thus, all components in Figure 1 would be given numbers from 100 to 199, components in Figure 2 would be given numbers from 200 to 299, and so forth.

Just for the record, every patent has only one Drawing. The Drawing may include many figures, but there is still only one Drawing. Many patent attorneys and even some judges are sloppy in this regard, and often refer to "the drawings" of a patent. Please don't do that. One of the hallmarks of a sophisticated patent attorney is that he/she speaks precisely, especially about patent matters.

H) Detailed Description

The Detailed Description section is not a mere excursus of the Summary. It has an entirely different purpose, namely providing a detailed description of the Drawing. Indeed some attorneys substitute the heading "Detailed Description Of The Drawing" or "Detailed Description of the Preferred Embodiment". The former appellation is preferred because the contents almost always include material other than the preferred embodiment(s). But however the section is named, the patent attorney should use this section to exemplify the inventive subject matter, not to delineate the "invention". The "invention" is delineated by the claims, not the detailed description.

---

241 MPEP § 608.02, drawing

The detailed description section usually occupies the majority of the application. This section can be as short as a few thousand words[242] or go on for hundreds of pages.[243] The length of the detailed description is a

The Detailed Description is a description of the Drawing, not the "invention"

function of how many embodiments are being described, and how complicated the embodiments are. Applications in relatively unpredictable fields such as biochemistry tend to require more embodiments than mechanical devices because it is so difficult to enable broadly generalized concepts. There is also a view that the length of the detailed description section is inversely correlated with how clearly the patent attorney understands what is inventive, and how the inventive subject matter differs from the prior art. Anyone can describe something in a long and complicated manner. It takes skill to describe things simply.

(1)   Enablement

The enablement requirement[244] forces a patent applicant to provide sufficient teaching so that a Person of Ordinary Skill in the Art (POSITA) can make and use the claimed invention without undue experimentation, using knowledge of one of ordinary skill in that art as of the filing date. As it turns out, that bar is not terribly difficult to step over. For one thing, it is not necessary for the inventor to teach how to practice the invention "well". It is sufficient that one of ordinary skill in the art can practice the invention at all. Thus, a teaching that allows the hypothetical POSITA to prepare a chemical compound at a 0.00001% yield, or produce a device that works some of the time,[245] still satisfies the enablement requirement. In addition, the experimentation can require several months and still not trigger a defect in enablement.

> "…whether undue experimentation is needed is not a single, simple factual determination, but rather is a conclusion reached by weighing many factual considerations". *Wands*, 858 F.2d at 737. Some of these considerations, commonly referred to as "the Wands factors", include "(1) the quantity of experimentation necessary, (2) the amount of direction or guidance presented, (3) the presence or absence of working examples, (4) the nature of the invention, (5) the state of the prior art, (6) the relative skill of those in the art, (7) the predictability or unpredictability of the art, and (8) the breadth of the claims".

In mechanical fields the enablement requirement can often be satisfied with a single sentence. The patent on the paperclip, for example, was completely enabled by the following: "It consists of forming same of a spring material, such as a piece of wire, that is bent to a rectangular, triangular, or otherwise shaped hoop, the end parts of which wire piece form members or tongues lying side by side in contrary directions". Similarly, the

---

242 U.S. 5509323 (Apr. 1996) "Transmission device, especially a reverse gear for boats"; this patent is only 3 pages, and the specification portion is only 1009 words.

243 U.S. 2003/0196788 (Oct. 2003) "Producing hydrocarbons and non-hydrocarbon containing materials when treating a hydrocarbon containing formation"; this patent has 1032 pages, 8959 claims, and 1,884 numbered paragraphs; U.S. 2004/0235205 (Nov. 2004) "Methods and systems for determining a critical dimension and overlay of a specimen"; this patent has 367 pages, 6,632 claims and 580 numbered paragraphs.

244 35 U.S.C. § 112, first paragraph

245 *Landers v. Sideways, LLC*, 142 Fed. Appx. 462, 465 (Fed. Cir. 2005)

patent on the yo-yo[246] was completely enabled by describing two small, connected blocks, with a string wound around the connector.

In some other fields, most notably chemical and biological fields, a simple description can be enabling to a narrow claim, but non-enabling to a broader claim. That is often the case when an inventor discloses a new chemical species where a marker is used to represent numerous choices. For example, a chemical formula is often written with letters, (e.g., W, X, Y, Z, R, R1, R2, R3) representing classes of ligands or other chemical groups (e.g., alkanes, alkyls, etc). In some cases the R groups can be extremely open ended, such as where the formula recites a particular group as representing "anything except hydrogen". In such instances the inventor may have adequately described how to manufacture the compound in the narrow case where the R group is a methoxy or ethoxy, or even a generalized ether, but not in the broader case where the R group is a phenyl or other aryl ligand. Under those circumstances a claim to a compound in which "R is an ether" might be acceptable, but the claim "R ≠ H" would not be acceptable.

Although "the scope of the claims must bear a reasonable correlation to the scope of enablement provided by the specification to persons of ordinary skill in the art",[247] "...the specification itself must necessarily describe how to make and use every possible variant of the claimed invention. The artisan's knowledge of the prior art and routine experimentation can often fill gaps, interpolate between embodiments, and perhaps even extrapolate beyond the disclosed embodiments, depending upon the predictability of the art".[248]

To circumvent problems resulting from insufficient enablement, it is common for applicants to include numerous examples. This can be a good idea, and might even be necessary to secure broad claims in Europe, Japan and elsewhere. Two warnings, however. First, one can easily go overboard in providing examples. Rather than willy-nilly including whatever examples one has concocted in the laboratory, it behooves the applicant and patent drafter to really focus on what relatively few examples would be used to cover the market space for the invention. Second, it is entirely proper to include "mind experiments", experiments that are contemplated but have never been performed. The only real caveat is that one cannot pass off a mind experiment as a real experiment. Doing so may lead the applicant down the dark path of inequitable conduct.[249]

(2)   Use Broad To Narrow Strategy To Describe the Figures

The detailed description section usually discusses the Drawing figures in series, one after another, and then moves on to give examples and data. The examples and data can also be merged into the discussion of the figures, and both ways are acceptable.

Sometimes the first figure or two are "prior art" figures. Prior art is more properly discussed in the background section, but from time to time the distinguishing features of the invention over the prior art are best understood by discussing specific examples of prior art in the Detailed Description. In those instances the Detailed Description section should begin with the prior art figures, and then move on to the figures showing aspects of the inventive subject matter.

> **Write the Detailed Description from broad to narrow; then list alternatives**

There are all sorts of strategies for discussing the figures. Some drafters list all the components right away, and then describe how those components interact with each other. Other drafters discuss a subset of only a few components in detail, then move onto discussion of another subset of components.

246 U.S. 261439 (Sept. 1952) "Climbing and spinning toy"
247 *Invitrogen Corp. v. Clontech Labs., Inc.*, 2005 U.S. App. LEXIS 24810 (Fed. Cir. 2005)
248 *Chiron Corp. v. Genentech, Inc.*, 363 F.3d 1247, 1253 (Fed. Cir. 2004)
249 *Novo Nordisk v. Bio-Technology*, 424 F.3d 1347 (Fed. Cir. 2005)

In most cases the clearest way to explain a figure is to begin the discussion with a broad overview of four or five major components, and then follow up with more detailed discussions of each of those components.

> Figure 1 generally depicts gumball machine 1 having a *gumball reservoir 10* (gumballs not shown), a *dispensing stage 20*, a *visualization stage 30* and a *base 40*. The general design has similarities to existing gumball machines such as that shown in US5452822, and to avoid needless duplication of text, US5452822 is incorporated herein in its entirety.

> Reservoir 10 is similar to that known in the art. It is usually made of a clear plastic and has a more or less spherical shape, although other materials and designs are also contemplated. Advertising or other designs may be included on or within the plastic. Reservoir 10 is held in place by a tensioning rod 12, which connects dispensing stage 20 with a cap 14. Nut 16 is threaded and mates with threads on the upper end of the tensioning rod 12.
>
> Dispensing stage 20 includes a gumball selecting mechanism (not shown) for selecting individual gumballs from the reservoir 10, and releasing them from chute 22. Such gumball selecting mechanisms are well known in the art. Stage 20 also includes a coin accepting mechanism 24 with hand crank 26, which is also well known in the art. Stage 20 may be entirely transparent, entirely opaque or anywhere in between.

(3)   Gumball Machine Example

In the example below, the attorney starts out with a general overview of an inventive gumball machine. Note that the inventive feature(s) need not be addressed at this early stage. (The bolding and italics is included here just to assist the reader). After describing the apparatus broadly, the attorney then goes on to discuss, in separate paragraphs, each of the components just listed.

Visualization stage 30 preferably includes a transparent plastic housing 32 and a transparent plastic funnel 34. The transparency is not absolutely necessary, and housings and funnels which are translucent, colored, opaque or partly covered with designs or advertising are also possible. Funnel 34 may have many different sizes and dimensions, depending on the overall size and shape of visualization stage 30, the size and mass of the gumballs, and the desired gumball path(s). Simple frusto-conical funnels are known in other fields, including piggy banks in which a coin travels a spiral trajectory while descending to a storage area. Other funnels and/or other surfaces may be used as well, including those having various bumps, ridges or other distortions.

An optional central tube or support (not shown) may also be used to assist in structural stability of the gumball machine 1, or to provide a passage through which deposited coins can fall to a coin box in base 40. Alternatively, deposited coins can remain in a coin box (not shown) within dispensing stage 20, they can simply fall through visualization stage 30 to a coin box (not shown) in base 40, or they can themselves be launched onto funnel 34, or a different funnel, and be captured in a coin box (not shown) in base 40.

Base 40 functions primarily to support the gumball machine 1, to provide a dispensing port 42 for dispensing gumballs, and in some embodiments to provide a storage area for deposited coins.

In practice, a customer would insert a coin into the coin accepting mechanism 24 and operate the crank 26. A gumball selecting mechanism (not shown) would then remove at least one gumball from the reservoir 10. The selected gumball(s) would then travel to chute 22, where it(they) would be trajected onto the funnel 34 with sufficient velocity to follow a spiral path such as path 50. The required velocity may be obtained by dropping the selecting gumball(s) a given distance, or by running them along a track, inside dispensing stage 20. Finally, the selected gumball(s) would be dispensed at dispensing port 42. As noted above, inserted coins may also travel from the coin accepting mechanism 24 to the coin box (not shown) by traveling through or along the inner surface of funnel 34. There may even be multiple funnels, such as a coin funnel stacked within or outside of the gumball funnel.

(4)   Crankshaft Example

Very often the inventive subject matter is a relatively narrow component or aspect of something much more complicated. In those instances the detailed description section should begin by listing only the few components of interest, and then discuss in broad terms how those components work together. The entire introductory comments are thus kept simple and understandable. In the example below, the invention involved an internal combustion engine in which the pistons move in a special manner. The drafter appropriately starts out by listing only those components of an internal combustion engine that are important to understanding the invention.

Only after presenting an overview of the components does the drafter go into detail about each of the listed components.

Turning to Fig. 1, an internal combustion engine has four pistons 20 coupled to a compound crankshaft 10 (remainder of engine not shown). Both pistons 20 and segments 1-5 would likely be supported by, or carved out of, an engine block , which is also not shown.

Each of the pistons 20 has piston rings 24 which reciprocate inside piston cylinders 22. Crankshaft 10 comprises segments 1-5, each of which includes at least one ring gear 14, an eccentric gear 60 and a crank arm 16. Each of the eccentric gears 60 meshes with one of the ring gears 14, and is further connected to one of the crank arms 16. Adjacent crank arms 16 (those having no intervening eccentric 60) are interconnected by crank pins 18, and the crank pins 18 are coupled to pistons 20 via connecting rods 26. Connector pieces 50 (see figures 2-4) interconnect adjacent eccentric gears 60 (those having no intervening crank pin 18) of inside segments 2-4, and connect eccentric gears 60 of outside segments 1 and 5 to shaft 12. In this manner reciprocating motions within each of the pistons 20 are coupled with rotation of drive shaft 12.

In crankshaft 10, each of the ring gears 14 has internal teeth 30 (see figures 2-4) disposed in a ring, the geometric center of which defines a central axis 32. The central axes 32 of segments 1-5 are preferably collinear with each other, and with drive shaft 32, but such co-linearity is not necessary to practice the invention.

Each eccentric gear 60 cooperates in a planetary relationship with a corresponding ring gear 60 such that eccentric gears 60 rotate about peripheral axes 34 (see also figure 3) while revolving in a circular path about the central axis 32 of the ring gear 14. Because of the planetary relationship, ring gears 14 are referred to as fixed gears, and eccentric gears 60 are referred to as non-fixed gears. Ring gears 14 have twice as many teeth as the eccentric gears 60, such that each of the eccentric gears 60 makes one complete rotation about its peripheral axis 34 for each complete revolution about the central axis 32.

Each of crank arms 16 has an effective length greater than Lo. This causes the crank pins 18 to trace out approximately elliptical patterns, and further causes the crank pins to travel about the central axis 32 in a direction opposite to the rotation of shaft 12. The eccentricity of the elliptical path taken by each of the crank pins 18 is determined by the effective length of the corresponding crank arm 16 relative to Lo. For an effective arm length of 3Lo, which is depicted in figure 1, crank pins 16 move in an elliptical path with an eccentricity of approximately 2

Under those circumstances, the up and down movement of the crank pins 18, (i.e., the stroke length), will be approximately twice the corresponding side to side movement. As the effective arm length is increased further, the eccentricity of the path of the crank pin 16 approaches unity.

The strategy of describing embodiments in a broad-to-narrow fashion can be applied to all types of inventions. In chemical or electrical patents, for example, the figures are often schematics having dozens of components. Describing those components from left to right or top to bottom may be convenient for the drafter, but can be terribly confusing for the reader. It is almost always better to separate out the various components into a relatively small number of sections, deal with those sections from a high level of abstraction, and only afterward delve into the details of individual sections at some lower level of abstraction.

(5) Address Each Component Separately

The basic drafting strategy discussed above forces the drafter to contemplate numerous alternatives. If this is done correctly, the detailed discussions will provide extremely strong support (both enablement and description) for broad claims. The real question is how to do this "correctly". How can a drafter possibly list all the relevant alternatives?

(a) Parameter Method

One method is to write down (on paper or computer) all relevant parameters for the component being described, and then list all contemplated alternatives for each of those parameters. If the component is a pencil, the relevant parameters might be dimensions (height, width, and length), composition of housing, and composition of the "lead" or core. Other examples are listed below.

Component	Parameters
bristles of a hair brush	dimensions, number, diameter, materials, arrangement, and movement of the bristles
bolt	dimension, composition, thread size, coating, hardness, brittleness
providing a solvent	method, timing, choices

Figure - Parameter Method Of Developing Alternatives (I)

Once the parameters are listed, the drafter can readily record alternatives that come to mind for each of those parameters. In the case of the bolt, for example, the parameter of composition likely has alternatives of steel, wood, plastic, composites, and so forth. For the same bolt the parameter of coating likely has alternatives of none, oil, zinc, or plastic. In table format the analysis for a bold might look like the following:

Component	Parameters	Alternatives
bolt	dimensions	≤1 inch, 1 inch, 1.25 inches, 1.5 inches, 1.75 inches, ≥2 inches
	composition	steel, wood, plastic, composites
	thread size	very fine, fine, course
	coating	none, oil, zinc, or plastic
	hardness	≥6, ≥7, ≥8
	brittleness	≤4, ≤3, ≤2.5

Figure - Parameter Method Of Developing Alternatives (II)

At this point the drafter is in a position to write a paragraph describing that particular component. For example, the bolt component may be described as follows: Bolt 32 is preferably a standard 1 inch steel bolt, having course threads, and no coating. However, other alternatives are contemplated. For example, bolts can have lengths of 1 inch, 1.25 inches, 1.5 inches, 1.75 inches, and 2 inches. Bolt 32 can also comprise steel wood, plastic, and composites. The thread size can vary from very fine, to fine and course. Bolts can be non-coated, or have oil, zinc, or plastic coatings. Hardness can vary from 6, 7, to 8 on the Moh's scale, and brittleness can vary from 4, 3, to 2.5 on a suitable brittleness scale.

(b) Rationalize The Listing Of Alternatives

Of course simply listing parameters and alternatives rapidly devolves into intractably long and boring lists. Not only is that staccato writing style difficult to read, there is also a danger that even a very thorough effort will still leave gaps in the description. It is simply impossible to contemplate all the alternatives all the time. A stronger description weaves the rationale of alternatives into the description. For example, the above description of a bolt could be re-written as follows:

> Bolt 32 is preferably a standard 1 inch steel bolt, having course threads, and no coating. However, all suitable bolts are contemplated. For example, bolts may have any appropriate length from 1 inch to 2 inches, depending on the thickness of plates 12, 14.

Standard size bolts arc preferred to reduce cost, including 1.25 inch, 1.5 inch, and 1.75 inch bolts. It is also contemplated that bolt 32 can have any desired composition, from steel or other very strong materials to relatively soft materials, including wood, plastic, and composites. The thread size is really a design parameter, and all threading sizes are viable, including very fine, fine, and course threads.

Suitable bolts may be coated or non-coated. Bolts coated with plastic may be useful due to added resistance to acid environments, while those coated with zinc may be important to prevent oxidation. Other contemplated coatings include oil. Hardness and brittleness of bolt 32 is again a design choice, dependent upon numerous factors including expected vibration and other environmental factors, cost, and so forth. In particularly preferred embodiments, hardness can vary from 6, 7, to 8 on the Moh's scale, and brittleness can vary from 4, 3, to 2.5 on the brittleness scale.

In this improved writing style, for example, the drafter explains why different lengths might be used. That improved description allows a litigator to later argue that the inventor contemplated any length that was needed to hold together certain parts. Also, the reference to standard lengths, modified by the caveat that standard sized are preferred, allows a litigator to later argue that the inventor contemplated non-standard lengths. Similarly, note that the composition alternatives, steel, wood and so forth, are listed from the perspective of relative strength. That additional information allows a litigator to later argue that the inventor contemplated bolts having whatever strength is needed.

Examiners often reject claims on the grounds that the claimed elements are merely design choices. The reference to thread size as merely a design choice turns that same distinction back against the patent office, and guides the inference that all thread sizes are contemplated. Still further, the explanation of reasons behind coating choices can be read as an inference that other coating choices are also contemplated as appropriate for specific environmental choices. The brittleness and hardness alternatives are again set forth as merely design choices.

Explain *why* the preferred components are preferred

(c) Including Functional References

It is also possible to improve the thoroughness of the description, by focusing on how the alternatives work rather than what the alternatives are, or why certain alternatives are listed. For example, a very simplistic description of a pencil might be as follows:

Pencil housings can be made from any suitable material. Contemplated materials include relatively stiff and impermeable materials such as wood and plastics, as well as relatively flexible and/or impermeable materials such as paper....

> Employing all of the above approaches, the description of the pencil housing may thus be expanded to state:

To expand that description using a functional perspective, a drafter could list the two alternatives that he thought contemplated for the housing composition (namely wood and plastic), and then ask himself how those materials operate as housings -- in other words, what function does a housing serve, and what characteristics of the housing are important to satisfy those functions. Having done that the drafter would quickly realize that wood and plastic operate as housings because they are stiff, impermeable, and extend continuously about the pencil core. That observation would then lead the drafter to contemplate housings that are flexible, permeable, and do not extend continuously about the core. At the very least the patent attorney could add paper to his list of suitable housing materials. For example, instead of merely listing wood and plastic as alternatives, the drafter might state:

> It is contemplated that pencils can have a housing made from wood or plastic, and a core comprising graphite, wax, or polymer. Pencils can be any suitable length, from less than two inches to more than ten inches....
>
> Pencil housings can be made from any suitable material. Contemplated materials include wood, plastics, and other compositions that provide sufficient stiffness, impermeability, and continuous covering for soft cores. Also contemplated are paper and other materials that are sufficiently flexible to be wrapped about the core. Such materials can provide needed protection to the core, while still facilitating "sharpening" without the use of a cutting blade.

In general, good patent drafting arises from considering the inventive subject matter from several different perspectives. Describing the inventive subject matter from different levels of abstraction (such as the broad to narrow approach discussed above), and including the rationales behind inclusion of the various alternatives (such as the "why" and "how" approaches detailed above) are among the most powerful ways to vary perspective. Yet another tool is to use express definitions to force the reader to recognize that contemplated embodiments are not limited to the alternatives listed.

(d) Avoid Sounding Too Hypothetical

One of the pitfalls of writing a detailed description to cover a great number of alternatives and permutations is that the text begins to sound too hypothetical. In the paragraph below, for example, a reader could be forgiven for wondering whether the applicant invented anything at all.

> Typically, the control device 400 sends a signal to the injectors 300, instructing the sensor(s) to release a certain amount of treatment chemical. Variations upon this method are also contemplated as long as the injectors 300 are somehow activated.

For example, perhaps a signal could be sent to the injectors 300 instructing the injector 300 to a specific amount of treatment chemical immediately. Or, less preferably, perhaps a signal can be sent to the injectors 300 indicating the desired output of the injector 300 over a period of time (i.e. for the next hour).... Such control can be direct or indirect.

For example, instead of saying that some step "could" or "might" be accomplished, it is probably better to say that the step "can" be accomplished incidentally. Many drafters use this.

Use of the term "may", as in "the rod may be two to three inches long" is very common practice, but technically incorrect. "May" refers to permission, e.g., "may I go to the rest room". When discussing whether something is or is not possible, the correct term is "can".

In Figure 3 the control device 400 sends a signal to the injectors 300, which in turn causes the sensor(s) to release a certain amount of treatment chemical. There are, of course, many variants to the signal, and all such variations are contemplated. In preferred embodiments the signal instructs injectors 300 to immediately release a specific amount of treatment chemical. In less preferred embodiments the signal instructs the injectors 300 to release the desired amount of treatment chemical over a period of time (i.e. for the next hour).... Such control can be direct or indirect.

The paragraph above should be rewritten so that is sounds more definite. It is especially important to eliminate words such as "somehow", "perhaps", and "could" as shown below:

(6)   Definitions

(a)   Define Key Terms Tautologically

In the two-legged chair example discussed in a previous section, the word "connectors" replaces "nails, screws, bolts, and dowels". But what does that buy us? Does the term "connectors" include all possible types of connectors, including glue? It does if the patent attorney defines his terms tautologically rather than by simply listing the known choices.

A tautology is a classification scheme that covers all possibilities. One of the main tricks of drafting patents is to list the known choices on a piece of paper, and then classify them in some manner. The list of "nails, screws, bolts, and dowels", for example, can readily be classified into those that are threaded and those that are not threaded. This is immediately a tautology because everything must be either threaded or non-threaded. However, abstracting just another step, one can see that both threaded and non-threaded connectors are examples of a broader class of mechanical connectors.

> **Tautological claiming is key to ensuring that all commercially relevant embodiments are disclosed**

Abstracting still further, one can see that a sister class to mechanical connectors also falls within the class of chemical connectors. From that one can very quickly think of all the various types of chemical connectors, glues, adhesives, and so forth.

But we're still not done. If there are mechanical and chemical connectors, there is probably a third category, which could be called non-mechanical and non-chemical connectors. As long as one can think of a genus of that class, it makes sense to try to claim the entire class. In this case one could conceivably hold a chair together using magnets. Claiming this class provides the final piece of the tautology tautological claiming. From a purely logical perspective, all connectors in the universe must be (a) mechanical, (b) chemical, or (c) non-mechanical, non-chemical, because that last category (non-mechanical non-chemical) is a catchall that includes everything that is not in one of the other two categories!

ELEMENTS SUBJECT TO VARIATION SHOULD BE DESCRIBED TAUTOLOGICALLY

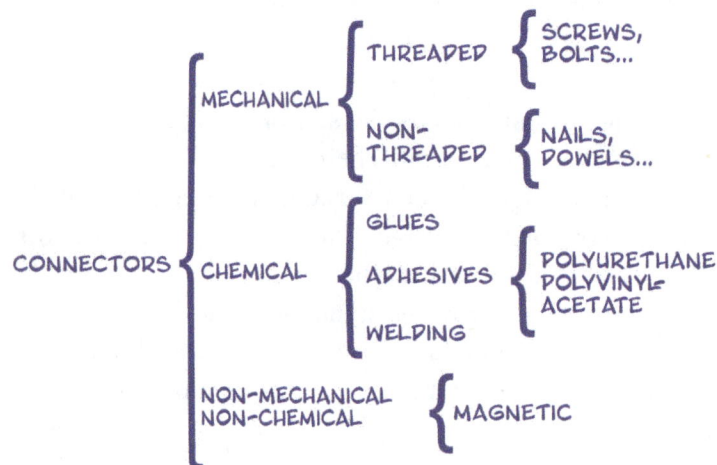

Figure - Tautological Claiming Of A Connector

Here's another tautology. In this case the inventor wants to claim a new type of balloon catheter used in repairing clogged arteries. The preferred material is a biocompatible polymer known as polyester terephthalate, but the inventor wants to ensure that the claims cover all types of electrometric materials. He also wants to ensure that he will have plenty of leeway to narrow the scope during prosecution if necessary.

Work through the examples to understand tautological claiming

The way to do this is to describe the most preferred material as polyester terephthalate (polyester t- for short), and then list all the alternatives he can think of. In this case we know that polyethylene-t, dimethyl-t, and polytrimethylene t- would all be satisfactory. The task is to define all of those compounds as species in a class of homopolymers, and further define one of the species a subclass called "other". That works as long as one can identify at least one member in the subclass, and the art is sufficiently determinative. One can then hive off polytrimethylene -t so that there is least one member in the other subclass.

Of course, if there is a class called homopolymers, there must be a class called heteropolymers. One can claim that class as long as one can think of at least one species. In this instance one could create block-copolymers, graft-copolymers and blends of the various homopolymers as shown above.

And of course both homopolymers and heteropolymers fall within the family of polymers, and that leads us to appreciate that there must be a family of non-polymers. A little research on the Internet reveals that prepolymers and quasi-polymers are considered to be non-polymers. Now polymers and non-polymers can be viewed as subset of a super group called elastomers. Since the quintessential characteristic of a balloon is that it is elastic, one can confidently use the term "elastomeric material" in the claims, knowing full well that the term will cover every suitable type of material. Indeed, if one defines elastomers as described above, it is logically impossible to have missed anything.

CLAIMING OF A BALLOON MATERIAL

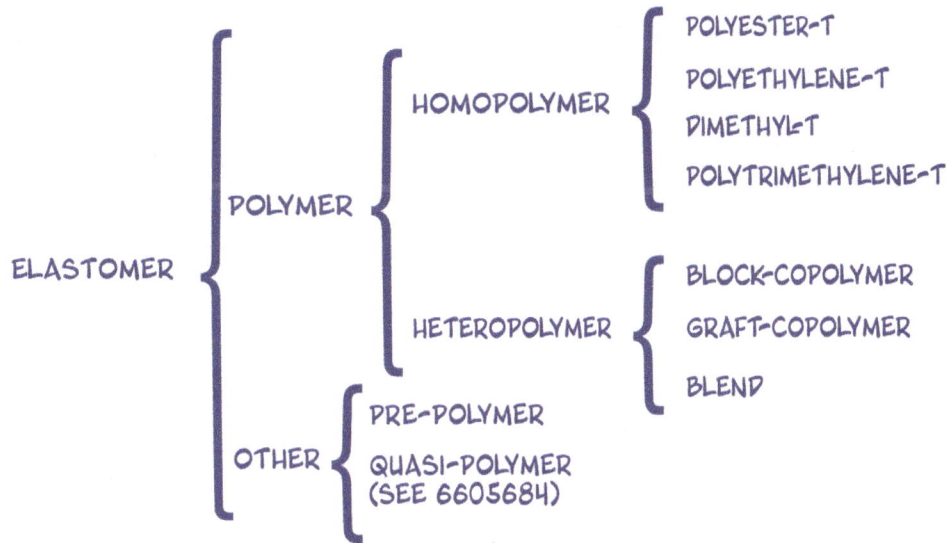

Figure - Tautological Claiming Of A Balloon Material

A bonus of this approach is that it provides plenty of wiggle room in case one needs to narrow the scope of the claims with respect to the balloon material. For example, if the examiner rejects the claims based upon a reference that teaches homopolymer materials, one could probably still claim heteropolymer materials. If the examiner cites references that teach co-polymers, one could probably still have a good case for claiming elastomers other than copolymers. This is all in stark contrast to an application that merely recited polyester, polyethylene, dimethyl, and polytrimethylene terephthalates.

Of course, in order to properly support broad claims through the use of tautologies, one has to draft the claims before the specification. One could work the other way around, by drafting the specification and examples before the clams, but that leads to either short applications that cannot support broad claims,[250] or very expensive, long applications with dozens and dozens of examples.

(b) Benefits of Expressly Defining Terms

It is very common to expressly define the terms used in patent applications, especially in fields where the art is regarded as being relatively unpredictable. In the biochemical field, for example, a patent attorney might describe a novel mechanism for delivering a drug to a target tissue. If the same mechanism were suitable for use with hundreds of different drugs, the invention would be the targeting mechanism rather than the drug. The first inclination would be to claim the mechanism for use with "drugs" in general, but that approach would be dangerous because it leaves no room for back-pedaling in the event the examiner finds prior art in

---

250 *LizardTech, Inc. v. Earth Res. Mapping, Inc.*, 424 F.3d 1336, 1345-7 (Fed. Cir. 2005) ("(A) patentee cannot always satisfy the requirements of section 112, in supporting expansive claim language, merely by clearly describing one embodiment of the thing claimed.)

which the mechanism was used for a particular drug or class of drugs. By defining drugs as listed below, the drafter gives himself all sorts of options for claiming subsets of drugs, such as particular classes of drugs, or even individual drugs.

> Suitable drugs are typically biologically active compounds or mixture of compounds that have a therapeutic, prophylactic or other beneficial pharmacological or physiological effect. Examples of drugs that may be used in combination with the block co-polymer of the present invention include anti-arrhythmic drugs, anticoagulants, antidiabetics, antiepileptics, antifungals, antigout, antimalarials, antimuscarinic agents, antineoplastic agents, antiprotozoal agents, thyroid and antithyroid agents, anxiolytic sedatives and neuroleptics, beta blocking agents, drugs affecting bone metabolism, cardiac inotropic agents, chelating agents, antidotes and ...

> antagonists, corticosteroids, cough suppressants, expectorants and mucolytics, dermatological agents, diuretics, gastro-intestinal agents, general and local anaesthetics, histamine H1 receptor antagonists, nitrates, vitamins, opioid analgesics, parasympathomimetics, anti-asthma agents, muscle relaxants, stimulants and anorectics, sympathomimetics, thyroid agents, xanthines, lipid regulating agents, antiinflamatory drugs, analgesics, antiarthritic drugs, antispasmodics, antidepressants, antipsychotic drugs, tranquillizers, narcotic antagonists, antiparkinsonism agents, cholinergic agonists, anticancer drugs, immunosuppressive agents, antiviral agents, antibiotic agents,

Definitions can be included in the background, summary, or detailed description sections. They can be collected together and segregated from the remainder of the discussion in some manner, or they can be separated and integrated into the discussion. The better approach seems to be dependent upon the extensiveness of the definitions. Where the definitions are logically or conceptually inter-related, they should probably be segregated from the remainder of the discussion. This recommendation holds true especially for very extensive definitions. Using biochemistry as an example once again, the definitions of alkanes, alkenes, alkynes and so forth are all logically or conceptually interrelated, and should be listed together.

Important claim terms should be expressly defined

A good way to address this problem is to draft the specification only after first drafting the claims. That way the person drafting the claims can review the claims to identify critical terms, and think through the definitions of those terms even before beginning to draft the specification. Definitions are preferably kept short, typically no more than a few sentences. Typical formats are shown below.

As used herein, the term "apples" means....

The term "apples" is used herein to mean...

(c)   Intrinsic Evidence Is Primary Source For Interpretation

The outcomes of patent infringement litigations often turn on interpretation of a few key terms recited in the claims. The problem is often exacerbated by the courts' unfamiliarity with the particular technologies involved, and especially their unfamiliarity with the peculiar lexicons of the relevant fields. In the past the courts tended to rely heavily on extrinsic evidence, including testimony of expert witnesses, dictionaries, and so forth. But the modern trend is to interpret claim terms according to their common meanings (in the field) as clarified by the specification and file history. In a widely cited 2004 case,[251] *Phillips v. AWH*, the Federal Circuit clarified *en banc* that dictionaries and other extrinsic sources can still be used to interpret claim terms, but only in the context of the intrinsic evidence, and that the "dictionary first" method of interpreting claims[252] placed too much reliance on extrinsic sources.

> "The main problem with elevating the dictionary to such prominence is that it focuses the inquiry on the abstract meaning of words rather than on the meaning of claim terms within the context of the patent. Properly viewed, the "ordinary meaning" of a claim term is its meaning to the ordinary artisan after reading the entire patent…. The risk of systematic overbreadth is greatly reduced if the court instead focuses at the outset on how the patentee used the claim term in the claims, specification, and prosecution history, rather than starting with a broad definition and whittling it down"[253]

Applying that rule in a subsequent case,[254] *Nystrom v. Trex*, a unanimous Federal Circuit withdrew an earlier opinion to finally decide the claim term "board" was limited to "wood cut from a log", and could not properly be broadened "to encompass relatively obscure definitions that are not supported by the written description or prosecution history".

> "What Phillips now counsels is that in the absence of something in the written description and/ or prosecution history to provide explicit or implicit notice to the public--i.e., those of ordinary skill in the art--that the inventor intended a disputed term to cover more than the ordinary and customary meaning revealed by the context of the intrinsic record, it is improper to read the term to encompass a broader definition simply because it may be found in a dictionary, treatise, or other extrinsic source".[255]

(d)   Problems Arising From Expressly Defining Terms

Problems can arise when a term is expressly defined one way in the specification, but defined in an inconsistent manner elsewhere in the application, in another patent, application, or other publication that is incorporated by reference. A classic example is where a patent drafter defines a computer as including a housing having a display, a keyboard, operating electronics, and a battery, but later on refers to a cable that couples the housing to the display. If the display is part of the housing, how can the display be coupled to the housing with a cable?

One also needs to be careful about definitions in families of patent applications. Definitions of terms in a parent application are very likely to be applied to the same terms in a daughter CIP application even though the specifications may be very different from one another, and a different definition may be more appropriate.

> **But be careful to avoid "catchas" when expressly defining claims**

---

251 *Phillips v. AWH Corp, et al.*, 415 F.3d 1303 (Fed. Cir. 2005).

252 The so-called Texas Digital line of cases, after Texas Digital Systems, Inc. v. Telegenix, Inc., 308 F.3d 1193 (Fed. Cir. 2002).

253 *Phillips v. AWH, Supra*, 415 F.3d at 1321.

254 *Nystrom v. Trex Company, Inc.*, et al., 424 F.3d 1136 (Fed. Cir. 2005).

255 Id. at 1145.

Still further, attorneys must also be careful about using weasel words in the definitions. To say that the term "preferred fruits" includes cherries doesn't help very much. Does it include apples? The weasel word "includes" can render the definition too broad to be particularly useful. A similar problem arises when a definition uses the terms "may", "can", "up to" and so forth. To define a fireproof fabric as one that "may withstand heat up to 1000 degrees F for up to ten minutes" is saying nothing at all.

In general, a drafter can be his/her own lexicographer, and can define terms to mean whatever he wants them to mean.[256] Making up new words to use in the claims is especially powerful because the drafter can take several paragraphs in the specification to explain a term, but would never want to place all that information in the claims. For example, U.S. 5723589[257] used the made-up term "Glinkoside" in the claims, and that term was coined and explained in detail in the specification. An existing word can even be defined to have a meaning inconsistent with the usual meaning. But be careful. While legally possible, the strategy can backfire in front of a judge or jury. The preferred route is to add a qualifier to an existing word. For example, a drafter could use the ordinary meaning of the term "melting", but might want to define melting as "melting quickly", and then define how quickly is "quickly".

(7)   Terms Having Special Meanings In Patent Law

Every technological field has its particular jargon, words that are used in a manner peculiar to field. For example, in human anatomy the terms "dorsal" and "ventral" relate to the relative positions of the body of a person who is "standing on all fours". Patent law is no different in having its own jargon.

> **"Connected" means something completely different from "coupled"**

A classic distinction in patent law is between the terms "connected" and "coupled". The term "connected" means that the pieces are physically touching, while the term "coupled" means that they are either touching or connected through one or more intermediate pieces that are physically touching. In the boxes below, for example, box A is connected to box B, and box B is connected to box C. But box A is only coupled to box C.

| A | B | C |

Figure - "Connected" Versus "Coupled"

Similarly, in a hydraulic system an actuating piston is fluidly connected to an intermediate piston, and the intermediate piston is fluidly connected to a following piston, but the actuating piston is only fluidly coupled to the following piston. Corresponding distinctions can also be made for electrical components in a circuit.

Another classic distinction is between "consisting of" on the one hand, and "comprising", "including" or "having" on the other hand. The term "consisting of" means that there are essentially no other components than that which is listed. The terms "comprising", "including" and "having" all mean that other components *could* be present. The collection of three coins that consists of a quarter, a nickel, and a penny, is properly said to comprise a quarter because other items could be, and in this case are, included. The term "consisting essentially of" is a watered down version of "consisting" that allows for minor additions. Thus, an alloy may be said to consist essentially of 60% Fe, 10% Cr, and 30% Ni, even though it has 1% other impurities. What is considered minor depends upon the field, the functional effects of the additional impurities or other components, and so forth. U.S. 6096313[258] provides an excellent example of an issued claim that is narrowed to the point

---

256 *Merck & Co.*, supra, 395 F.3d at 1370.
257 U.S. 5723589 (Mar. 1998) "Carbohydrate conjugated bio-active compounds".
258 U.S. 6096313 (Aug. 2000) "Compositions containing immunogenic molecules and granulocyte-macrophage colony stimulating factor, as an adjuvant".

of irrelevance through use of the term "consisting of". Including a substantial quantity of something as simple as water can circumvent the claim.

> 1. An immunogenic composition consisting of:
> (a) at least one peptide molecule, said at least one peptide molecule *consisting of* an amino acid sequence for a tumor rejection antigen, where said peptide molecule binds to an MHC molecule on a cell surface to provide a peptide--MHC complex; and
> (b) an amount of granulocyte macrophage colony stimulation factor sufficient to stimulate an antigen specific, CD8+ cytolytic T cell response against said peptide--MHC complex.

On the other hand, the Federal Circuit refuses to be held slave to overly legalistic constructions. In *Conoco v. EEI*,[259] the Court recently re-affirmed that "consisting of" does not necessarily exclude additional components or steps that are unrelated to the invention.

By the way, the term "comprising" is often misused in patent applications. Proper usage requires a whole that comprises various parts. Thus, an automobile comprises wheels, a body, an engine, and so forth. But the wheels do not *comprise* the automobile; they *compose* the automobile. Also, there is no excuse for using the prolix phrase "is comprised of". The phrase is anathema to readers with any measure of linguistic sensibility. Finally, avoid close repetition of the term "comprising" in a single sentence. It is unnecessarily confusing to write, "The field of the invention is reverse osmosis water filtration systems, particularly systems *comprising* a pressure vessel *comprising* concentric flow paths". The better wording is "The field of the invention is reverse osmosis water filtration systems, particularly systems *comprising* a pressure vessel *having* concentric flow paths".

More terms:
Channel
Depression
Vessel
Opening
Touching

There are numerous other terms that have (or should have) special meaning in patent law. Here are some of the more commonly used terms with special meanings.

• A "channel" implies an elongated depression having an open top. Channels need not be open on the ends. A "canal" is similar to a channel, with the added implication that the canal carries a liquid. A "tunnel" is similar to a channel, but is closed all the way around over its length, and is usually open on the ends. A passageway is fairly generic, and most likely includes channels, canals, tunnels, and so forth. A passageway, for example, can be open or blind. All of these terms imply a capacity for traversion, even if there is nothing traversing at a given moment in time.

• A "depression" implies a very shallow deformation of a surface. An "indentation" implies a deeper deformation, and a cavity implies an even deeper deformation, where the depth of the deformation is relatively great compared with the area of surface deformed. Depressions, indentations and cavities are blind, in that material cannot pass through to the other side of some object.

259 *Conoco, Inc. v. Energy & Envtl. Int'l, L.C.*, 2006 U.S. App. LEXIS 21036 (Fed. Cir. 2006), citing *Norian Corp. v. Stryker Corp.*, 363 F.3d 1321, 1331-32 (Fed. Cir. 2004)

• A "vessel" is an object having a cavity that can receive a material of some sort, whether gas, liquid, solid, plasma. Vessels can be open or closed at a given point in time. But presumably were or can be opened at some relevant period of time.

• An "opening" leads to a cavity of some sort, whether the cavity is a void (filled with a gas or possibly a vacuum) or is filled to some degree. A "hole" is a passageway that may or may not lead to a cavity. For example paper is generally regarded as being so thin that a hole in the paper is a passageway from one side of the paper to the other side, with no intervening cavity. Interestingly, the patent office usually rejects claim that recite a hole per se, on the grounds that a hole is not a physical limitation. Such rejections can be circumvented by reciting an object having an opening that defines a hole.

• The term "touching" means that there is no distance between the closest points of two objects or substances. The implication is that other than perhaps an irrelevantly thin film of dust or oil, the molecules of one object are as close as possible to molecules of the other object. A body of water can touch the shoreline. A wire can touch a spool. "Juxtaposing" is a softer term, implying very close proximity, but not necessarily touching. Juxtaposing does, however, have the added implication of two or more solid objects (as opposed to substances in general). The term "mating" refers to cooperation of at least two physical components, including a "male" member having a projection and a "female" member having an opening sized and dimensioned to receive at least a substantial portion of the projection. The teeth of gears can mate with each other, as can a jar and screw-on lid. The matching size and shapes of the male and female members are generally preexisting, so that an arrow fired into a bale of hay would not be considered to mate with the bale of hay.

More terms:
Fluid
Disclosed
Recites
"A" vs "The"

• A "fluid" means anything that flows under the relevant operating conditions. Water is a fluid at standard temperature and pressure, but in its ice form is only a fluid under very high pressures. Air and other gasses are fluids. Even window glass can be considered a fluid over sufficiently long time periods.

• The term "discloses" refers to things that have been made public through the disclosure. Inexperienced patent attorneys often state that a cited reference "discloses" a particular feature. That usage is improper because it implies that the feature was unknown in the field until the publication of the reference. Better words in that circumstance are "describes" or "sets forth" or "teaches".

• The term "recites" should be limited to statements about the contents of patent claims. A specification may *teach* or *disclose* or *discuss*, but a claim recites.

• The indefinite article "a" means at least one. If a claim recites "A device comprising a shaft, a bearing supporting the shaft...", the claim includes devices in which the shaft is supported by one, two, or any number of bearings.

• The definite article "the" specifically refers to something to which an indefinite article was previously used. In the claim fragment recited above, for example, the second instance of the term "shaft" is deemed to clearly refer back the shaft recited in the preamble. Use of the definite article "the" without corresponding use of the term "a" is deemed to be indefinite. Thus, the following would be improper: A device having a bearing supporting the shaft...." In that language it is completely unclear what shaft the attorney was talking about.

More terms:
Consisting of
"A or B"
"Said" vs "The"

• Many writers confuse metaphorical terms with similar terms that refer to physical or tangible senses. The term "Further" for example, should be used in the figurative or metaphorical sense, while the term "farther" should be reserved for physical distance. Similarly, the term "coterminous" should be used in the figurative or metaphorical sense, and "conterminous" reserved for physical and tangible senses. The same distinction applies to "consist in" (metaphorical) and "consist of" (physical).

• The phrase means different things in different contexts. The term "consisting of a or b" means that only A is present or only B is present. That language does not cover a combination of "A" and "B". On the other hand, the language "comprising A or B" means that at least A or B must be present.

• The phrase "A and/or B" contemplates three possibilities, "a", "b", and the combination of "a and b". Sometimes even the courts get these things wrong. In a 2013 case,[260] the Japanese Intellectual Property High Court (IPHC) held that "5-50 ppm of sodium (Na) and/or 5-100 ppm of potassium (K)" means that *both* Na and K must be present in the ranges recited!

> 1. An immunogenic composition *consisting of*:
>   (a) at least one peptide molecule, said at least one peptide molecule consisting of an amino acid sequence for a tumor rejection antigen, where said peptide molecule binds to an MHC molecule on a cell surface to provide a peptide--MHC complex; and
>   (b) an amount of granulocyte macrophage colony stimulation factor sufficient to stimulate an antigen specific, CD8+ cytolytic T cell response against said peptide--MHC complex.

• Attorneys are split on whether to use "said" or "the" as the definite article in a patent claim. Both usages are technically correct, and both are found in the patent literature. "Said" is certainly the old-fashioned format, and is thought by many to appear overly legalistic. Some attorneys adopted a middle path, using "said" when referring back to elements introduced in the preamble, and using "the" when referring back to elements introduced in the body of the claim. It is probably best to avoid all use of the term "said".

• The term "in" includes both "entirely within" and "at least partially within". For example, a "diaphragm disposed in the body" includes

More terms:
In
Entirely Within
Integral

---

260 *Kuraray Co., Ltd. v. Sekisui Chemical Co., Ltd.*, Case No. 2012 (Gyo-Ke) 10451 (Decision rendered on September 26, 2013)

both diaphragms contained entirely and partially in the body. Also, a trash bag is "in" a trashcan even though a portion of it is hanging outside of the trashcan.[261]

• The term "integral" does not necessarily mean that the elements are all connected. Consider, for example, the following claim:

> An apparatus comprising:
> an elongated base member for attachment to an
> underlying surface; and
> a plurality of elongated ***prongs extending integrally***
> ***from said base member*** at selected spaced
> intervals along the length of said base member.

A casual reader might well think that the phrase "prongs extending integrally from said base member" requires that the prongs extend directly from the base member. But that thought would be mistaken. A 1965 CCPA case held that the term "integral" is not limited to a fabrication of parts from a single piece of metal, but is inclusive of other means for maintaining the parts fixed together as a single unit.[262] The better drafting of the claim would recite one of the following:

> A bird deterrent comprising:
> a single injection molded piece having an elongated
> rail, a plurality of laterally extending prongs,
> and a plurality of superiorly extending
> prongs ....
> A bird deterrent, comprising an elongated rail of plastic,
> which is injection molded as a single continuous
> piece with a plurality of the laterally extending
> prongs alternating at greater and lesser angles
> relative to normal.

(8)   Using Numerals To Define Components In The Figures

Straightforward numbering of elements in the drawing is often critical to rapid understanding of an invention. Unfortunately, many patent drafters are so inconsistent in their numbering that understanding is hindered rather than facilitated.

The same component should be designated with the same number across all relevant figures. Thus, if a ball bearing in a horizontal cross-section is numbered 126 in Figure 1, then the same ball bearing in a vertical cross-section of Figure 2 should also be labeled 126. The rule does not, however, apply to corresponding components in different embodiments. Corresponding components should be labeled in a similar, but not identical, manner. For example, a corresponding ball bearing in a second embodiment in Figure 3 might be labeled 326.

Numbering of components in the figures should be consistent

Components should generally be grouped in logical fashion, with subcomponents sharing a digit. In the ball bearing example, Figure 1 might depict a bearing 120, having a bearing case 122, bearing track 124, and ball bearing 126. A shaft carried

---

261 *Cannon Rubber Ltd. v. First Years, Inc.*, 2005 U.S. App. LEXIS 28879, 10-11 (Fed. Cir. 2005) (non-precedential)
262 *In re Larson et al.*, 144 U.S.P.Q. 347 (C.C.P.A. 1965)

by the bearing might be labeled 130, and have ends 132 and 134. Dotted lines can advantageously be employed to designate subsections of an object for numbering purposes. Thus, in an electronic schematic, an RF stage may be designated 20, and individual components in the RF stage may be designated 22, 24, 26, and 28. This broad to narrow numbering scheme is consistent with the broad to narrow description strategy discussed above. A good draft format for numbering a device is as follows:

> In Figure 1 device 10 generally includes a _____ 20, a _____ 30 and a _____ 40.... The _____ 20 generally comprises a _____ 22, a _____ 24 a _____ 26 and a _____ 28.... The _____ 30 generally comprises a _____ 32, a _____ 34 and a _____ 36.

Be sure to skip at least every other numeral so that forgotten numerals can be adding in logical sequence later on. Arabic numbering is almost always used in preference to Roman or other numbering.

Letters can be used in combination with numbers to designate components. Usually letters are used to designate multiple instances of similar components. Thus, the two ends of shaft 130 can advantageously be numbered 132A and 132B, with the ring and fingers of a hand 350 being labeled 350B and 350D. Theoretically, letters can also be used to identify the same components at different time frames. A fresh whole apple may be designated 129 in Figure 1 at the start of a recipe, and the same apple 129A may be shown cored and peeled in Figure 2 at a later stage. Alternative embodiments may have different numbers or the same number with a letter qualifier. If one embodiment of an application is numbered 8, another embodiment might be numbered 18 or 8B.

It is a good idea to make a list of all numbered elements in the drawing for future reference. It may be very clear what numbers correspond to which components when the application is filed, but that clarity is often lost a year and a half later when someone is trying to understand the drawing to write a response to an Office Action. Keeping a current list of numbered elements also encourages consistency in writing the specification. Still better advice is to use Patent Optimizer[263] to check the specification and claims before filing.

(9)   Steer Clear of Saying "The Invention Is..."

In patent applications the "invention" is whatever is claimed. Each claim defines an invention, and the issues of validity and infringement are determined independently for each claim. Therefore, an application with 15 claims defines 15 inventions. If the very same subject matter were drafted into an application with 18 claims, there would be 18 inventions. Since an applicant rarely files a utility patent application limited to a single claim, the inventive subject matter is almost never limited to a single invention that could be called "the invention".

The point is that when one first files a patent application (provisional or formal), the drafter can't be sure what the invention is because he can't know what claims will eventually be allowed. Remember that the "invention" is what is eventually claimed. This is why experienced patent drafters often refer to "the claimed invention(s)" rather than merely "the invention".

Refer to "the inventive subject matter" rather than "the invention"

Moreover, by baldly stating in the application that "the invention is <<such and such>>" or "the unique feature is <<such and such>>" a patent drafter is making a false statement. There are almost certainly multiple inventions, and the drafter doesn't actually know what they are. Still further, if the ensuing patent is ever litigated, the defendant will often try to confuse the jury by comparing what the attorney said the invention was against what the claims being litigated actually say. After all, the drafter of the patent application said that "the invention is" or "the unique feature is", and in so doing used two definite terms, "the" and "is". At that point the patent holder very much wishes that the drafter had used much softer language.

What language could have been used? The drafter should have said, "the inventive subject matter comprises..." or "in one aspect of the inventive subject matter...." Note that the term "inventive subject matter" substitutes for "invention", and the vague terms "comprises" or "aspect" or "includes" substitute for the more definite term "is". These suggestions apply to all types of patent applications, including provisionals.

(10)   Writing Style

Many patent drafters are actually terrible writers. That bracing insight is not calumny, but a fact that can be verified by reading almost any patent on the U.S. Patent Office website. Even accounting for the obligatory reliance on technical jargon, and the need to provide sufficient detail to enable the invention, the sad fact is that most patents are drafted with little or no regard to good writing style. Anyone drafting a patent application should give serious study to the classic, *Elements of Style* by William Strunk, Jr., *The Redbook: A Manual on Legal Style* by Bryan A. Garner, or any of myriad other books that teach good writing. In addition, patent drafters would do well to follow the suggestions listed below.

(a)   Keep The Detailed Description Short

One of the most important rules in drafting patent applications is to follow the KISS principle - keep it simple, stupid. Long, complicated patent applications are annoyingly difficult to read, whether the reader is a patent examiner, a competitor, a judge or a jury. There may be some benefit to obfuscating the merits of the invention, but whatever the patent attorney is trying to hide comes out eventually anyway, and hiding the truth with surplus verbosity almost always turns out to be counter-productive. A patentee is much better served where the drafter uses his skills in deciding what to say, rather than in saying it in some clever, overly complicated manner.

Short and simple writing is best

Some patent drafters maintain that short, simple detailed description sections are dangerous because the attorney can too easily omit critical information needed for enablement or best mode. Others disagree. If the application is drafted as outlined above, with the claims being drafted first, followed by summary, background, and detailed description, the patent drafter knows exactly what needs to be supported, and how to do it. Moreover, possible problems with enablement are better addressed by citing appropriate references in the Background section, than blathering on for page after page with detail that is already known to those in the field. For this and many other reasons, patent drafters should include the closest known references in the Background section, and incorporate those references into the application by reference. That strategy effectively includes in the application all sorts of information that can later be drawn upon to establish enablement and sufficient description. An even better strategy is to state in the Specification that all references are incorporated by reference.

Note that a patent application need not *expressly* identify the best mode within the patent application, as long as he does not "disguise" it.[264] Thus, one can properly disclose ranges of practical temperatures, dimensions, speeds, etc, as long as the best mode falls within the ranges, and the ranges are not too broad.

---

264 *Wellman, Inc. v Eastman Chem. Co.*, 642 F3d 1355, 1359 (Fed Cir 2011)

Of course there are instances in which a very detailed description is desired. We have had many instances in which a patent portfolio is the main asset of a company, and where a detailed specification with an early priority date provides an opportunity to draw out additional inventions years later. The bottom line here is that a Specification should be drafted according to the needs and resources of the patentee.

(b) Use Headings Liberally

Good use of headings can greatly simplify an application. In long applications with numerous examples, patent attorneys often supplement the standard section headings such as Background, Summary of the Invention, and so forth with an additional heading for Examples. Other subheadings are also desirable. For example, in describing a complicated device, it is often very helpful to include subheadings that delimit descriptions of major sections of the device. In describing a pair of running shoes, subsection headings may advantageously be used to delimit descriptions of the sole, the heel counter, and the body.

Use lots of headings and subheadings

Liberal use of subheadings helps keep separate ideas separate. Subheadings also help ensure that the drafter finishes the discussion of one topic before moving on to the next topic.

(c) Keep Sentences Short And Simple

Run-on sentences can be deadly. It also means poor writing since a long sentence often means that the author is combining several different thoughts. Splitting them up is advantageous in that it forces the author to focus on the individual ideas. In any event shorter, one-thought sentences greatly aid comprehension of the reader. Sentences in excess of forty words should definitely flash a warning sign, as should sentences with more than three or four commas.

A powerful way to simplify the text is to reduce the number of words. Say "to prevent" rather than "in order to prevent". Say "lubricant" rather than "lubricating medium". Also, omit unnecessary description. Instead of saying "which mechanically attaches firmly to the drill stem and directly adjacent to the lower end of the drill stem or bit coupling hub" just say "which mechanically attaches adjacent the lower end of the drill stem".

Simplify!

Employing multiple terms to describe the same thing is a clear warning sign that the terms being used are too complicated. If the proper language is "drill stem guide assembly" then always call it the "drill stem guide assembly". Don't start substituting the "drill stem guide device", the "drill stem guide" or "the assembly". Moreover, unless one really needs to say "drill stem guide assembly", it is better to call out the item as a "drill stem guide" or perhaps a "guide".

Another trick is to avoid long strings of adjectives. Rather than referring to an element as "a floating stem guide bearing ring", refer to the item as simple a guide bearing ring, and clarify that the guide bearing ring preferably floats with respect to... "

Often, entire sentences can be simplified. The following is excessively verbose:

Materials or molecules that absorb fluids are versatile, and can be utilized in many applications. Some examples of products used to absorb fluids include paper towels, diapers, sponges, and surgical pads and gauzes. In many of these applications, the more absorbent a product is, the more desirable that product becomes. That may be true for several reasons, including increasing efficiency, reducing environmental waste, convenience, and reducing costs.

The same thing can be stated in a simpler manner:

> Materials or molecules that absorb fluids are quite versatile. Commonly used absorbent products include paper towels, diapers, sponges, and surgical pads and gauzes. In general, greater absorbency is more desirable due to increased efficiency and convenience, and reduced environmental waste and cost.

Here is another example. The text is confusingly worded, with no stylistic, conceptual, or other benefit.

> In systems wherein the filtration units are separated by anti translation devices ("ATDs") and/or other connectors, it is contemplated that it can be advantageous to include any monitoring units, flow control apparatus, and/or pressure control apparatus in or near such ATDs and connectors, particularly when such ATDs and connectors are used to route water within the system.

The very same concepts are better worded using simpler language, and two sentences. Note that the revised text still uses passive voice ("can advantageously be placed"), but that usage has become accepted through decades of use.

> Position monitoring units, flow control apparatus, pressure control apparatus and/or other connectors can advantageously be placed in or near anti translation devices ("ATDs"). This is especially true where the connectors are used to route water within the system.

At the risk of beating the horse to death, here is yet another example. The following text is just pathetic, especially where the author repeats the confusing phrase "Being able to...."

> The present invention is directed to a water filtration system comprising a plurality of filtration units wherein the flow of feed water to the filtration units can be monitored and can be controlled such that the flow of feed water to individual units or to subsets of units can be determined, and can increased or decreased, possibly independently of the overall flow of feed water through the system. Being able to control flow to filtration subunits allows compensation for changes in efficiency of the filtration units over time. Being able to monitor the flow into subunits allows for identification of units that are in need of replacement.

The following language is much clearer:

> The present invention is directed to a water filtration system comprising a plurality of serially disposed filtration units, in which the flow of feed water to individual filtration units can be monitored and controlled. Among other things the ability to monitor and control the individual flows allows an operator to compensate for changes in efficiency of the filtration units over time. In extreme cases, flow to downstream units can be terminated entirely where such units are in need of replacement.

(d) Consolidate Similar Ideas, And Separate Distinct Ideas

One of the easiest ways to spot fuzzy thinking is to spot where a speaker/writer combines ideas that should not be combined. In the passage below there are really two separate concepts merged together. The first concept is the versatility of absorbent products, and the second concept is absorbency.

> Materials or molecules that absorb fluids are quite versatile. Commonly used absorbent products include paper towels, diapers, sponges, and surgical pads and gauzes. In general, greater absorbency is more desirable due to increased efficiency and convenience, and reduced environmental waste and cost.

A better way to delineate these two concepts is to separate them -- first describing the versatility concept and providing examples, and then tackling the absorbency concept and providing examples.

> "Materials or molecules that absorb fluids are quite versatile. Commonly used absorbent products include paper towels, diapers, sponges, and surgical pads and gauzes. Other products are used to absorb fluids dropped by motor vehicles".
>
> In general, greater absorbency is more desirable due to increased efficiency and convenience, and reduced environmental waste and cost. Although the materials discussed above may be useful for a variety of applications, none of them are capable of extremely large amounts of fluid, such as 250 times their weight or more.

The principle of separation applies to structures, uses, methods of manufacturing, and so on. For example, the structure of a device and its use are two different concepts. When discussing structure of a device, just discuss the structure of the device. When discussing possible uses of the device, limit the discussion to the uses.

The benefits of consolidating similar ideas, while separating distinct ideas, go far beyond improved readability. They go to the heart of patenting because they help the drafter clarify in his/her mind exactly what is the invention. In the absorbent materials application being discussed, the invention comprises irradiation of starches and other polymers to make them more absorbent. With that in mind, it is perfectly reasonable to wonder why there should be any discussion at all of the various types of absorbent products in the prior art.

The really important feature is absorbency, not types of products or even versatility in types of products. Moreover, the discussion regarding types of products should focus on products that require especially high absorbency, and for which the current materials are not completely adequate. Still further, since the invention relates to activating polymers using radiation, it would be useful to end the background section by discussing the closest references, namely previously known processes for activating particles. A better description that includes all of these principles is set forth below. Note that the text (a) focuses on absorbency rather than versatility; (b) addresses particular types of products as they relate to the need for absorbency; and (c) ends the background section by processes for activating particles.

> There is, however, a need for materials that provide absorbencies in excess of 250 times their weight. For example, U.S. Pat. No. 6,439,492 issued to Leiggi (Aug. 27, 2002) teaches an absorbent pad comprising a main enclosure having an absorbing element used to absorb fluids dropped by vehicles. The absorbent pad comprises a porous layer disposed on the top of the pad and an impermeable layer on the bottom of the pad and an absorbent layer in the middle. Given the amount of fluid that may be dropped from an automobile, it would be helpful to provide greater absorbencies than that taught by Leiggi.
>
> One method of increasing absorbency is to include activated double bonds. U.S. Pat. No. 5,863,958 issued to Dyer et al. (Jan. 26, 1999). Dyer et al. teach polymers made from 1,3,7-octatriene or like conjugated polyenes and a crosslinking agent having at least 2 activated double bonds. One example is ethylene glycol dimethacrylate. Dyer et al. teach that those polymers can be used to make absorbent foams that are useful in absorbent articles such as diapers, as well as latexes that are useful as binders and adhesives.

The flip side of overly long and complicated paragraphs is the use of single sentence paragraphs. Such paragraphs detract considerably from readability of the specification, and also impede the persuasiveness of any points the writer is trying to make. For example, if a patent drafter is reciting the difficulties experienced by the prior inventors in solving problems in the art, and is trying to establish the consequent brilliance of the current invention, the strength of his argument will be considerably lessened by the disjointed nature of single sentence paragraphs.

(e) Keep To The Point

One of the most annoying characteristics of fuzzy thinking is that the writer tends to include all sorts of irrelevant material. For example, in a paragraph intended to introduce the types of materials that are known to provide absorbencies up to 20 times the weight of the material, an inexperienced patent drafter might be tempted to say all of the following:

Materials that absorb about 20 times their own weight are well known. U.S. Pat. No. 6,293,935 issued to Kimura et al. (Sept. 25, 2001) teaches an absorbent article with liquid shrinkable elements. The absorbent article comprises a liquid permeable top layer, a liquid impermeable back layer, and a liquid retentive absorbent member interposed between the top and back layers. The absorbent member has absorbent layers and liquid shrinkable members, which can elastically shrink when that member absorbs liquid. The absorbent member may comprise polymers, including starch, crosslinked carboxymethylated cellulose, and polyacrylic acid, which are claimed to be capable of retaining 20 or more times as much liquid as their own weight.

Most of that discussion is a waste of paper. It is irrelevant to the discussion that the Kimura article contains liquid shrinkable elements. It is even more irrelevant how the layers of such an article are arranged. If the Kimura reference were included in the discussion at all, the correct, simpler description would be as follows:

Materials that absorb up to about 20 times their own weight are well known. U.S. Pat. No. 6,293,935 issued to Kimura et al. (Sept. 25, 2001) teach the use of a wide range of polymeric materials, including starch, crosslinked carboxymethylated cellulose, and polyacrylic acid.

(f)   Keep Descriptions Broad, But Without Overreaching Statements

Although weasel words should not be used in definitions, they should be used when describing characteristics of specific embodiments. For example, instead of saying that the "coking drums operate at 500 °C", say that the "coking drums typically operate at about 500°C", or between 450°C and 550°C. Other good weasel words are "optionally", "advantageously", and "preferably".

On the other hand, a patent attorney should avoid overreaching statements. Inexperienced patent drafters often make global statements such as "Scientists throughout the world have been addressing this problem for decades". There is just no benefit to such statements, and indeed the recitation of specific facts ("throughout the world" and "for decades") may lead to falsehoods. It is better practice to simply state "Scientists have been addressing this problem for some time". Another useful practice is to liberally employ softening terms, "may", "can", "substantially", "frequently", "typically", "generally", "often", "usually", "commonly", "one of the main... is", and so forth.

Avoid unnecessary global statements

The flip side to this warning is that patent drafters should consider using definite language whenever the statement is substantially without potential fallacy. For example, when discussing liver transplants, there is no need to waffle by saying that "Other disadvantages to liver transplantation may include costliness, risk of rejection of the new liver by the patient's immune system, and risks of complications during and after the transplantation". The truth of the matter is that the listed disadvantages exist. Leaving out the qualifier "may" in such instances makes the application sound at least somewhat definite.

One should also be careful about how examples are described. As mentioned elsewhere, use of the term "such as" is dangerous because the reader is left to wonder what characteristics the examples share, and how those examples relate to the class being discussed. Thus, the statement "connectors such as nails and screws" is vague, and perhaps unwittingly limited to mechanical type connectors. If a patent drafter insists upon using "such as" language, he should at least insert a comma before the "such as" to state "connectors, such as nails, screws". A better way of listing examples is to switch the language around, listing the examples first. The patent drafter might, for example, refer to "nails, screws, and other connectors". Similarly, a claim could very properly recite, "the top is nailed, screwed, or otherwise coupled to the sides". Still another good way of listing examples is to expressly state that the examples are only examples. Thus, a patent attorney could also properly state "the top is coupled to the sides by any suitable means including, for example, nails or screws".

(g) Be Precise

Be precise. Use the right words!

Broad claiming can be entirely consistent with precise wording. Indeed, one could argue that the broader the claims, the more important it is for the patent drafter to use terms in a precise manner. Listed below are several admonitions that have proven valuable over the years.

• Be careful about using "ten dollar" words just because everyone else seems to be using them. What, for example, does "rotationably" mean, other than simply "rotatably"? And yet that very term is used in at least six different patents. Yes, longer word forms can be appropriate, but only where they have a slightly different meaning from the shorter form. For example, "downwardly" conveys a movement that is less direct than "down".

• Avoid pleonasms. Don't say "I saw it with my own eyes". Just say, "I saw it".

• The term "contained" typically means that something is completely included inside something else. Thus, a tiger can be contained within a cage. But many drafters loosely recite electronics or other objects contained within a housing. The problem is that the claim can be readily circumvented by including some of the electronics outside the housing, or even in the wall of the housing. In those cases the housing does not contain the electronics; it houses at least a portion of the electronics.

There are several word and phrases that have figurative and physical counterparts.

• "Further" should be used for figurative distances, as in "that statement was even further evidence of impropriety". "Farther" should be reserved for physically measurable distances, as in "the store is 2 miles farther down the road".

• The term "desirable" refers to objects. A house or a ring can be desirable. The term "desirous" refers to a state of mind. A person can be desirous of living in the house.

• The term "determinately" means conclusively, precisely, with proof and limits. "Determinately" is the antonym of "indeterminately". The term "determinedly" means with firm resolve.

• Be careful of word "enclosing". A flange might surround and juxtapose the opening of a pipe, but it does not "enclose" the opening.

• Avoid using the term "like" to expand the scope of a category. For example, if a specification describes a laptop computer, and then states that "computers like that tend to break down", the term "like" adds nothing whatsoever to the description. The problem is that the reader has no idea what characteristics are necessary or sufficient to warrant inclusion in the category of computers "like" the one just described. Is it the size of the display, the battery reserves, or the fragility of interfaces that places a computer in the category? This mistake is common in ordinary language as well. A newscaster will often make reference to an actor "like" so and so. Is the newscaster referring to a person of that particular height, weight, gender, fame, current income, number of movies released this year, or some other characteristic? Use of the term "like" in that sense is meaningless.

• The use of the phrase "such as" raises similar issues. Consider the phrase "All suitable metals are contemplated, such as copper and bronze". What does the writer mean? Is there an implication that the only suitable metals are copper and copper alloys? The better practice is to use the term "including". The phrase above is properly reworded as "All suitable metals are contemplated, including copper, and bronze".

• Avoid using the term "like" when the meaning is "as". Instead of "like with horizontal homojunction MOSFETS", say "as with horizontal homojunction MOSFETS".

• The term "regularly" is not the same as "from time to time". The former denotes some measure of greater frequency, whereas the latter denotes less frequency. Both of those terms are distinct from "random" or "arbitrary".

• The words "therefore" and "therefor" are not interchangeable. The word "therefore" is used to introduce a logical conclusion, as in the phrases: "Those limitations are completely unnecessary for allowance, and are therefore superfluous" and "It is therefore relatively easy for a judge or jury to determine infringement".[265] Therefor is reflexive term, meaning "for that" or "for it". Proper uses include "ordering goods and enclosing payment therefor" and "a refund therefor".[266]

• The words "which" and "that" are not interchangeable. Use "which" after a comma, and "that" when there is no comma. For example, write "laptop *computers that* have large displays can be quite expensive in the long run because tend to crack", but "laptop *computers, which* often crack due to their large displays, can be quite expensive in the long run". Unless the context requires use of "which", you are generally better of using "that".

By the way, there are several word usage sites on the Internet that can be accessed to improve one's linguistic acumen. Grammarly is a free, cloud-based typing assistant, that will check a variety of language aspects as you write. The site also has a blog with tips.[267]

---

265 https://www.merriam-webster.com/dictionary/therefore
266 https://www.merriam-webster.com/dictionary/therefor
267 https://www.grammarly.com/

(h) Avoid Excessive Use of Logical Connectors

Logical connectors "moreover", "however", "therefore", "consequently", "thus", and "not", and pronouns "that" or "it" force a reader's mind to follow the writer along a logical argument. Their use is certainly appropriate in some instances, but unnecessary use of logical connectors can render even a good argument difficult to follow. Consider the following sentences.

Wording Dependent on Logical "Not"	Better Wording
One method of decreasing the amount of jerking experienced from the sudden stops in the conveyor is to allow the conveyor to slow down before coming to a stop. However, that still may not allow the device to run at higher speeds, and may result in a slower metal stitching or punching process.	One method of decreasing the amount of jerking experienced from the sudden stops in the conveyor is to allow the conveyor to slow down before coming to a stop. Even with conveyor slowing in place, the metal stitching and punching processes may still run too slowly.

Figure - Wording Comparison For Logical Connectors (I)

The last sentence on the left is difficult to understand. First, the "however" forces the reader into looking for an exception to the preceding statement. In the exception frame of mind the reader is immediately struck by the pronoun "that", which refers to some entire proposition set forth in the previous sentence. The reader's mind now has to go back and determine what "that" referred to, and prepare to receive an exception. What indeed does "that" refer to? Does it refer to the method, the reduction in amount of jerking, or allowing the conveyor to slow down before coming to a stop. Already confused, the reader is struck by the "not" logical connector, which forces his mind to conclude that the exception is being described in terms of a negation of an act. What a mess. The replacement sentence on the right omits all three logical connectors, and clarifies that slowing the conveyor fails to solve the problems.

Here's another example.

Wording Dependent on Logical "Thus"	Better Wording
Similar rotary elements may exist for embossing and perforating sheets of metal, but they, too, tend to have similar disadvantages. For example, the tooth that embosses the metal is likely to begin to emboss at an angle off-normal to the sheet. Thus, rotary elements used for embossing sheets of metal tend to be deformed.	Similar rotary elements may exist for embossing and perforating sheets of metal, but they, too, tend to have similar disadvantages. For example, the tooth that embosses the metal is likely to begin to emboss at an angle off-normal to the sheet. The off-angle approach tends to deform the sheet.

Figure - Wording Comparison For Logical Connectors (II)

In this instance the logical connector "thus" is employed to hide a logical disconnect. It is the sheets that become deformed, not the rotary elements. The replacement sentence clarifies that fact with simpler to understand language.

(i)   Use Active Voice

A writer's use of passive voice is an easy problem to spot, and an easy one to fix. Look for sentences that describe an action but are silent as to the identity of the actor. Thus, the statement that "it was determined that the temperature could be raised to 200 °C" is in passive voice because the sentence is silent as to the actor. Who made that determination? If the inventors made that determination then simply state that "The inventors then determined that the temperature could be raised to 200 °C".

Some writers believe that passive voice is perfectly acceptable. While acceptable from time to time, frequent use of passive voice increases ambiguity, and is a hallmark of a sloppy mind. Consider the following sentence.

> When the person in distress activates the remote alarm switch, when the remote alarm switch is removed from the individual by a forceful or unauthorized action, or when the signaling unit is removed from the proximity of the remote alarm switch, then the portable signaling unit sends a data transmission to the central dispatch station.

The writer's use of passive voice has no benefit, and obfuscates the meaning of the passage. The following re-write in active voice is much clearer.

> In the Hoffman device, the portable signaling unit sends a data transmission to the central dispatch station when any of three conditions occur: (1) the person in distress activates the remote alarm switch, (2) the remote alarm switch is removed from the individual by a forceful or unauthorized action, and (3) when the signaling unit is removed from the proximity of the remote alarm switch.

(j)   Avoid Legalistic And Overly Complicated Terms

Legalistic and overly complicated terms should be omitted from patents whenever a simpler term will suffice. Consider the following language:

> The present invention relates more particularly to a device having a flywheel that moves the proximal end of a drive shaft in a circular motion, and wherein an intermediate portion of the drive shaft is constrained in movement such that the distal end thereof moves in a manner similar to the proximal end.

OK. It is perhaps understandable that the language is written in "patentese", in which the entire concept is squished into a single sentence. But is it really necessary to use the term "thereof"? The same attorney went on to write that:

> Rather, the proximal and distal ends of the drive shaft preferably move along circular paths without substantial rotation thereof.

> Movement of the drive shaft is constrained at a point intermediate the proximal end and the distal end thereof. The point where motion of the drive shaft is constrained may be proximate the center of the length of the drive shaft, or may be between the center of the drive shaft and one of the ends thereof.
>
> Constraining the motion of the drive shaft preferably prevents undesirable rotation thereof, as discussed above.

Enough already. The world can do without so many instances of "thereof". The same goes for other legalistic terms such as "wherefore", "hereinafter", and "aforesaid".

(k) Stay Away From Pronouns.

Pronouns can cause terrible problems because they introduce unnecessary ambiguity. For example, in the following sentence, the reader has to wonder what is meant by the phrase "it is applied?"

> To place the drill stem guide assembly 5 into use, it is applied to the top head closure 8 by lowering the drill stem 6 into the top head closure 8.

What exactly does the term "it" refer to? Admittedly that example is fairly egregious. But a great many patent applications use "it", "that" and so forth with abandon. Such language is admittedly very common in ordinary speech, and indeed in much legal drafting. But patent drafters are, or should be, held to a much higher standard than others in terms of their attention to clear expression. After all, a patent application reduces an entire invention to one sentence, even if that invention resulted from millions of dollars and many years of effort.

Patent attorneys often make up adverbs by adding the suffix "-ly" to adjectives. That is perfectly acceptable practice, although it does make for stilted-sounding language. One of the most popular of these made-up adverbs is "rotatably", as in "The blade is rotatably disposed on the shaft".

The connector term "v". should only be used in litigations, as in "Smith v. Jones". The term "vs". is used in all other contexts, for example "the relative benefits of IBM compatible vs. Apple compatible computers".

Technically, the term "may" refers to whether one has permission to do something, while the term "can" refers to physical capability. It is more proper to state, "The light conduction element can include any of numerous types of optical fibers…" than to say "The light conduction element may include any of numerous types of optical fibers…". On the other hand, [mis]use of the term "may" in patent law is so ubiquitous, that it has become an acceptable variant.

Be careful about confusing the terms "disclosed" and "described". Not all descriptions are disclosures. The term "disclosed" means that the relevant information was novel at the time of the disclosure. The term "discussed" says nothing about novelty. In general, it is advisable to employ the term "discussed" when referring to other people's writings, because that usage avoids admitting that the subject matter was novel at the time of that writing. By the same token it is usually advisable to use the term "disclosed" to refer to an applicant's own invention.

In addition to all of the above, a patent drafter should also remain cognizant of word usages that can be simplified. A recent draft referred to "modification of the particles' surfaces". It would have been much simpler (and clearer) to refer to the "surface modifications".

(I)   Punctuation

The detail with which patent drafters focus on punctuation must seem rather odd to non-attorneys. Among other things patent attorneys distinguish between such seemingly similar phrases as "the soup contains corn, potatoes, ham, or beef" and "the soup contains corn, potatoes, ham or beef". The last comma in the first phrase clearly establishes that the soup contains four choices: (1) corn, (2) potatoes, (3) ham, and (4) beef. The second phrase is susceptible to that interpretation, but is indefinite because it also supports an alternative interpretation that the soup contains corn, potatoes, and then either ham or beef. The better practice is to insert the Oxford comma.

Patent drafters are also very much focused on distinctions between the injunctive and disjunctive joinders, "and" and "or". Continuing with the example above, a statement that "the soup contains corn, potatoes, ham, and beef" means that all of the listed components are included. A statement that "the soup contains corn, potatoes, ham, or beef" means that only one of the listed components is included. To establish that one or more of the listed components is included, one should say "the soup contains at least one of corn, potatoes, ham, and beef".

Proper punctuation is very important, especially in claims

Patent applications in the U.S. and other countries are published with the figure numerals in bold type. There is no requirement for a patent drafter to do so, and it can be incredibly time consuming to keep changing type style. A more useful practice is to bold the first instance in which a figure is being discussed at length.

Capitalization and abbreviation should be applied consistently. For example, if one uses the non-abbreviated format "Figure 1" early in a patent application, then the better practice is to consistently use the non-abbreviated format "Figure 2" rather than the abbreviated format "FIG. 2".

The general rule in the United States is that punctuation marks at the end of a sentence (question mark, period) should be placed inside the final quotation marks. The problem is that the proper usage can wrongly imply that the punctuation is part of the quote. That is confusing, especially in a field such as patent law where every word and every punctuation mark is significant. In patent drafting it is better to violate this particular rule, and place the punctuation mark outside the quotes.

As in other legal writing, it is important to avoid excessive use of commas. If a sentence has more than three or four commas, other than to separate elements in a list, the sentence should probably be reworded.

(11)   Useful Boilerplate Paragraphs For Common Portions Of The Detailed Description

There is no need to reinvent the wheel every time one drafts a patent application. In some fields of technology there are paragraphs that tend to be used over and over. In pharmaceutical applications, for example, applicants often include boilerplate paragraphs that describe the myriad possible chemical modifications, forms of the drug, routes of administration, contemplated indications (diseases), and so forth. Suitable paragraphs usually abound in the prior art documents, and can be readily modified and copied as appropriate. The following, rather compressed versions of much longer texts, are included to give the reader an idea of the degree of generality involved:

Conventional buffers such as phosphates, bicarbonates or citrates can be used for this purpose. Of course, one of ordinary skill in the art may modify the formulations within the teachings of the specification to provide numerous formulations for a particular route of administration. In particular, contemplated compounds may be modified to render them more soluble in water or other vehicle, which for example, may be easily accomplished with minor modifications (salt formulation, esterification, etc.) that are well within the ordinary skill in the art. It is also well within the ordinary skill of the art to modify the route of administration and dosage regimen of a particular compound in order to manage the pharmacokinetics of the present compounds for maximum beneficial effect in a patient.

In certain pharmaceutical dosage forms, prodrug forms of contemplated compounds may be formed for various purposes, including reduction of toxicity, increasing the organ or target cell specificity, etc. Among various prodrug forms, acylated (acetylated or other) derivatives, pyridine esters and various salt forms of the present compounds are preferred. One of ordinary skill in the art will recognize how to readily modify the present compounds to prodrug forms to facilitate delivery of active compounds to a target site within the host organism or patient. One of ordinary skill in the art will also take advantage of favorable pharmacokinetic parameters of the prodrug forms, where applicable, in delivering the present compounds to a targeted site within the host organism or patient to maximize the intended effect of the compound.

It is generally contemplated that the compounds according to the inventive subject matter will be formulated for administration to a mammal, and especially to a human with a condition that is responsive to the administration of such compounds. Therefore, where contemplated compounds are administered in a pharmacological composition, it is contemplated that contemplated compounds can be formulated in admixture with a pharmaceutically acceptable carrier. For example, contemplated compounds can be administered orally as pharmacologically acceptable salts, or intravenously in a physiological saline solution (e.g., buffered to a pH of about 7.2 to 7.5).

Similarly, it should be appreciated that contemplated compounds may also be metabolized to their biologically active form (e.g., via hydroxylation, glycolsylation, oxidation etc.), and all metabolites of the compounds herein are therefore specifically contemplated. In addition, contemplated compounds (and combinations thereof) may be administered in combination with yet further antiviral and/or antibacterial agents. Suitable additional drugs therefore include various antibiotics (e.g., beta-lactam antibiotics, tetracycline antibiotics, oxazine antibiotics, etc.), various antiviral compounds (e.g., polymerase inhibitors), and/or compounds that stimulate the immune system.

Other text is so broad that is can be used over and over regardless of the field of the invention.

Before the present invention is described in further detail, it is to be understood that the invention is not limited to the particular embodiments described, as such may, of course, vary. It is also to be understood that the terminology used herein is for the purpose of describing particular embodiments only, and is not intended to be limiting, since the scope of the present invention will be limited only by the appended claims.

Where a range of values is provided, it is understood that each intervening value, to the tenth of the unit of the lower limit unless the context clearly dictates otherwise, between the upper and lower limit of that range and any other stated or intervening value in that stated range is encompassed within the invention.

The upper and lower limits of these smaller ranges may independently be included in the smaller ranges is also encompassed within the invention, subject to any specifically excluded limit in the stated range. Where the stated range includes one or both of the limits, ranges excluding either or both of those included limits are also included in the invention.

Unless defined otherwise, all technical and scientific terms used herein have the same meaning as commonly understood by one of ordinary skill in the art to which this invention belongs. Although any methods and materials similar or equivalent to those described herein can also be used in the practice or testing of the present invention, a limited number of the exemplary methods and materials are described herein.

Here are some useful generic boilerplate paragraphs.

> As used herein and in the appended claims, the singular forms "a", "an", and "the" include plural referents unless the context clearly dictates otherwise.
>
> All publications mentioned herein are incorporated herein by reference to disclose and describe the methods and/or materials in connection with which the publications are cited. The publications discussed herein are provided solely for their disclosure prior to the filing date of the present application. Nothing herein is to be construed as an admission that the present invention is not entitled to antedate such publication by virtue of prior invention. Further, the dates of publication provided may be different from the actual publication dates, which may need to be independently confirmed.

Of course some applicants go overboard with boilerplate. An application published in 2010 had 109 paragraphs of boilerplate.[268]

One boilerplate paragraph that should often be used at the conclusion of the Detailed Description section is something along the lines of the following:

> Thus, specific compositions and methods of <<insert title of invention or a few word description of the main concept>> have been disclosed. It should be apparent, however, to those skilled in the art that many more modifications besides those already described are possible without departing from the inventive concepts herein. The inventive subject matter, therefore, is not to be restricted except in the spirit of the disclosure. Moreover, in interpreting the disclosure, all terms should be interpreted in the broadest possible manner consistent with the context. In particular, the terms "comprises" and "comprising" should be interpreted as referring to elements, components, or steps in a non-exclusive manner, indicating that the referenced elements, components, or steps may be present, or utilized, or combined with other elements, components, or steps that are not expressly referenced.

Such language can be useful later on to support an argument that the claims should not be limited to the examples set forth in the Detailed Description. It never hurts to reiterate that the scope of a patent is defined by its Claims, not its Specification, and that the examples given in the disclosure are not the only contemplated embodiments.

---

268 U.S. 2010/0211431 (Lutnick)

(12) Hyperlinks

The Patent Office doesn't allow hyperlinks in applications. The error is not critical, however, and the Applicant will merely be required to delete the hyperlink in a response to Office Action. See MPEP § 608.01. A "hyperlink rejection" is also a bit odd, since by December 2009 the Patent Office had already granted over 12,000 patents with embedded hyperlinks.

Applicants are not allowed to incorporate material by reference using a hyperlink. 37 C.F.R. § 1.57(d).

I) Abstract

The Abstract can usually be drafted in only a few minutes, by copying the language from the summary section into the abstract, and collapsing one or more entire paragraphs into single sentences. Here is an example.[269]

Note that in U.S. Prosecution, the abstract is limited to 150 words.

Text from Summary	Text from Abstract
In the present invention apparatus and methods are provided in which filter containing production modules are mechanically coupled in series, while the filters contained in the production modules are fluidly coupled with the feed, filtered and waste fluid flowpaths in parallel. Among the many different possibilities contemplated, each production module can advantageously contain not only a filter, but all three flowpaths, so that a series of coupled modules can be installed, accessed, and removed as a single unit. It is further contemplated that coupled modules can be deployed in a space efficient manner, such as by insertion into a deep or shallow well, a tower, along the ground, into the side of a hill or mountain, or even under a road or parking lot. It is still ether contemplated that adjacent production modules can be designed to mate with one another using a slip fit joint, and that the production modules can be maintained in mating relationship through connections to supporting cables or rods.	A filtration system includes production modules (305) which are mechanically coupled in series, and which contain filters that are fluidly coupled in parallel, so that a series of coupled modules can be installed, accessed, and removed as single unit. Coupled modules can be deployed a well, a tower, along the ground, into the side of a hill or mountain, or even under a road or parking lot. Adjacent production modules can mate with one another using a slip fit joint.

---

269 U.S. 6521127 (Feb. 2003) "Modular filtration systems and methods".

Note also that abstract shown has component numbers or other figure references. This is not required in the

Abstracts in the foreign countries typically need component numbers, but not in the U.S.

U.S., but the PCT, EPO, and many foreign countries follow the convention of correlating drawing components with elements in abstract. In many jurisdictions the patent examiners require the applicant to make that correlation, but it can be advantageous to let the examiner add the figure references. Among other things, doing so shows that the examiner understood the specification, and recognized that (often broader) terms used in the specification could be fairly correlated with the Drawing and Detailed Disclosure.

The U.S. and other jurisdictions also object to, or at least frown upon, use of awkwardly worded "patentese" in the Abstract. For example, examiners often object to the use of the stilted term "preferred embodiments" in the Abstract. A patent drafter can readily substitute terms such as "preferred device", "example", and "exemplary method".

In the United States, the Abstract must be placed on its own page, must be a single paragraph, and cannot contain images. In the U.S., the PCT, and many countries, the Abstract is limited to 150 words and 25 lines.[270] The easiest way to calculate the length of a draft abstract is to block it using word processing software, and then have the computer calculate the number of words. In Microsoft Word, one needs only block the entire paragraph of the abstract, click on Tools, then click on Word Count.

The Abstract can be used to give meaning to the claims

For years the Abstract could not be used to interpret a patent claim. In that respect the Abstract was only formally deemed to be part of the application. That law has now changed. Under 35 U.S.C. § 1.72(b) the Abstract can be used for interpreting the scope of the claims.[271]

J)   Paper, Spacing etc.

Patent applications in the U.S. can properly be submitted on the common 8 ½" x 11 inch paper, on the European style A4 paper, or on legal paper. It is best to stick with the first two. Legal paper is difficult to fit in some files, in briefcases, and is just all around a big headache.

Since some foreign applications *must* be filed on A4 paper, many firms are starting to use A4 paper for all their applications. The idea is to avoid the need for reformatting the pages when filing PCT and abroad. That is a viable choice, although one that hasn't been generally adopted. For one thing clients don't usually want A4 paper, so one is always having to either cut off part of the document, or shrink it down to 91% size to accommodate an 8 ½" x 11 inch image.

U.S. uses 8.5 x 11 or A4 paper with minimum 1.5 lines spacing

Patent applications in the U.S. must have either double or 1½ line spacing.[272] 1½ line spacing is preferable because it provides better readability. Double spacing allows so little text on a page that it tends to adversely affect comprehension.

Line numbering is optional, and can be readily implemented on Microsoft™ Word™ by clicking on File/ Page Setup/Layout/Line Numbers, and then selecting Add Line Numbering, and change Count By to the numeral 5. Note that the Specification and Abstract pages should have line numbering that restarts on each page, but the Claim and drawing sheets should not. Line numbering for claims starts anew at the beginning of each claim.

270 MPEP § 608.01(b) abstract of the Disclosure
271 *Hill Rom Co. v. Kinetic Concepts, Inc.*, 209 F.3d 1337, 1341 n.* (Fed. Cir. 2000); 37 C.F.R § 1.72.
272 37 C.F.R § 1.52(b)

The much better choice is to use paragraph numbering, especially on provisional applications because those are published without line numbering. Paragraph numbering is usually set in bold, in square brackets, with left zero padding (e.g. [027]), and can be automatically generated by a word processor.

Full justification of text is entirely optional, however, left justification is easier to read.

K) Proofread

Proofread! Then proofread again! It's really embarrassing to have a patent issue that includes comments that have nothing to do with the application. Here's what U.S. 9346394 included in the specification:

> "In one embodiment, the sensor 408 works with a microprocessor described elsewhere in this patent. In another embodiment the sensor 408 works with a relay in a known manner I'm sorry babe, but I may actually have to be here late. I've got to get this patent application filed today. Thankfully, Traci is willing to stay late to help me get it done."

Glossary

Abandoned Application	An application that is no longer pending. Applications can go abandoned because the applicant expressly abandons them, or because the applicant failed to respond to a final rejection. A parent application of often, but not always, abandoned when a child application is filed.
Active Patent	A patent that is still in force; i.e., it has not lapsed or gone abandoned.
Allowable Claims	A claim that is deemed allowable by the patent office. Each claim of a patent application can be allowed or rejected independently of all other claims.
Angel Investor	An affluent individual who provides capital for a business start-up, usually in exchange for convertible debt or ownership equity.
Apparatus Claim	A claim to a physical thing, such as a machine or a chemical composition. This contrasts with method claims, which are drawn to steps in a process.
Application	A filing for a patent. A utility application can have a status of pending or abandoned. A formal patent application has a specification, usually at least one claim, and usually at least one page of drawing. The specification usually has a title and the following sections: field of the art, background, short description of the drawing, detailed description, and examples. A provisional application can be very short, having perhaps only a few paragraphs and a drawing.
Application Filing	The date on which an application is filed. Filed applications are pending.
Assignee	A person, company or other entity to which title (i.e., ownership) in a patent application or a patent has been transferred.
Best Mode	The best way that an inventor knows how to practice his invention.
Boutique Law Firm	A small (usually then than 20 attorneys) law firm that specializes in a particular area of law.
Child Application	An application that claims priority to one or more parent applications.

CIP Application	A child application that contains additional disclosure relative to the parent. CIP applications have multiple priority dates, one to the filing date of the parent with respect to subject matter disclosed in the parent, and another to the filing date of the CIP with respect to the additional disclosure (termed "new matter").
Claim Drafting	The writing of patent claims, especially with an eye to broadly protecting a patentable invention.
Claims	Numbered sentences following the patent specification, which define the scope of the claimed invention(s). Each claim covers a slightly different but overlapping scope.
Co-Inventor	An inventor that shares inventorship with another person. Intentional failure to list a co-inventor on a patent application may render any ensuing patent unenforceable.
Commercialize	Placing something into the stream of commerce. Patent and patent applications can be commercialized in many different ways, including selling the patent or application, licensing the underlying technology, or selling products or services that utilize the technology.
Commercially Viable Solution	An embodiment of an invention that is commercially significant. There are almost always many embodiments that are technically feasible, but commercially unimportant. One of the goals of patent drafting is to secure for the applicant patent rights to as many of the commercially viable embodiments as possible.
Continuation Application	The term is strictly construed to mean a child application that supersedes the parent application. The USPTO used to refer to these continuations as FWC (file wrapper continuations) and used to issue a new serial number. The office then changed the name to RCE (Request for Continuing Application) and continued prosecution without changing the serial number. The latest incarnation is called a CPA (Continuing Patent Application), which also uses the same serial number as the parent, but now there is no pretense that the continuing application is anything other than a reincarnation of the parent. The term "continuing application" somewhat confusingly includes continuations, divisionals, and continuations-in-part.
Daughter Application	A spin-off from an existing application. Possible daughter applications are divisionals, continuations, and continuations-in-part.

Dependent Claims	A claim that is dependent on at least one other claim. The limitations of a dependent claim are those contained within the dependent claim, as well as all limitations contained within any claims upon which the dependent claim is directly or indirectly dependent. Thus, if claim 3 is dependent on claim 2, and claim 2 is dependent on claim 1, then claim 3 contains all the limitations of claims 1, 2, and 3.
Disclosure	This term usually refers to information that an inventor provides to a patent attorney or agent to assist in writing a patent application. The term can also refer to information in a patent or other document that is used as prior art against a later filed patent application.
Divisional Application	A child application having the same specification as, and claiming priority to, a parent application. A divisional is usually employed to prosecute claims that were withdrawn or canceled from the parent.
Drafting Charges	Amount charged for writing the text of a patent application. The term is also sometimes used to mean costs associated with preparation of the drawing.
Drawing	The figures of a patent. Technically there is only one drawing, even though the drawing may extend over several pages.
Elements	Words or phrases of a patent claim that refer to a portion of the subject matter being claimed. Thus, in a claim to a chair, the elements may be the legs, seat, arms, back, coverings, connectors, and so forth.
Embodiment	Implementation of an idea. Embodiments can be actual (in which case the technology is used in the physical world), or constructive (in which case the law deems an embodiment to have been made by virtue of one having filed a patent application with an adequately detailed disclosure).
Enforceability	The ability to prevail against an infringer in a court of law on a claim of patent infringement.
Examiner	The person at the patent office who reviews the prior art, and makes determinations as to patentability. Examiners are not concerned with enforceability.
Expired Patent	A patent that is past the end of its life span. In the United States, patents issuing from applications filed after June 7, 1995, have a life span extending for 20 years from their earliest claimed priority date, plus whatever extensions may apply.

Family	A group of at least two patents and/or patent applications that are linked by virtue of priority claims to one another. A patent family often has three or more "generations".
Filing Costs	Filings fees plus charges for completion and submission of the various papers that accompany a patent application.
Filing Date	The date that a patent application is considered to have been received by the patent office. The filing date is the same as the priority date if there is no priority claim
Filing Fee	The fee charged by the patent office to accept a patent application for processing.
Foreign Application	An application that is filed outside of the country having original filing. Thus, if a patent is originally filed in the United States and later in Japan, the Japanese application is a foreign application.
Formal Application	An application other than a provisional application. This usually means a utility or PCT application. Formal applications must have at least one claim, whereas a provisional application need not have any claims.
Grandchild Application	An application that claims priority to both a parent application, and a parent of the parent.
Green Fields Patenting[SM]	A patenting strategy that focus not on what the inventor thinks he invented, but on what the inventor (or assignee) wants to stop others from doing. Used synonymously with Blue Sky Patenting [SM].
"In Force" Patent	A patent that has not been invalidated, by expiration (reached the end of its life span), by lapsing (failure to pay a maintenance fee), or invalidated by a court or the patent office.
Improvement	An embodiment of an invention that was not disclosed in a prior application.
Independent Claims	A claim that is not dependent on any other claim. All of the limitations of the claim are therefore contained within the independent claim.
Informal Application	A provisional application. Such applications are informal in that, among other things, they do not need to include any patent claims.
Invalidated Patent	A patent that can no longer be used as a basis for bringing a patent infringement action. In many cases some, but not all, claims in a patent are invalidated.

Invention	An idea that is new, useful, and non-obvious over the prior art. Years ago the patent office required a working model or other evidence that the idea was actually reduced to practice before a patent would issue. Currently, mere ideas can be patented as long as the patent application can describe to one of ordinary skill in the art (the technology field) how to make and use the claimed invention.
Invention-Centered Approach	A strategy that focuses on claiming an invention by its technical merits, rather than a market-centered approach.
Inventor	A person who conceived or helped conceive of an invention. A patent application can name multiple inventors. The head of a department, or other person who might well be listed on a journal article, is only an inventor for patent purposes if he/she actually contributed to the conception of the invention. Similarly, a person who helped build a prototype is not necessarily an inventor, despite the fact that he/she may have contributed far more physical effort and time than an inventor. Inventors can be listed on a patent application in any order.
IP	Intellectual Property, which is generally considered to include patent, trademark, copyright, and trade secret rights.
Issuance Of A Rejection	During the course of a patent prosecution, the patent office sends out official notices regarding claims that are being argued. Sometimes the claims are allowed, and sometime they are rejected. It is very common to get rejections, and simply means that more work needs to be done to either amend the claims, or convince the patent office that the claims are allowable.
Lapsed Patent Application	A patent application that has gone abandoned for failure to timely pay respond to take a required action, such as respond to an office action or pay a fee.
Lapsed Patent	A patent that has gone abandoned for failure to timely pay issue fees.
Large Entity	In the United States, an assignee that has at least 500 employees. Many countries do not distinguish between large and small entities.

License	A license is a contract or other legal arrangement that gives a licensee (a person, company, government or other entity) a right to do something. In the case of patents, a license provides a right under a particular patent or set of patents. A license under one patent does not necessarily mean that the licensee can legally practice the claimed invention. The reason is that the licensee might also be infringing a claim of a different patent.
Limitations	Patent claims are typically parsed into phrases covering the different recited elements. If a claim recites "a computer having a power circuit, a processor, and a memory", that portion of the claim has three limitations on the computer, namely that it has (1) a power circuit, (2) a processor, and (3) a memory".
Market-Centered Approach	A patenting strategy that focuses on claiming the commercially viable embodiments that preclude competition, rather than on the technical merits of the invention. Compare with invention-centered approach.
Means-Plus-Function Claims	A claim that includes at least one element that is defined by its function rather than a physical limitation (e.g., "means for opening a door" rather than "a door knob"). Means-plus-function claims do not necessarily have to include the term "means for".
Method Claims	A claim drawn to steps in a process rather than a physical thing *per se*. Method claims usually begin each phrase with a word ending in "ing", such as "enclosing", or "providing" or "connecting".
Method Of Use Claim	A type of method claim in which the applicant focuses on the manner in which some¬thing (often a pharmaceutical or machine) is used.
Monopoly	A monopoly is a situation where one entity controls the rights to do something. For example, if a pharmaceutical company has a monopoly on selling a drug, then that company is the only one that can sell the drug. There are laws against monopolies in the United States, but patents are an exception to those laws.
Multiple Dependent Claims	A claim that is alternatively dependent upon more than one claim. A typical format would be "A device according to any of claims 1, 3, 4, or 7, in which ...."
Office Action	A formal communication from the patent office. Some office actions are favorable, some are unfavorable (rejections and objections), and some are informational only.

One Year Deadline	There are two one-year deadlines. A PCT application can only claim priority to an earlier filed application if the PCT application is filed within one year of the earlier filed application. Also, a provisional application will go abandoned unless a formal application is filed within one year of the provisional's filing date, and claims priority to the provisional.
Owned Patents	Patents are initially owned by the inventor(s). The ownership rights, however, are usually assigned to a company, university or government agency for commercialization purposes. Patent rights can be split in many ways, according to market, geography, time span, or in myriad other ways.
Parent Claim	Patents and patent applications have both independent and dependent claims. Independent claims stand alone, while dependent claims include all the limitations of a parent claim from which they depend. Thus, if claim 2 recites "The device of claim 1, wherein ...", then claim 2 is dependent on claim 1 and includes all of the limitations of claim 1. In that instance claim 1 is the parent of claim 2.
Parent Application	An application which a daughter application is spun off.
Patent	A patent is basically a right to sue others for making, using, selling, importing or exporting something that falls within the scope of claimed subject matter. In the most basic sense, a patent is a deal struck with the government. An inventor discloses the details an invention, and the government grants a limited monopoly to that invention.
Patent Agent	A person who has passed the patent bar with the U.S. patent office, but has not passed the attorney bar of any state or District of Columbia, and very likely did not go to law school. Patent agents have all the same rights and responsibilities as patent attorneys with respect to dealings with the patent office.
Patent Application	An application for a patent. Patent applications are "pending" until they are either abandoned, or they mature into a patent.
Patent Attorney	A person who has passed the patent bar, as well as the attorney bar of one of the states or District of Columbia.
Patent Drafter	The person or persons who draft the patent application. Even though the inventor may assist in the process, the task of correctly drafting a patent application ultimately falls to the responsible patent attorney or agent.

Patent Mill	An office that files a large number of patent applications, with an emphasis on quantity rather than quality. Patent mills can make millions of dollars per year, while providing almost universally bad results for their unsuspecting victims.
Patentability Search	A search undertaken to determine whether, or how broadly, an idea can be patented. Documents relevant to patentability are called "references". Patentability searches should usually be undertaken by inventors and their patent attorneys or agents before patent applications are even drafted, and in any event patentability searches are always undertaken by the patent office in determining patentability. Patentability searches are entirely different from right-to-practice searches.
Patentable Idea	An idea that is new, useful and non-obvious over the prior art (i.e., over what is already known), and that is sufficiently definite in the mind of the inventor(s) that it can be enabled (i.e, described in an adequate level of detail) in a patent application. Years ago the patent office required a working model or other evidence that the idea was actually reduced to practice before a patent would issue. Currently, however, mere ideas can be patented.
Patentable Invention	Same thing as patentable idea.
Patent Office	The national or regional authority charged with receiving and processing patent applications. In the United States the patent office is the USPTO.
Patent Prosecution	The back and forth arguing between the patent applicant (or practitioner) and the patent office prior to an application being issued or abandoned. Unless an application is speeded up in some way, patent prosecution can often take three or more years. Current statistics can be found at http://www.uspto.gov/ dashboards/ patents/ main.dashxml.
Patent Rights	A U.S. patent provides the owner with the right to stop others from making, using, selling, importing and exporting with respect to the claimed area of technology. Interestingly, having a patent does not necessarily mean that the owner can practice the technology. It simply means that the owner has a right to sue others for doing so.

PCT	Patent Cooperation Treaty; an international treaty signed by the United States, and administered by WIPO. The PCT receiving office for the United States is the United States Patent and Trademark Office (USPTO). Patent applications are examined through the PCT procedures, but the PCT never issues any patents.
Petition To Make Special	A formal petition before the USPTO to speed up processing of a patent application based upon satisfaction of particular requirements.
POSITA Or PHOSITA	A Person of Ordinary Skill In The Art. Generally speaking, this is a hypothetical person who knows everything that is known in the field of an invention, anywhere in the world, at any time prior to the filing or other priority date of an application, and who has only an ordinary level of creativity. Ideas that would have been obvious to such a hypothetical person should be rejected by the patent office on the grounds of obviousness.
Preferred Embodiment	A preferred implementation of the subject matter of a patent or patent application. Patent applicants in the United States are required to satisfy the "best mode" requirement, which means that they must describe whatever implementation of the claimed invention(s) that they consider to be "best" at the time that the application is filed.
Primary Application	The oldest formal application in a family of patent applications. Subsequent (secondary) applications in the family usually focus on various subsets of the disclosure of the primary application.
Prior Art	Knowledge that is sufficiently close to the claimed subject matter that it is considered to be relevant to patentability. Prior art can be US or foreign patents, newspaper, journal or other publicly accessible documents, web pages, advertisements, and so forth. Prior art is defined by statute (35 U.S.C. § 102) for purposes of determining anticipation, but is slightly different for purposes of determining obviousness.
Priority; Priority Date	A legal fiction by which something is treated as if it had occurred earlier in time. The claims of a divisional patent application, for example, have a filing date of the divisional application, but for purposes of determining patentability are treated as if that filing date were the filing date of the parent application.
Prototype	A sample or model built to test a concept or process. A working prototype of an invention is not needed to file a patent application on the inventive concepts underlying the invention.

Provisional Application	An informal patent application. Provisional applications are never examined. Unless they are used as a parent in a formal application, they are microfilmed and placed into storage at the on-year anniversary. In the latter case the provisional is then considered to be "dead" (expired).
RCE	See Request For Continued Examination.
Reductionistic Thinking	A process of reducing a complex idea, system, etc., to simpler parts or components that contain the essence of the idea or system.
Rejected Claims	Claims that the examiner considers to be unpatentable over the prior art, either because the claims are anticipated, obvious, and/or for some other reason. Claims that are merely objected to, rather than rejected, contain a technical defect that can usually be overcome relatively easily.
Request For Continued Examination	During patent prosecution, the patent office typically issues a non-final office action, and then a final office action. To get another two bites at the apple, an inventor, attorney or agent can simply file a Request For Continued Examination, and pay additional fees.
Restriction Requirement	A statement by the patent office that the pending claims are deemed to address more than one invention. Restriction requirements are very commonly issued where an applicant has some claims directed to a method and some claims directed to an apparatus.
Retained Patents	Patents are usually assigned to a company, university or government for commercialization. An inventor can, of course, keep ownership of a patent, and try to commercialize it himself. Such patents are "retained" by the inventor.
Right-To-Practice Search	A search undertaken to determine whether practice of a given technology will likely infringe the patent rights of another.
Royalty	Money or other value, usually paid to a patent holder in exchange for a license to a patent. Royalties are typically paid monthly or quarterly, and can be fixed fee, scheduled fee, or dependent on sales or other conditions.
Scope Of Equivalents	A patent claim covers both that which is literally encompassed by the language of the claim, and also that which is equivalent. The idea behind the doctrine of equivalents is that an infringer should not be able to circumvent a patent claim by making an insubstantial modification.

Small Entity	In the United States, an assignee that has less than 500 employees. Many countries do not distinguish between large and small entities with respect to fees.
Tautological Claiming	A claiming strategy in which an independent claim recites a broad subject matter, and dependent claims recite successively narrower subsets of that subject matter.
USPTO	United States Patent and Trademark Office
Utility Application	A patent application that claims a useful invention. Contrasts with a design application, which claims the ornamental appearance of something.
Venn Diagram	A diagram that uses circles and ovals to represent applications of set theory.
White Space	The conceptual space around an idea, which is not already known by others.
White Space Patenting	A patenting strategy that seeks to claim all the commercially viable white space around an inventor's idea.
WIPO	World International Property Organization.

Index

D

E

F

G

H

I

About the Author

Robert D. Fish, Esq. has been a patent attorney for more than 30 years, practicing White Space and Green Fields Patenting[SM]. He is currently head of Fish IP Law, LLP, in Orange County California.

Mr. Fish and his team at Fish IP have secured over 15,000 patents, and over 6000 trademark registrations. Together they have attracted a world-class clientele in a diverse array of technologies, including pharmaceuticals, stem cell and other non-pharmaceutical treatment modalities, medical devices, chemical extractions and assaying technologies, human-machine interfaces, augmented reality software and devices, business methods, cryptography, plasmas and other high energy technologies, and oil and gas processing.

Fish IP has worked with over 150 law firms in foreign countries, with several firms in China, S. Korea, UK, EP, and Australia / New Zealand relying on Fish IP for their US prosecution.

Mr. Fish has been involved in several patent enforcement programs, which include in-bound and out-bound licensing, arbitration, and litigation. Mr. Fish has litigated in several state and federal courts, including California, Pennsylvania, Massachusetts, Nevada, and Delaware) and has overseen cases in several European countries

Other Titles in the Series

Cost-Effective Patenting (2002)

Strategic Patenting (2007)
  Building Strong Patent Portfolios

Green Fields Patenting (2011)
  Patenting the Future

Patent Magic (2011)
  Prosecution Strategies and Practice Tips

Internet Websites

www.FishIPLaw.com

www.PatentBeast.com